THE IRRECONCILABLES

THE FIGHT AGAINST
THE LEAGUE OF NATIONS

by Ralph Stone

THE UNIVERSITY PRESS OF KENTUCKY

Standard Book Number 8131-1199-4
Library of Congress Catalog Card Number 70-94073

COPYRIGHT © 1970 BY THE UNIVERSITY PRESS OF KENTUCKY

A statewide cooperative scholarly publishing agency serving Berea College, Centre College of Kentucky, Eastern Kentucky University, Kentucky State College, Morehead State University, Murray State University, University of Kentucky, University of Louisville, and Western Kentucky University.

Editorial and Sales Offices: Lexington, Kentucky 40506

To Jeanne

CONTENTS

Acknowledgments   ix

Introduction   1

1   The Origins of the Fight   4

2   Seizing the Initiative   24

3   Confrontation with Wilson   52

4   The Fight outside the Senate   77

5   Reservations: A Strategy for Victory   100

6   The Treaty's First Defeat   128

7   No Compromise and No Treaty   147

Conclusion   178

Appendix   183

Bibliographical Essay   189

Index   197

ACKNOWLEDGMENTS

BEGUN ORIGINALLY in graduate school at the University of Illinois, this volume owes most to the man who directed my doctoral dissertation, J. Leonard Bates. His encouragement and sound criticism helped immeasurably at the time; even more have I benefited since that time from the example of his own careful scholarship and from his warm friendship. An early draft of the manuscript was read by Norman Graebner who offered several excellent comments. Two of my colleagues at Miami, Robert Merideth and Robert Reid, provided searching reviews of a recent draft, and I have adopted many of their suggestions.

I have been fortunate in receiving the cooperation of a number of persons who aided my research. Especially do I wish to thank Mrs. Marion H. Graham, the daughter of Senator Lawrence Sherman, Mrs. Garvin E. Tankersley, the daughter of Senator Medill McCormick, and Mrs. James A. Reed, the wife of Senator James Reed. All of them welcomed me into their homes and allowed me access to the papers of these senators.

Librarians and archivists across the country were unfailingly generous of their time. The Miami University librarians merit special mention as those from whom I have received the most extensive assistance. The Faculty Research Committee at Miami provided funds that freed me for two summers of writing. Mrs. Patricia McGuire was responsible for most of the typing. Judy Shaw assisted greatly in reading proof and preparing the index.

My wife, Jeanne, read the manuscript, typed portions of it, and, above all, maintained a cheerful disposition throughout everything.

INTRODUCTION

ON THE NIGHT of November 19, 1919, a happy crowd of people, including several senators and their wives, gathered for a victory party at the Washington home of Alice Roosevelt Longworth, daughter of the recently deceased former President, Theodore Roosevelt. They had come from the Capitol where, a short time before, the United States Senate had rejected on three separate votes resolutions to approve the Treaty of Versailles, the first twenty-six articles of which would have brought the United States into the League of Nations. Four months to the day later, on March 19, 1920, after the Senate had reconsidered its previous action and agreed to debate the Treaty once again, another party was held at Mrs. Longworth's to mark what was to be the final defeat of the Treaty.[1] That afternoon the Senate had failed by a margin of seven votes to give it the necessary two-thirds approval. Of all those who celebrated this result, none had cause to feel more jubilant than a small band of sixteen senators, sometimes referred to as the bitter-enders or battalian of death, but better known as the irreconcilables, who had fought for the complete rejection of the Treaty, irrespective of any qualifying reservations. They were: William E. Borah of Idaho, Frank B. Brandegee of Connecticut, Albert B. Fall of New Mexico, Bert M. Fernald of Maine, Joseph France of Maryland, Asle J. Gronna of North Dakota, Hiram W. Johnson of California, Philander C. Knox of Pennsylvania, Robert M. La Follette of Wisconsin, Joseph Medill McCormick of Illinois, George H. Moses of New Hampshire, George W. Norris of Nebraska, Miles Poindexter of Washington, James A. Reed of Missouri, Lawrence Y. Sherman of Illinois, and Charles S. Thomas of Colorado.[2] Fourteen of the group were Republicans; Reed and Thomas were the only Democrats.

1

The Senate's action was one that few contemporary observers would have predicted at the outset of the great debate. Championed by a President who boasted an impressive record of legislative accomplishments, favored by a large percentage of the American people, and approved in some form by eighty senators, the Treaty seemed certain to be passed. Even today historians continue to wonder at the combination of forces that produced the result. Many explanations, of course, have been advanced: Woodrow Wilson's stubborn refusal to compromise, Henry Cabot Lodge's hatred of Wilson, partisanship by both political parties, executive-legislative rivalry born of the Constitution's separation of powers, and sincere ideological disagreements.

Most accounts of the Treaty fight have been devoted to explaining why those who wanted or professed to want the Treaty approved were unable to reach an agreement. As a consequence of this emphasis, the sixteen senators who were openly committed to the Treaty's defeat have been relatively ignored, and their position distorted or misunderstood. This is unfortunate, since within the group were several of the outstanding senators of the twentieth century. In addition, a closer look at the irreconcilables and their interaction with Lodge and Wilson clarifies the position of these two protagonists. It is my hope, too, that this study will contribute to a better overall understanding of the League fight.

The bitter-enders often appear in historical accounts, as they did in their own time, as an ideologically homogeneous minority set off from the mainstream of American thought. They were and are pictured as blind obstructionists, more interested in destroying than in building, relying on blatant demagoguery to accomplish their ends. Their contribution, it is said, was nil; they submitted no viable alternatives to what they opposed, nor did they clarify the issues presented by the Treaty. Even their negative achievement in defeating the Treaty is explained away by the mistakes of Wilson, the schemings of Lodge, and by larger impersonal forces.

The irreconcilables naturally viewed themselves in quite a different light. They considered their opposition to the Treaty to be responsible. They believed they were positive, willing to present alternatives, and no more guilty of demagoguery than the Treaty's

1. Alice Roosevelt Longworth, *Crowded Hours* (New York, 1933), 292, 303.

2. There is much confusion about the number and identity of the irreconcilables. Different authors list twelve, thirteen, fourteen, fifteen, sixteen, nineteen, and "a dozen or so." The sixteen named above were the only senators to vote against the Treaty, to be paired against it, or to have it announced they would have voted against it on each of the four resolutions of approval.

defenders. Moreover, they saw themselves as courageous in voting their convictions. Many of their fellow senators, they believed, would have preferred to vote against the Treaty but did not do so for fear of the political consequences. The irreconcilables also thought that the American people, temporarily shocked by the horrors of war into a willingness to accept almost any "peace" treaty and any league of nations, would change their mind once they had heard specific arguments against *the* Treaty and *the* League and had gained the perspective of time. In later years, as the United States continued to remain outside the League, the irreconcilables liked to point out that they had been vindicated, that they had performed a valuable educative function in addition to having defeated the Treaty when it was presented. But the irreconcilables by no means drew the same lessons from their experience. They, in fact, called attention at the time to their own ideological and political diversity, whatever others might say.

The gap between the way the irreconcilables saw themselves and the way they have been seen by their critics is wide. In part this is because a few prominent irreconcilables have been singled out for more attention than the others and, by implication, these few have been judged representative of the group as a whole. If, however, one also examines the less well-known bitter-enders, the picture of the battalian of death is neither so bright as the bitter-enders themselves proclaimed nor so dim as their critics would maintain. The gap will never be closed, but it can be narrowed.

In presenting the irreconcilables as a group assuming a particular stand on the Treaty of Versailles, I have not endeavored to reconcile their individual positions at this time with what they said and did on other issues at other times in their careers, except in the immediate period preceding the Treaty debate. Sixteen biographical studies would no doubt clarify to some degree each man's position in 1919-1920, but that would be a different approach than the one I have taken. The appendix contains brief sketches of the men as they appeared in 1919. My purpose rather is to analyze both their ideas and their methods of implementing them as they pertained to the struggle over the Treaty, a struggle which in itself is an important chapter in recent American history and which for most of the participants marked the high point of their careers.

1 *THE ORIGINS OF THE FIGHT*

THE STRUGGLE over the Treaty of Versailles, and most particularly the League of Nations, emerged from the issues raised following the outbreak in July, 1914, of the First World War. Issues concerning neutral rights, military preparedness, freedom of the seas, secret diplomacy, and the Senate's role in making foreign policy were debated with a close awareness of their meaning for the postwar settlement. There was also the matter of a world organization, which had received critical attention well before the United States entered the war in April, 1917. In the debates over these issues, the irreconcilables in many cases manifested attitudes and opinions that would characterize their opposition to the Treaty of Versailles; in a few cases significant changes in outlook occurred over the course of several years. But in either instance there were fundamental divisions and disagreements among the group in wartime that continued into the Treaty fight.

In 1914 ten of the sixteen had been elected to the Senate: Borah, Brandegee, Fall, Gronna, Norris, La Follette, Poindexter, Reed, Sherman, and Thomas. Four more—Fernald, France, Johnson, and Knox—took office before April, 1917, in time to vote on the war declaration. The final two—McCormick and Moses—were not elected to the Senate until 1918, although McCormick served as a representative from 1916 to 1918.

The irreconcilables' reaction to the initial stages of the war apparently differed little if at all from that of most Americans: shock and dismay mixed with a conviction that the United States must remain neutral. Woodrow Wilson's proclamation of neutrality on August 8, 1914, and his early efforts to implement it won acceptance, enthusiastically in a few instances, more often in a matter-of-course way or by silence.[1] There were a few scattered criti-

cisms of Wilson when 128 Americans lost their lives following the sinking of the British liner *Lusitania* by a German submarine on May 7, 1915. Borah, for example, charged that not enough had been done to prepare for such a crisis, and Fall wanted "just punishment" meted out to Germany if it disregarded Wilson's note warning against future transgressions of American rights.[2] But these were not criticisms of Wilson's basic policy. At this date no irreconcilable wished to break relations with Germany, much less to declare war. Instead, there was a continued desire to maintain a neutral posture.

This general consensus, however, left many questions to be debated. Neutrality was feasible as long as it maintained the nation's security and honor. But what constituted security and honor? Were these objectives sometimes contradictory? And if agreement were reached on their meaning, how could they be accomplished? Could they be accomplished by greatly increasing military strength? Or did added military power paradoxically reduce security by increasing tensions that led to counterarmaments? Was the demand for military preparedness solely a response to the security needs of the country? Or was it the result of special interests seeking their own selfish ends? Would the emphasis on preparedness mean a neglect of pressing domestic problems and even lead to a large military establishment that endangered the very foundation of democracy? How firmly should the United States adhere to traditional policies, such as freedom of the seas, in view of changed military conditions, notably submarine warfare?

Such questions were staggeringly complex, and the complexities were compounded when these questions were linked, as inevitably they were, to the subject of peacemaking. The man ultimately responsible for the answers to these questions was the President; yet the burden also fell on senators and representatives who were compelled to make decisions on the great issues of the day.

The irreconcilables divided into two factions on the issues surrounding neutrality. The first, small in numbers but more intellectually cohesive, opposed increased military preparedness and favored neutrality. The second, larger numerically but not nearly

1. Arthur S. Link, *Wilson: The Struggle For Neutrality, 1914-1915* (Princeton, N.J., 1960), 6-7. Generalizations about the group's attitude on any specific issue rest primarily on information concerning those who were in Congress at the time. The irreconcilables actually had little to say about Wilson's neutrality policies until the spring of 1915. Like Wilson, they often seemed more interested in the Mexican revolution than in World War I.

2. *New York Times*, May 9, 16, 1915.

so united in its thinking, supported preparedness and, after March, 1917, opposed neutrality.

The smaller group was made up of three middle western Republican progressives, close personal friends who held a common political philosophy and who had fought together in many victorious causes before 1914: Robert La Follette of Wisconsin, George Norris of Nebraska, and Asle Gronna of North Dakota. After 1914 they continued to occupy common ground, but now, as foreign affairs assumed more importance, their victories became fewer. The peace progressives, as they may be called, strongly supported Wilson's early efforts to maintain neutrality.[3] La Follette, defending the President against fellow Republicans who questioned his commitment to neutrality, declared in February, 1915: "Wilson will not plunge this country into war. At the head of the nation that stands for peace, he has guarded our neutrality with noble care."[4] But La Follette soon grew disillusioned with Wilson as the noble guardian of peace. By the autumn of 1915, the President was pursuing a more anti-German, pro-British policy and at the same time he had authorized increased arms production.[5] His actions distressed the peace progressives, and they now branded him as one of the self-seeking, bellicose, pro-Ally preparedness crowd. As more and more progressives came to accept the President's new course, these three peace progressives found themselvs to be an ever-smaller minority, deserted by most of their comrades, fighting a losing battle. But the more hopeless their cause, the more convinced they were that egregious errors were being committed.

Their criticisms were many. They argued that war would mean economic slavery for the masses, the restriction if not curtailment of long-needed domestic reforms, an atmosphere of militarism incompatible with American freedoms. The preparedness movement, they believed, was the result of "an artificial, cold-blooded, selfish propaganda" campaign waged by the financial and commercial interests of the country.[6] These interests, hiding their greed behind

3. The phrase is used by Robert Seager in "The Progressives and American Foreign Policy, 1898-1917: An Analysis of the Attitudes of the Leaders of the Progressive Movement Toward External Affairs" (Ph.D. diss., Ohio State University, 1954), 314. Seager includes Hiram Johnson among the peace progressives. I have chosen to place him in the other group both because of his vote for war and because of his later views on the Treaty. His position was closer to Borah and Reed than to La Follette, Norris, and Gronna.

4. Belle Case La Follette and Fola La Follette, *Robert M. La Follette*, 2 vols. (New York, 1953), 1: 502, 517.

5. Arthur S. Link, *Wilson: Confusions and Crises, 1915-1916* (Princeton, N. J., 1964), 15-24.

6. *Congressional Record*, 64 Cong., 1 sess., 11330-31 (July 20, 1916).

the facade of patriotism, sought to convince Americans that their security depended on an immediate and extensive program to enlarge the military forces. Another insidious threat to America's neutrality, according to the peace progressives, was the practice of secret diplomacy. Secret diplomacy had frequently led to war, they claimed, because it permitted a few men—military leaders hungry for glory or politicians willing to sacrifice anything for "a relatively unimportant diplomatic victory"—to control the destiny of the masses of people who were essentially peace-loving.[7]

Contrary to what some preparedness advocates insisted, said the peace progressives, the nation was not endangered by the European war. America's natural geographic isolation, though not so formidable as before, was still sufficient to protect it from any potential invader. Besides, as Gronna remarked in July, 1916, European nations would soon lie prostrate, their soldiers slaughtered and their treasuries exhausted.[8] If the United States merely continued its pre-1914 rate of military growth, its strength would be equal or superior to that of any of the belligerents by the end of the war.

In addition to these largely negative arguments against going to war, La Follette, Norris, and Gronna marshaled positive arguments emphasizing the international benefits to be gained from neutrality. By remaining neutral, so began this part of their position, the United States would be able to exert a powerful influence in behalf of international peace and justice. As early as February 8, 1915, La Follette proposed an international conference of all neutral nations to promote the following objectives: the early termination of war; the limitation of armaments and nationalization of factories producing armaments; the halting of the international arms traffic; "the ultimate establishment of an international tribunal where any nation may be heard on any issue involving rights vital to its peace and the development of its national life, a tribunal whose decrees shall be enforced by the enlightened judgment of the world"; the establishment of a federation of neutral nations to maintain and preserve commercial rights; the taking of any future action "to establish permanent world peace."

Only the neutral nations, La Follette stated, possessed the impartiality and good will necessary for mediation that might end the war. He envisioned no physical force to support this mediation. Yet "the moral effect of a combination of all neutral nations, backed by the united voice of 800,000,000 people," would be immeasurable.

7. Ibid., 3887 (March 10, 1916), 11352 (July 21, 1916).
8. Ibid., 11352 (July 21, 1916); also see Norris's remarks, 11188 (July 17, 1916).

If neutrals were not moved by "broad humanitarian considerations" to undertake mediation, a concern for their own sovereign rights, integrity, and peace should impel them to act. America's policy of neutrality must not be misconstrued, however, as mere selfish indifference. Rather, according to La Follette, it was "based on sympathetic love and understanding. As a people we are intensely interested in the cessation of a war that is slaying our kindred, bringing indescribable desolation to the lands we love and to the homes of our fathers." The United States did not wish "to see the map of Europe changed by might of conquest." Instead it believed that each of the European nations should preserve its "natural autonomy; that each should have the largest opportunity for self-development, the largest share in the world's progress; and that each should be given, as of right, access to the highways of the sea."[9] La Follette thus advocated several of the same goals that Wilson would support: self-determination, freedom of the seas, a peace without victory, and arms limitation.

George Norris, La Follette's fellow progressive from Nebraska, held similar opinions about the benefits of neutrality. By staying out of war, Norris declared, the United States would retain the respect of others for its integrity, generosity, and sympathy for and protection of the weaker nations. Free of suspicion—"our entire national life has been emblematic of an unselfish respect for the right of other nations"—America could offer "the proferred hand of universal brotherhood" with the expectation that it would be gratefully received.[10]

Norris's peace proposals were embodied in an amendment to the naval appropriation bill of July, 1916. The amendment directed the President to halt ship construction until he had "made an effort to secure an agreement for . . . a permanent international court of arbitration" to be established after the war. In addition, Wilson was asked to advise the belligerents that the United States would participate in peace negotiations and support not only an international court but also arms limitation and an international navy, composed, partly, of American ships, to enforce the court's decrees. That Norris was ambivalent on the subject of an international navy

9. Ibid., 63 Cong., 3 sess., 3230 (February 8, 1915); and for an elaboration on his proposals, 3631-63 (February 12, 1915). Also see La Follette and La Follette, *La Follette*, 2: 954; Ellen Torelle, *The Political Philosophy of Robert M. La Follette* (Madison, Wis., 1920), 413-14; Padriac C. Kennedy, "La Follette's Imperialist Flirtation," *Pacific Historical Review* 29 (May 1960): 291-93.

10. *Cong. Record*, 64 Cong., 1 sess., 10932 (July 13, 1916).

became clear as he continued his address. "A treaty of peace that would turn the navies of the world into scrap iron and provide for a few vessels that should be international in their service, for the purpose of doing police duty, will bring about a never-ending peace." In all likelihood, he said, an international navy would never be called into service. Instead, "we could trust to the honor of the nation and to the enlightened public sentiment of the civilized world" to enforce the court's judgments.[11]

Asle Gronna, the third peace progressive, never matched his more articulate colleagues in presenting positive suggestions for peacekeeping, but he agreed with them on limiting preparedness and he voted with them on most domestic issues. This last point is noteworthy because many of their ideas on international affairs were derived from what they had learned, or thought they had learned, as domestic reformers. Protecting America's foreign policy from predatory warmongering businessmen, they thought, was much like protecting domestic institutions from these same businessmen. Similarily, open diplomacy would do in foreign policy what reforms such as the initiative, referendum, and recall did at home, namely, give the people larger voice in their affairs.

The peace progressives' reliance on public opinion as the means of enforcing peace reflects their faith in reason and democracy, but it seems at odds with a lesson they had learned in domestic politics: moral force alone could never check the foes of reform. This inconsistency in regard to sanctions is not explained away merely by saying they were provincial Midwesterners unaware of how the world had shrunk. Norris, for example, based his proposals on the interdependency of nations. The growth of trade, he observed, had brought economic interdependency; advances in science, technology, and especially in communications led to social, political, and cultural interdependency. His conclusion that "when we are brought into this close relationship the scales fall from the eyes, prejudice flees from the heart, and we realize that humanity is the same everywhere," may seem absurdly utopian and naive, but it did not spring from provincialism.[12] Rather than provincialism, the peace progressives' inconsistency in endorsing force in domestic affairs and abjuring it in international affairs was due to the con-

11. Ibid., 11185-91 (July 17, 1916), 10933 (July 13, 1916). Also see George Norris, *Fighting Liberal* (New York, 1945), 204; an early statement of Norris's peace views is an article written after his return from the International Peace Conference at Brussels in 1905, copy in the George Norris Papers (Manuscripts Division, Library of Congress), Box 10.

12. *Cong. Record*, 64 Cong., 1 sess., 10931 (July 13, 1916).

tradiction in their conception of the United States vis-à-vis the rest of the world, a contradiction apparent in Norris's remarks. While professing that humanity was the same everywhere, Norris at the same time viewed America as unique, standing above those less fortunate nations senselessly engaged in a war that had little to do with mankind's real concerns. The United States must not only remain free of that war; it must also show the way to a better day. Hence, to become committed to the necessity of military power as a means of enforcement would be to admit the United States was not unique and that interdependency had not caused prejudice and other such evils to disappear.

While La Follette, Norris, and Gronna were not the only ir-reconcilables to believe in America's uniqueness and moral superi-ority—indeed, this belief was shared by Wilson and his Senate sup-porters—both their vision of the future and their plan to attain it were special. More idealistic than their fellow bitter-enders, having greater expectations, these three would remain hopeful and even openminded about President Wilson's peace plans (as distinct from his preparedness and war messages) long after other irreconcilables had rejected them; but their disappointment and disillusionment, when it eventually came, would be the greater.

Of the twelve irreconcilables who favored increased preparedness and voted for war in 1917, seven were in the Senate at the time of the key preparedness debates of 1915 and 1916. Of these seven, Frank Brandegee and Miles Poindexter headed the drive for an enlarged army and navy. While far apart on many issues—Brandegee was an acid-tongued tory from Connecticut, Poindexter a Bull Moose Progressive from Washington[13]—they voted as one on preparedness. It was Brandegee, however, who delivered the more biting speeches, in particular against the peace progressives. His ideas, juxtaposed to those of La Follette, Norris, and Gronna, show clearly the split among the irreconcilables during the war and anticipate their later division over the Treaty.

Brandegee denounced the peace progressives' ideas on world peace no less than their opposition to preparedness, as demonstrated in his speech of February 22, 1915, a week after La Follette had urged the neutral nations to unite for peace. Brandegee considered it foolhardy even to discuss the possibility of universal peace. "I

13. After 1916 Poindexter moved far to the right, to "the shoot- 'em-at-peep-o'-day and bathe-'em-in-buckets-of-blood right." William Hard, "The Irreconcilables," *New Republic* 22 (March 31, 1920): 148; Howard W. Allen, "Miles Poindexter and the Progressive Movement," *Pacific Northwest Quarterly* 53 (July 1962): 114-22, traces the rise and decline of Poindexter's liberalism.

should consider myself a candidate for a madhouse if I should undertake to shape the policy of this great Nation upon any such conception as that." To talk, as these men did, "about the beauties of beating swords into plowshares and setting a good example to people who are . . . cutting each other's throats" was to talk nonsense. Moreover, he stated, the peace progressives were ignorant of their own nation's history if they thought America had risen to greatness by espousing high-sounding principles. "Grown men" should know "how we have established our institutions, how our fathers . . . have had to fight with the strong arm to maintain what they thought was right and to maintain the very life . . . of this country." Misreading history was a risky if common practice; even more dangerous, according to Brandegee, was the habit of wishful thinking about the future. It was this confusing what ought to be with what was, this avoidance of hard fact, of reality, that caused the peace progressives to make their ridiculous proposals.

Brandegee considered his ideas, in contrast to those of the peace progressives, to be based on the hard facts of reality. "I am not discussing what may happen thousands of years hence, perhaps when all the rest of the races of the world have been educated to the point of Christianity and the kindness and sweetness which ought to characterize people if they practice what they preach." Senators must talk about existing conditions, and he for one was not willing to sit quietly "with the pillars of the temples of the world smashing and tumbling all about my ears and lull myself to sleep with any dolce far niente talk about universal peace and sympathy and the concordance of nations." Such talk he regarded "in its effect, though, of course, not in its intention as treason to this country."[14]

During the debate over the naval appropriation bill of July, 1916, Brandegee again attacked "the pacifists and that school." He was unhappy with the notion advanced by some opponents of preparedness that America enjoyed the love and respect of other nations, that the European powers after the war would be divided and exhausted, and that therefore the United States would be safe if it continued in its current state of military readiness. Such thinking, he said, rested on an unrealistic appraisal of international politics. His own analysis of the future foresaw danger: "The alliances of the European and Asiatic powers are shifting sand. . . . At the close of this war, with all the restraints torn down, with international law made a 'scrap of paper,' with the wreck of Europe lying at their feet, there is nothing at all to prevent Germany and

14. *Cong. Record,* 63 Cong., 3 sess., 4270 (February 22, 1915).

Japan . . . making an alliance, and we may be driven to fight on both coasts of this country."[15]

Miles Poindexter, while less astringent in his language, concurred in Brandegee's judgments on preparedness and peace. It was absurd, he said, to talk of the United States rescuing Europe from its alleged state of depravity. Such moralistic effusiveness might satisfy many Americans, and it was "theoretically perhaps defensible upon some high plane of brotherly love; but we all know that international relations are not . . . determined by principles of brotherly love." America's rivals did not conduct their relations on any such principles. "On the contrary, it can not be denied that matters of self-interest govern."[16]

Apart from Brandegee and Poindexter, the other five irreconcilables who supported preparedness did so with less consistency and fewer criticisms of the peace progressives. William E. Borah, for example, accepted the view that nations attached little importance to past friendships and moral obligations, and that therefore a larger navy was imperative; but he was as fervent as La Follette in condemning secret diplomacy. Lawrence Sherman, one of the two irreconcilables from Illinois, voted for almost all significant preparedness legislation, but, like the peace progressives, he also claimed that unscrupulous economic interests on the East Coast exaggerated the need for armaments. Moreover, again like the peace progressives, he believed for a time in America's ability, as a neutral, to rebuild the shattered foundations of international law and morality after the war. Nevertheless, he was more nationalistic and more willing to use force to preserve peace than were La Follette, Norris, and Gronna. James Reed and Charles Thomas, the two Democrats, showed the least consistency. On sixteen roll call votes Reed supported preparedness on eleven occasions and voted against it on five. Thomas, who split his votes evenly for and against, frequently denounced advocates of greatly increased preparedness, such as Brandegee; but he favored at least moderate preparedness measures, most of which the peace progressives opposed. Albert Fall was a strong proponent of preparedness, but he missed most of the key roll call votes.[17]

15. Ibid., 64 Cong., 1 sess., 11377-78 (July 21, 1916).
16. Ibid., 1145 (January 17, 1916).
17. For Borah and Sherman, see the following references in *Cong. Record*: 63 Cong., 2 sess., 9728 (June 3, 1914); 64 Cong., 1 sess., 1438 (January 24, 1916), 3470, 3474-81 (March 3, 1916). Sherman's views on international law may be seen in his speech "The Duty of Neutrals in Creating a World Court," delivered before the World Court Congress meeting in New York City on May 3, 1916, copy in Lawrence Sherman Papers (in possession of his

Before 1917, then, the irreconcilables disagreed on two principal questions: the degree of preparedness that was necessary and wise, and the action, if any, to be taken by the neutral United States in creating postwar peace machinery. The peace progressives saw the two questions as intertwined and almost of equal importance, whereas the remaining irreconcilables tended to regard preparedness as the paramount question, and thought the general discussion of peace premature and the specific proposals unrealistic. La Follette, Norris, and Gronna were sympathetic toward Wilson's interest in arranging a negotiated peace but alienated by his preparedness bent. The faction led by Brandegee and Poindexter generally supported the President's preparedness measures, but were reluctant to broach subjects such as self-determination, disarmament, and a postwar association of nations.

Notwithstanding their differences over preparedness and postwar questions, the irreconcilables were agreed until 1917 that the United States should remain neutral. This agreement disappeared, however, when Germany announced in January, 1917, that its submarines would sink neutral as well as enemy ships. Wilson now severed diplomatic relations with Germany and shortly thereafter asked Congress for authority to arm American merchant ships. The peace progressives, certain that this action would draw the United States into the war, helped lead a filibuster at the close of the Sixty-fourth Congress which prevented the armed-ships bill from coming to a vote. Wilson was incensed as perhaps he never before had been as President, and he denounced the filibusterers as "a little group of willful men" who had "rendered the great government of the United States helpless and contemptible."[18] The filibuster actually proved meaningless, for the administration found authority elsewhere to arm the ships. After another month during

---

daughter, Mrs. Marion W. Graham, Daytona Beach, Fla.). The seventeen roll call votes I have used are as follows: *Cong. Record*, 63 Cong., 2 sess., 9641 (June 2, 1914); 64 Cong., 1 sess., 4609-10 (March 22, 1916), 6198 (April 15, 1916), 6359 (a), 6359 (b), 6368, 6371 (a), 6371 (b), 6374 (April 18, 1916), 11192 (July 17, 1916), 11367, 11372-73 (a), 11373 (b), 11378, 11384 (July 21, 1916), 11564-65 (July 25, 1916). The votes alone do not show the wide difference between Reed and Thomas. Reed was highly critical of the peace progressives, although he also on occasion attacked Republican proponents of preparedness. See *Cong. Record*, 63 Cong., 2 sess., 9379 (May 28, 1914); 64 Cong., 1 sess., 5420 (April 4, 1916), Appendix, 127-32; 63 Cong., 1 sess., 5945 (November 20, 1913), 2 sess., 16310-11 (October 8, 1914); 64 Cong., 1 sess., 5203-04 (March 31, 1916).

18. Ray Stannard Baker and William E. Dodd, eds., *The Public Papers of Woodrow Wilson: The New Democracy, 1913-1917*, 2 vols. (New York, 1925-1927), 2: 435.

which several American ships were sunk, Wilson went before Congress to deliver his war message. It was answered by the passage of resolutions in both houses of Congress overwhelmingly in approval. All the irreconcilables but La Follette, Norris, and Gronna cast yea votes.[19]

Before the final roll call, old arguments were reiterated and harsh words exchanged. Norris, in rhetoric reminiscent of William Jennings Bryan's Cross of Gold speech, denounced the munitions-makers and profiteers: "I would like to say to this war god, you shall not coin into gold the lifeblood of my brethren." James Reed replied with a savage attack, accusing Norris of nearly treasonable language in saying the dollar sign had been put on the American flag. It was not a war for profits, said Reed, but for preserving American sovereignty and dignity. Borah, in explaining his vote for war, denied the peace progressives' contention that this act would end America's policy of "no entangling alliances," or that the nation had surrendered its future to England. Nor did he, like some prowar progressives, see it as a crusade for humanity: "I hold fast and firmly [he said] to the doctrine that our own national security, our own national honor, the right of our own people and the lives of our own citizens are alone, when challenged and assailed, sufficient to justify me in voting for a declaration of war. I join no crusade; I seek or accept no alliances; I obligate this Government to no other power. I make war alone for my countrymen and their rights, for my country and its honor." Joseph France, newly elected irreconcilable from Maryland, demurred: "To me this was no holy war until we entered it; now it has become such." "I do not subscribe to any of the doctrines of materialism," he declared. Beneath the battle, the blood, and the sacrifice, "beneath all the vast ebb and flow of human events, a divine purposiveness moves resistlessly on to the achievement of great and ethical ends." (France would by 1919 move very close to the peace progressives.) Brandegee had some final words for the antiwar irreconcilables: "They are not talking about our country. They proclaim what they say is a higher doctrine. They belong to the brotherhood of man, no man's country, and they are wandering around in circles of futility closely approaching treason." Thus were the bitter-enders divided as America entered the war.[20]

19. *Cong. Record*, 65 Cong., 1 sess., 261 (April 4, 1917), 413 (April 5, 1917).
20. Ibid., 214, 215, 253 (April 4, 1917). For Brandegee and France see *Cong. Record*, 64 Cong., 2 sess., 4866 (March 3, 1917); 65 Cong., 1 sess., 2049 (May 10, 1917).

From 1914 to 1917 the leading topics of debate in the country were preparedness and neutral rights. But at the same time, countless Americans were looking ahead toward the war's end, when the question of how to preserve the peace would replace that of how to avoid, or, once in, how to win the war. Various organizations existed to give serious consideration to the subject. The best known and most influential was the League to Enforce Peace. It was founded in 1915 by William Howard Taft, Hamilton Holt, A. Lawrence Lowell, and others, for the purpose of establishing a postwar association of nations. These men believed that the old and, in their eyes, discredited balance of power "system" must yield in favor of an association of nations that would rely primarily upon physical force, not public opinon, to "guarantee" peace.[21]

In May, 1916, Woodrow Wilson spoke to a League to Enforce Peace meeting in Washington, D. C. The President outlined his views on the postwar settlement, listing self-determination, respect for the independence and integrity of small as well as large nations, and freedom from wars of aggression as fundamental prerequisites of a stable peace. Above all he wanted to see the United States take the lead in a "universal association of the nations to maintain the inviolate security of the highway of the seas for the common and unhindered use of all the nations of the world, and to prevent any war begun either contrary to treaty covenants or without warning and full submission of the causes to the opinion of the world—a virtual guarantee of territorial integrity and political independence."[22] In the months following this address Wilson reiterated his desire for a league.

There was little congressional reaction to Wilson's ideas until December, 1916, when the President sent a note to the belligerent nations asking them to state their terms for an armistice. Both sides, the note read, had professed to be fighting for similar objectives: ending aggressive wars, giving small nations equality, and abandoning balance of power politics for an association of nations. To accomplish these objectives after the war, Americans stood ready to "cooperate . . . with every influence and resource at their command."[23]

Three days after the President's note, a resolution was introduced

21. Ruhl J. Bartlett, *The League to Enforce Peace* (Chapel Hill, N. C., 1944), 42-45.

22. Baker and Dodd, eds., *The New Democracy*, 2: 184-88.

23. *Cong. Record*, 64 Cong., 2 sess., 633-34 (December 21, 1916). The note was sent on December 18, 1916.

in the Senate which endorsed Wilson's words as expressing the overwhelming sentiment of the American people.[24] This resolution touched off the first Senate debate on a league specifically suggested by the President and committing the United States to its purposes. Appropriately, the man who introduced it was Gilbert Hitchcock of Nebraska, who later became minority leader for the Democrats and in 1919-1920 had responsibility for steering the Treaty of Versailles through the Senate; and the senator who first opposed the resolution was William E. Borah, sometimes called the original irreconcilable, and one of Hitchcock's most persistent critics during the Treaty fight.

Borah quickly obtained recognition after the resolution. Warning his colleagues that the resolution carried "tremendous consequences," he announced that he would object to it, causing it to be referred to the Foreign Relations Committee. Two weeks later Hitchcock's resolution was reported out. Gone were the overall endorsement of the Presidential note and the reference to public sentiment. Borah was still not satisfied. His remarks, however, were directed not so much against the resolution as against the broad concept of a league of nations.[25]

He began by saying that Wilson's note of December 18, together with his address before the League to Enforce Peace and other speeches, initiated "an entire change of policy with reference to our foreign affairs." He was especially concerned with that part of the President's note which pledged America's "every influence and resource" to accomplish the belligerent nations' stated objectives. One of those objectives, according to Wilson, was a league of nations, which would presumably guarantee the "territorial integrity and political independence" of its smaller and weaker members. Therefore, said Borah, Wilson's pledge "if it means anything at all," means "that the Army and the Navy of the United States . . . will be at the command of any plan agreed upon between the Government and the nations of Europe for the protection of the small nations of that country [sic]." But the worst part of the President's plan was that the United States would agree "to authorize other nations to make war upon [it] if we refuse to submit some vital issue of ours to the decision of some European or Asiatic nations. This approaches, to my mind, moral treason." Borah had two reasons for calling Wilson's proposal "moral treason." In the first place, a league of nations denied the validity of the

24. Ibid., 635 (December 21, 1916).
25. Ibid., 636 (December 21, 1916), 791 (January 3, 1917).

Monroe Doctrine and "no entangling alliances." In the second place, and more to the point, collective security was not a realistic substitute for past policies. It did not take into account the forces of nationalism and self-interest. To assume the United States would sacrifice its soldiers and money to enforce peace between countries whose quarrels might have little bearing on its own security and well-being was highly dubious. For Borah, then, the issue was already drawn: the league idea presupposed a fundamental change in America's foreign policy, and he wanted his fellow senators to declare themselves for or against it. "I insist the question is plainly here, and I do not propose that it shall be put aside. I want you to take the responsibility or renounce it."[26] This would be his theme throughout the later debates of 1919-1920.

Though Borah was the only irreconcilable to speak extensively on the Hitchcock resolution, other senators had questions about the President's note. Was it Constitutional? Did Wilson have the authority to ask the belligerents to state their peace terms? Or, contrariwise, did the resolution project the Senate into an area reserved for the President? More meaningfully, in view of the future struggle over the Treaty of Versailles, several senators wondered if the resolution might not be an effort on Wilson's part to get an early commitment to the league idea before submitting an actual proposal to the Senate in a treaty. Still other senators believed that the Committee-amended resolution did not make explicit the Senate's approval of only that part of the December 18 note in which peace terms had been requested. After further discussion and amendment, the resolution came to a vote. By the substantial margin of 48 to 17, it passed. Borah, apparently satisfied that it was innocuous, and having voiced his opinion on the underlying issue, voted for it. Also supporting it were Norris, La Follette, Thomas, and Reed. Brandegee, Poindexter, and Sherman voted no; the remaining bitter-enders abstained and gave no public indication of their preferences.[27] While the vote itself had little meaning other than to show the continued division among the battalian of death, the debate on the resolution was a brief sign of what Wilson could expect in the not-distant future.

26. Ibid., 892-96 (January 5, 1917). Borah received praise for his speech from men of such opposite viewpoints as William Jennings Bryan and Theodore Roosevelt. Interestingly, Henry White, Wilson's choice as one of the commissioners to the peace conference in 1918, wrote to Borah endorsing the speech. Bryan to Borah, January 11, 1917, Roosevelt to Borah, January 15, 1917, White to Borah, January 9, 1916 [sic], William E. Borah Papers (Manuscripts Division, Library of Congress), Boxes 182, 183.
27. Cong. Record, 64 Cong., 2 sess., 883-84, 896-97 (January 5, 1917).

Another sign came on January 22, 1917, when Wilson clarified and enlarged upon some of his recent statements about a peace settlement. Though addressing the Senate, the President "would fain believe" he was speaking to "the silent mass of mankind everywhere," whose desires were those of the United States: a "peace without victory," a peace of fairness, justice, equality, self-determination, freedom of the seas, and arms reduction. To maintain such a peace, the United States was prepared to join an association of nations in which entangling alliances would give way to a concert of power, in which the Monroe Doctrine would become "the doctrine of the world."[28]

Wilson's speech was received warmly by Democratic legislators, coolly by Republicans; but there were exceptions, notably among the irreconcilables. On the Republican side, La Follette was conspicuous by his kind words for the address. More typical of Republican irreconcilables was Sherman's assessment of Wilson's ideas as "humanitarian in purpose but impracticable in operation." Among Democrats Reed stood out because of his hostile remarks. The Missouri bitter-ender wanted nothing to do with an organization which, he implied, would be controlled by European monarchies. The other Democratic irreconcilable, Charles Thomas, reacted quite differently. He was, in fact, inspired by Wilson's address to prepare a speech of his own, his first of any substance devoted to the subject of peace.[29]

Thomas thought the President's speech was "one of the most lofty conceptions of a peace founded on righteousness that has ever fallen from the lips of a statesman." It was the kind of a peace the United States should help to preserve, "with arms, if necessary." Its principles showed recognition of America's evolution from eighteenth- and nineteenth-century isolationism to its present status as a world power. Yet Thomas was also skeptical. He doubted that the warring nations shared these conceptions of a just peace. He questioned the permanency of any peace settlement that avoided the problem of trade barriers between nations. Finally, he wondered whether man, at his present stage of moral evolution (if indeed he had evolved morally), was prepared to accept the Wilsonian ideals. For, he continued, "human nature is the same as it always has been. Man is a fighting animal. He is a selfish animal." As were individual men, so were nations. "The things which have caused war in the past are the things which will cause war in the future.

28. Arthur S. Link, *Wilson: Campaigns for Progressivism and Peace, 1916-1917* (Princeton, N. J., 1965), 265-68.
29. *New York Times*, January 23, 1917; *Washington Post*, January 22, 1917.

Competition between peoples, the racial hatreds existing everywhere, the suspicions and resentments engendered through commercial strife, . . . and, above all, increasing armaments." Nevertheless, Thomas concluded on a less pessimistic note, Wilson's speech should not be dismissed. It had focused the world's attention upon the great subject of peace; and future generations, in "the leaven of time," would possibly adopt its suggestions as standards of conduct.[30]

The "Peace without Victory" address generated considerable discussion for about ten days. Once Germany announced the resumption of unrestricted submarine warfare, attention switched to the imminence of war. It is significant that this ten-day period—from January 23 to February 1—was marked by increasing displeasure, mainly among Republican senators, with Wilson's ideas and even more with his methods of presenting them. After February, 1917, the shift in the debate to breaking relations with Germany, the Zimmermann telegram, the armed-ships bill, and finally to war itself and all that it involved, tended to obscure (perhaps for some later scholars, certainly for many of the participants) this growing opposition. The irreconcilables who at this time registered their dissatisfaction were later fond of reminding Wilson of their earlier protests.

Sherman spoke most articulately for those who distrusted the President's conduct toward the Senate and who suspected that his December peace note, the subsequent Hitchcock resolution, and the "Peace without Victory" address were part of a scheme "to forstall and foreclose independent action on the part of the Senate." Was it not Wilson's purpose, Sherman asked, to appeal to public opinion in advance of Senate action so that the league idea "might sink unanswered into the minds of the general public . . .? Was it not . . . for the purpose of preventing dispassionate action by the Senate, making us accept whatever treaty shall be hereafter transmitted to us, and compelling us to ratify it by the coercion of the public opinion sought to be created?"[31] Not all the bitter-enders, however, were critical. It is noteworthy that Sherman's remarks were immediately challenged, not by a Democrat, as might have been expected, but by George Norris, a Republican peace progressive. Norris got up to say that he, for one, did not suspect the President of devious motives in his recent address to the Senate.[32]

Other irreconcilables were letting it be known they had serious

30. *Cong. Record,* 64 Cong., 2 sess., 2371-72 (February 1, 1917).
31. Ibid., 1884 (January 24, 1917).
32. Ibid.

doubts about the idea of a league. Philander Knox replied to an inquiry from the League to Enforce Peace with a polite rejection of its purposes.[33] Albert Fall indicated his concern in an exchange of words in the Senate with Democratic Senator John Shafroth, who had proposed the establishment of an international court with the power to enforce its decrees. Fall wanted to know where the authority to declare war would reside. Could the court order the United States to fight or would Congress retain that power? Shafroth obviously had not given this question much thought: he first replied that a Constitutional amendment would be necessary to transfer the power to the court, but upon further questioning by Fall, he grew evasive and would not admit that Congress would relinquish its authority.[34] Here in 1917 was a preview not only of the substance of the 1919 Treaty debate but also of the style: an irreconcilable on the offensive, probing for weaknesses in the enemy's arguments. By 1919 the defenders of the Treaty of Versailles were better prepared to answer questions, especially those about collective security. But the irreconcilables were also more skilled; moreover, in 1919 the debate was concerned with a document of 268 pages, a voluminous source from which to draw questions.

The 1917 debate over a league faded quickly following Germany's submarine challenge. After the United States declared war, harmony, not debate, was the watchword. While the irreconcilables generally followed the President's leadership, they did not forsake all criticism of his policies. Particularly as the war progressed, many of them attacked the waste and inefficiency, restrictions on civil liberties, and partisanship toward favored economic groups. They contended, further, that Wilson had not defined clearly and precisely America's war aims. He was guilty, they charged, of vague generalities and inconsistencies, in short, of muddled thinking. In private their remarks became more pointed. Wilson was a "rotten" administrator and a "wretched" executive, Medill McCormick wrote.[35] Hiram Johnson privately viewed the President as an

33. John H. Latane, ed., *Development of the League of Nations Idea: Documents and Correspondence of Theodore Marburg,* 2 vols. (New York, 1932), 1: 63.

34. *Cong. Record,* 64 Cong., 2 sess., 1881-82 (January 24, 1917); and see ibid., 1951 (January 25, 1917) for a resolution introduced by Borah to reaffirm the Senate's "faith and confidence in the permanent worth and wisdom" of the policies of the Founding Fathers. Borah saw "a vast amount of influence and money" behind the league proposition. Borah to T. N. Williams, January 31, 1917, Borah Papers, Box 182.

35. McCormick to Richard Lloyd Jones, January 15, 1918, Medill McCormick Papers (in possession of his daughter, Mrs. Garvin E. Tankersley, Washington, D. C.).

"absolute dictator and czar." Johnson would refrain from saying publicly all that he felt so as not to detract from the war effort. But, he vowed, "there are some of us who will hold him to a strict accountability in the future, and while his shall be the power, his, as well, shall be the responsibility. While today, he is undoubtedly able to get by with our people with policies and with expressions wholly at variance with each other, I firmly believe the day of reckoning is coming."[36]

In January, 1918, discussion of peace terms revived, following Wilson's address to Congress in which he presented, in fourteen points, "the program of the world's peace, [and] therefore . . . our program." As in his "Peace without Victory" address Wilson stressed altruism. "What we demand in this war . . . is nothing peculiar to ourselves." The fourteen points for peace included "open convenants openly arrived at," freedom of the seas, removal of trade restrictions, reduction of armaments, impartial settlement of colonial claims, and, points six through thirteen, self-determination for various European subject peoples and nations. The fourteenth point was almost an imperative: "a general association of nations must be formed" to guarantee "political and economic independence and territorial integrity to great and small states alike."[37]

The Fourteen Points address, perhaps the most famous address Wilson ever made, occupied an important place in the Treaty fight. It became a key document, a point of reference for all factions in the struggle. Significantly, it provoked almost no unfavorable comment at the time. This fact later permitted Wilson to accuse the irreconcilables of gross hypocrisy for their opposition to the Treaty. The bitter-enders would answer this accusation in a typical and effective fashion by countercharging that the Treaty of Versailles did not embody the principles stated in the Fourteen Points. Or they could change tack to suggest that Wilson was the one guilty of hypocrisy because he had espoused millenial ideals that he knew could never be fully attained; or if he actually did believe they could be attained, he was either a blind visionary or an incompetent diplomat. Some irreconcilables could also say they had either withheld comment at the time of the address or had made certain qualifications in their acceptance of it. They claimed—and with justification in most cases—that had it not been wartime their reaction would have been less sympathetic, and they cited as evidence their pre-war attacks on a league.

36. Johnson to Meyer Lissner, April 9, 1917, Johnson to Joseph Scott, June 25, 1917, Hiram Johnson Papers (University of California Library, Berkeley).
37. *New York Times,* January 9, 1918.

While the bitter-enders could make a good case for themselves in this particular controversy, it is nonetheless true that their statements during the war often contradicted those made in 1919-1920; even taking only what they said during the war itself, one finds many inconsistencies. Still, they were no more inconsistent than other senators, and, on the whole, probably less so. Much of this inconsistency resulted from the temptation, yielded to by almost everyone, to give simple answers to complex questions. Much of it was due to genuine confusion and not to deliberate obfuscation. The bitter-enders' complaints that Wilson did not formulate clearly the nation's wartime goals reflected their own uncertainty and groping. Partisan politics, in the case of Republican irreconcilables, and personal bias against Wilson on the part of both Republicans and Democrats, also accounted for some of the contradictions. As the war turned for the better in the summer of 1918, senators felt less need for cooperation with the President. The approach of the congressional elections in November, 1918, further reduced the spirit of harmony. The result was that grievances, either real or fancied, were allowed fuller expression.[38]

Beginning approximately in June, 1918, the Senate started to take a close interest in the problems and opportunities that peace would bring. Mainly the discussion centered around Constitutional and parliamentary questions concerning the process of treaty making, the pressures that the executive branch could exert on the Senate, and vice versa, and the wisdom of Senate consideration of the peace treaty in open as opposed to closed sessions.

The irreconcilables continued to be divided. They split almost down the middle on a Borah-sponsored amendment providing for open sessions on the treaty. The familiar pattern of the prewar votes was still present: La Follette, Norris, and Gronna on one side (for the amendment), Brandegee and Poindexter opposed.[39] The peace progressives, in spite of their earlier dire prophecies that entering the war would ruin America's chance to promote international reforms, had not yet given up all hope. They still shared many of Wilson's ideals, but for the moment they preferred

38. Ibid.; *Cong. Record,* 65 Cong., 3 sess., 71 (December 4, 1918); Hiram Johnson to G. D. Williamson, June 25, 1918. For one example of the inconsistency, in this case Senator Sherman, see Ralph A. Stone, "Two Illinois Senators Among the Irreconcilables," *Mississippi Valley Historical Review* 50 (December 1963): 446-48.

39. See *Cong. Record,* 65 Cong., 2 sess., 7287 (June 3, 1918), 7424-31 (June 6, 1918), 7571-78 (June 10, 1918), 7611 (June 11, 1918) for debate and 7657 (June 12, 1918) for the vote on the issue of open and closed sessions.

to wait quietly to see if he could make good on his promises. The remaining irreconcilables who had supported military preparedness and voted for war were neither so reticent nor so sympathetic toward the President's peace proposals. Yet even they were far from united, as is evidenced in the respective views of Joseph France and Miles Poindexter. In July, 1918, France wrote an article in which he commented on the past history of the United States and what its future course would be. First, there were pioneers; then colonies, "hand touching hand; next a confederation, hands clasped in fellowship, mutually sacrificing, cooperating for liberty"; then came a federation, slowly struggling toward union; finally, "the long awaited consummation of the plan, the true and final integration of these states into that mighty nation which, with her full found and invincible powers, now so valiantly puts on her armor and assumes this weighty responsibility for the welfare of the world; may this be our national evolution."[40] Poindexter harbored far different feelings than his idealistic colleague from Maryland. To a constituent in Seattle, he wrote: "There is abroad in the land a strange, new doctrine of internationalism, which would surrender the national independence and sovereignty which our fathers fought to establish and preserve." In opposing "this un-American and dangerous doctrine," the Republican party had its greatest "opportunity . . . for national service."[41]

The disagreements among the irreconcilables would not stop with the war's end. Indeed, the possibility that these sixteen men would ever come together on one issue seemed remote. Yet they would soon find themselves fighting a common enemy to the bitter end.

40. Joseph I. France, "American Idealism in the War," *Annals of the American Academy of Political and Social Science* 78 (July 1918): 32-33.

41. Poindexter to J. E. Chilberg, June 14, 1918, Miles Poindexter Papers (University of Virginia Library, Charlottesville, Va.), Series 3, file 7-656.

2 SEIZING THE INITIATIVE

IN PROPORTION to their numbers, irreconcilables spoke more often, both in the Senate and elsewhere, than other groups in the Senate. Their greater activity was especially noticeable in the period from October, 1918, until the Covenant of the League of Nations was published on February 14, 1919. Not only did they criticize Wilson's ideas about the nature of the peace settlement, but they also faulted his decision to attend the peace conference and his failure to name either a senator or a prominent Republican to the peace commission. In addition, they condemned his appeal to the voters to elect a Democratic Congress in November, 1918, as a partisan maneuver which betrayed his own promise that politics should be adjourned until the war had ended. Whenever they lacked a specific action or idea to attack, the bitter-enders could always launch tirades against Wilson's superciliousness toward those who disagreed with him. Their main purpose was to voice objections so often and so loudly that the American people would demand careful consideration of any peace treaty the President negotiated. If such objections were not voiced, the people might accept any kind of peace settlement, so horrified were they by the suffering of the war.

The irreconcilables always carried the attack to Wilson and his supporters. From the outset of the great debate, they were on the offensive. During the first few months of the fight, the irreconcilables concentrated their substantive criticisms on the Fourteen Points. Instead of attacking them "in their entirety," as Theodore Roosevelt urged, they singled out one or at most two or three points, usually including the fourteenth.[1] In October, for example, much attention was devoted to point three, which called for "the removal, so far as possible, of all economic barriers and the establishment of an equality of trade conditions among all the nations consenting to the peace and associating themselves for its maintenance." Poindexter feared this meant "an economic free-trade league."[2] He based his fears on his belief that the idea of a league was primarily of British origin, that Wilson and his personal adviser, Edward M. House, seemed to favor free trade, and that southern cotton growers exerted an undue influence on the administration, as demonstrated by the absence of price controls on cotton in contrast to the restrictions on wheat.[3] (During the 1918 election campaign, Republicans would repeat with telling effect the charge that Wilson was too partial to southern interests at the expense of other sections.) Other senators expressed doubts similar to Poindexter's and also wondered if the Constitutional power of Congress to levy duties and regulate commerce would be invalidated by a league.

Democratic senators, apparently uncertain themselves what Wilson meant, had difficulty answering these queries. Therefore, the President made public a letter to Furnifold Simmons, chairman of the Senate Finance Committee, in which he stated that a league would not have the power to destroy a nation's tariffs. Rather, a league would urge equitable tariffs consonant with the most-favored-nation principle: namely, a nation should not raise its tariff for one nation and lower it for another. Although the President's letter cleared away the confusion regarding the idea of free trade, it still did not define what the league's role would be in determining violations of a most-favored-nation principle and how this principle would be enforced. Wilson, however, regarded his explanation as sufficient. He believed those who questioned were not honestly seeking information but only wanted "to pervert this great principle for partisan purposes . . ., to divert the mind of the nation from the broad and humane principle of a durable peace."[4] This was surely an accurate judgment of some of his questioners, but the President, as he often did later, failed to distinguish carefully between those who were apprehensive about specific features of a league and those who condemned the entire concept. It was, of course, extremely difficult to know where some senators stood, but greater efforts to that end might have been made. The ir-

1. Theodore Roosevelt to Miles Poindexter, October 24, 1918, Miles Poindexter Papers (University of Virginia library, Charlottesville), Series 4, file 55. Copies of the telegram were also sent to Henry Cabot Lodge and Hiram Johnson.

2. *Congressional Record*, 65 Cong., 2 sess., 11158 (October 7, 1918).

3. Poindexter to the editor of the *Jamestown* (N. Y.) *Morning Post*, September 20, 1919, Poindexter Papers, Series 6, file 20.

4. *New York Times*, October 29, 1918.

reconcilables were obviously pleased whenever Wilson attributed irreconcilability to senators who were not thus committed. Anything which served to antagonize others toward his manner as well as his ideas could only aid their cause.

That there were irreconcilables at this juncture who were willing not only to question the President's ideas but also to suggest alternatives to them was demonstrated in the speech of the Pennsylvania senator, Philander Knox, on October 28. Knox, too, had questions about free trade as well as freedom of the seas, but he was more concerned with the idea of a league. Objecting to the notion that the war had been fought to establish a world organization, he argued that America had intervened in order to defeat Germany and obtain "restitution, reparation, and guaranties" against any such future attack. "Guaranties" meant not a league of nations but assurance that Germany was militarily unable to make war. As for a league, which he said should be considered as a separate question, Knox recognized a new interdependence of nations arising from technological changes and resting upon the common purpose of the alliance against Germany. This interdependence would not be promoted through the creation of a league "if concurrence upon too many and too Utopian proposals and too great abnegation and too difficult obligations are made the *sine qua non* of its preservation." But a league could and should be created out of the present Allied coalition, whose single purpose would be to enforce peace. It would examine controversies that threatened war, suppress conflicts that broke out, despite all efforts, and throw its weight on the side of justice and equity. He admitted that the kind of league he advocated would encroach somewhat on a member nation's sovereignty; but he believed it would be more unified in membership, simpler, more direct in its goals, and hence more likely to endure than any conception which envisioned all the earth's peoples combining for a multitude of objectives.[5]

Knox's speech was important for two reasons. His suggestion, subsequently presented as a resolution, that the making of peace with Germany deserved consideration apart from the establishment of a league, may well have been the origin of one part of the important Round Robin resolution some four months later, in March, 1919, a statement signed by thirty-nine Republicans. Knox's other suggestion, for continuing the wartime alliance, was also endorsed in some form by many Republican senators (including eight bitter-enders) and by the Democratic irreconcilable Charles

5. *Cong. Record,* 65 Cong., 2 sess., 11485-88 (October 28, 1918).

Thomas. Thus, at the outset, the Pennsylvania senator—who was respected by his colleagues for his brains, his shrewdness as a parliamentarian, and his experience in foreign affairs gained as Taft's Secretary of State, not to mention his service as Attorney General under Roosevelt—marked himself as one of the battalion of death's ablest spokesmen. Knox lacked the oratorical skills to be a highly effective speaker, but the irreconcilables had no shortage of "voices" to spread the word. In fact, at this very time many of them were out on the stump taking part in the midterm congressional election.

While Woodrow Wilson may have regretted the partisan tone of debate on his Fourteen Points, he could not have been very surprised; nor could he wholly escape blame for the situation. In May, 1918, the President had said that "politics is adjourned" until the war was over. But neither party had really agreed. Both had been looking toward the election for months and as it approached the charges and countercharges grew more fervid.[6] Everyone regarded the election as more than normally important. The outcome would decide which party controlled the Congress that would pass upon the peace treaty. The treaty's fate, in turn, would affect the Presidential election of 1920.

On the eve of the contest, the Democrats' margin was only three seats in the House and ten in the Senate. It appeared likely that the Republicans would win the House and they had a good chance of capturing the Senate, where the fate of the treaty would be decided. With this prospect before them, Democrats had been strongly urging the President to make an appeal for the nationwide election of Democrats. They pointed out that previous Presidents had made similar appeals; that Roosevelt and Taft were openly asking for the election of a Republican Congress and denouncing the administration; and that, above all, there must be harmony between the executive and legislative branches if the peace negotiations and treaty ratification were to be successful, and such harmony could occur only if the Democrats retained control of Congress.[7]

Wilson needed little convincing. Not unaware of the furor an appeal would arouse, he nevertheless issued a statement on October 25. In it he asked the electorate, if it approved of his leadership,

6. Seward W. Livermore, *Politics Is Adjourned: Woodrow Wilson and the War Congress, 1916-1918* (Middletown, Conn., 1966), passim.
7. Joseph Tumulty, *Woodrow Wilson As I Know Him* (Garden City, N. Y., 1921), 323. Ruhl J. Bartlett, *The League to Enforce Peace* (Chapel Hill, N. C., 1944), 100.

so to indicate by sending Democratic candidates to Washington. He acknowledged that Republicans had been prowar, but they had also been antiadministration and had tried to subvert his policies. The voters were warned that a Republican victory would be interpreted abroad as a repudiation of his leadership.[8]

The statement brought quick retorts from Republicans in general, and irreconcilables in particular. Roosevelt and Taft, for example, accused the President of betraying his own pledge against playing politics. Knox found the statement "unjust, not to say outrageous," and predicted the voters would reject Wilson's implication that Republicans were less capable than Democrats of handling postwar problems.[9] Sherman declared that Wilson had removed his mask and revealed himself "as a grossly partisan Democrat caught in an attempt to rule the American people in their internal and domestic affairs."[10] La Follette saw the statement as the culmination of the President's attempt to dominate the legislative branch. All through the war, the senator wrote, Republicans and Democrats alike had "groveled at his feet." Congress was becoming "a mere automaton."[11] La Follette's vexation, heightened surely both by the savage criticism he had undergone for his vote against war and by the virtual estrangement from his own party, was understandable but not well founded. As if in rebuttal of the image of Congress as automaton, the press reported on October 27 that Republican senators were planning to make a full-scale assault on the Fourteen Points, concentrating on the "free-trade" proposition.[12]

It was widely believed at the time, and it has often been repeated since, that Wilson's appeal caused many normally Democratic voters to switch their allegiance or to stay at home in protest. Other forces, however, chiefly sectional and economic, were of greater consequence, as recent research has demonstrated.[13] International affairs figured very little in individual state races. Nevertheless, if Wilson's appeal had little or no effect on the election, its uses in the League fight, from the irreconcilables' point of view, were considerable. Whenever the League's opponents were charged with partisanship, they could and did reply by pointing to

8. Ray Stannard Baker and William E. Dodd, eds., *War and Peace: Presidential Messages, Addresses, and Public Papers, 1917-1921* (New York, 1927) 1:286-88. Arthur Walworth, *Woodrow Wilson*, 2d ed., rev. (Boston, 1965), 2:201.

9. *Brooklyn Daily Eagle*, October 28, 31, 1918.

10. *Chicago Tribune*, October 28, 1918.

11. Belle Case La Follette and Fola La Follette, *Robert M. La Follette* (New York, 1953), 2:899.

12. *New York Tribune*, October 27, 1918.

13. Livermore, *Politics Is Adjourned*, 224-47.

Wilson's statement. If there was partisanship, it was not theirs; and if it was, the President, they said, had cast the first stone. His pre-election appeal was evidence of his intolerance of differing views, his attempt to intimidate and coerce the Senate. By itself such an accusation, or counteraccusation, would not have been very effective. But in conjunction with numerous other allegations, it established, or so the bitter-enders hoped, a pattern of partisanship, truculence, and unyielding obstinacy.

The final election results gave the Republicans a total of forty-four more House seats than the Democrats and a narrow majority of two in the Senate. Among the victorious Republicans were no fewer than six irreconcilables: McCormick and Moses, both of whom won election to the Senate for the first time; and Borah, Fall, Fernald, and Norris, who were reelected. McCormick's solid victory was at the expense of the Democratic party whip, James Hamilton Lewis, one of the few Democrats in the Senate who had consistently challenged the irreconcilables in debate before March, 1919, when his and other defeated candidates' terms expired. Moses, who was to be a key liaison man between the irreconcilables and Lodge, squeaked through by only a thousand votes. Borah, on the other hand, safely ensconced in Idaho politics, overwhelmed his opponent. Amazingly, in view of Borah's previously stated opposition to the league proposal, Wilson privately supported his reelection. "I have appreciated very much Borah's friendly and helpful attitude and know that his support can be counted on," the President wrote.[14] Wilson apparently never lost his respect for Borah, even after there could be absolutely no doubt of their differences over the League of Nations. Probably Wilson saw in Borah a kindred integrity and commitment to high goals—in short an irreconcilability when it came to defending great principles.[15] The President's attempt to prevent Albert Fall's reelection was in marked contrast to his endorsement of Borah. When Secretary of the Treasury William Gibbs McAdoo, following a trip to New Mexico where he consulted with local Democrats on how to remove Fall, wrote the President that there was "a chance to finish the unspeakable" senator, Wilson made public a letter condemning Fall. After Wilson's letter was published, Fall de-

14. Wilson to ex-Senator Frederick Dubois, August 1, 1918, cited in Marion C. McKenna, *Borah* (Ann Arbor, Mich., 1961), 147.

15. Thomas A. Bailey, *Woodrow Wilson and the Great Betrayal* (New York, 1945), 65. See also the letter from Thomas M. Woodward to Borah, May 11, 1920, informing him "how much some of the President's personal friends appreciate the impersonal character of your opposition," Borah Papers, Box 552.

fended himself by saying he had supported administration war measures but would approve "no Bolsheviki German peace."[16] Fall won the election by less than two thousand votes. Norris, the only one of the three peace progressives up for reelection, survived a Nebraska primary battle in which his opponent had been backed by the chairman of the Republican National Committee, Will Hays.[17] Theodore Roosevelt, still not forgiving Norris for his stand against war, had to be restrained from publicly denouncing him. In the general election Norris won comfortably, aided by a United States Tariff Commissioner, William Kent, a good friend of Wilson whose actions the President would not publicly disavow.[18] Bert Fernald was reelected without much opposition from Maine's weak Democratic party.

With the exception of Moses, who was running to fill out an unexpired term ending in 1920, these newly elected or reelected irreconcilables looked forward to six years of political security. Fully a third of the Senate was secure in this way, of course. But for those who opposed the League, which remained popular in some form until its final defeat, the thought of not having to face reelection until 1924 may have been more meaningful. By then new issues were likely to arise that would replace the League in importance. These facts were well summarized by Albert J. Beveridge, former Indiana senator whose encouragement and advice were of great assistance to the battalion of death. To McCormick, Beveridge wrote: "You are in an almost perfect strategic position. You have six years before you and, at the present moment, can do just what you like, regardless of trumped up, artificial and wholly temporary public clamor. Moreover, should they succeed in putting this League through I think that there can be no doubt that, within two or three years there will be such a revulsion of public feeling, such a profound disgust with the whole thing, that the man who fights it now will be stronger and the man who favors it now will be weaker."[19] While it is certainly debatable whether McCormick and the others would have been less extreme in their opposition to the League had they not been in this "almost perfect

16. Livermore, *Politics Is Adjourned*, 204-205. *New York Times*, November 2, 1918.

17. George Norris to Will Hays, November 28, 1919; Hays to Norris, December 6, 1919, Will Hays Papers (Indiana State Library, Indianapolis).

18. Richard Lowitt, "Senator Norris and His 1918 Campaign," *Pacific Northwest Quarterly* 57 (July 1966): 113-19; Livermore, *Politics Is Adjourned*, 194.

19. Beveridge to McCormick, May 6, 1919, Medill McCormick Papers (in possession of his daughter, Mrs. Garvin E. Tankersley, Washington, D. C.).

strategic position"—irreconcilables who did face reelection in 1920 were no less militantly anti-League—the thought that Beveridge expressed must nevertheless have been reassuring.

Although the Republicans had won the election, potentially disastrous problems faced them. The biggest problem was securing unity among the senators. For the party to organize the new Senate, the cooperation of every one of the forty-nine Republicans was necessary. Much depended on the votes of La Follette, Norris, and Gronna.[20] Would these three progressive, antiwar middle westerners work with the Republican leaders, who were, especially in the person of Henry Cabot Lodge, conservative, prowar easterners?

There were reasons to think the three peace progressives might not cooperate. Norris, for example, was still irritated at the opposition of some party leaders to his nomination in the recent primary. One of his first acts after the November election was to prepare a resolution which would democratize senatorial committee membership rules by prohibiting a senator who was chairman of one of the major committees from serving concurrently on any other such committee. Regular Republicans were expected to oppose the resolution.[21] Another potentially disruptive figure in Republican ranks was La Follette. A motion to expel him from the Senate for allegedly disloyal statements made in September, 1917, was being considered. At one time Lodge and many other Republicans had favored his expulsion. Were the motion now to receive Republican support, La Follette might bolt the party and take Norris and Gronna with him.[22]

Notwithstanding what may have seemed such unfavorable conditions for the Republicans, it was still optimistic to expect, as some Democrats did, a split in Republican ranks. How could La Follette, Norris, and Gronna side with Wilson's party? It was, after all, the President who had branded them "a little group of willful men" when they filibustered against the armed-ships bill; it was he who had led the country into war, who had been responsible for wartime

20. *New York Times,* November 10, 16, 25, 1918. Lodge's correspondence reveals his concern for unity. See Lodge to H. R. McMurtrie, November 23, 1918, Henry Cabot Lodge Papers (Massachusetts Historical Society, Boston). Sherman was pessimistic about Republican chances of organizing the Senate because of G.O.P. "family troubles" and the possibility that some newly elected Republicans might lose their seats due to alleged corruption.

21. *New York Times,* November 16, 1918; *Washington Post,* November 16, 17, 1918.

22. La Follette and La Follette, *La Follette,* 2:781, 792-93. *Brooklyn Daily Eagle,* December 3, 1918.

restrictions on civil liberties, who had permitted war profiteers to exist unchecked by sufficiently high taxes, and whose administration had been guilty of numerous other actions which they opposed. Even had they borne less resentment toward the President, it was unlikely that Wilson would extend the olive branch in their direction. He had his own unpleasant memories, some of which were ascribable to these senators. Moreover, he was confident, in spite of the election setback, that the American people agreed with his ideas on peace as well as war, and that he could mobilize their support to overcome any parliamentary disadvantage. Finally, it would have been quite uncharacteristic of Lodge had he not been willing, as he soon showed he was, to make certain concessions to the progressives to prevent a party schism.

Shortly after the election, on the day the Senate Privileges and Elections Committee was meeting to consider the charges against La Follette's alleged disloyalty, Lodge invited La Follette into his office for "a little talk" about the parliamentary situation. Afterward the two men were seen walking down the corridor, Lodge with "his arm on La Follette's shoulder." That evening La Follette wrote to his family that he planned to support the party when it came time to organize the Senate, "and thereafter—. . . vote on all questions according to my convictions in an absolutely independent way." Some two months later a motion to dismiss the charges against the Wisconsin senator was passed by a 50 to 21 count. Thirty-three Republicans voted for the motion and only one opposed it, as against seventeen Democrats in support of it and twenty opposed. All the Republican irreconcilables except four who did not vote, voted for La Follette, as did the two Democratic irreconcilables. Three weeks later Norris's resolution to democratize committee membership rules was accepted in a modified form by the Republican senators.[23] Thus, while a progressive revolt was not completely ruled out, Lodge had made its occurrence much less likely.

There was one other discouraging, or at least uncertain, problem confronting Republicans, especially the irreconcilables. Even if they overcame their divisiveness, they could not take control of the new Congress immediately. The Sixty-fifth Congress would expire on March 4, 1919; the Sixty-sixth was not scheduled to begin until

23. La Follette and La Follette, *La Follette*, 2:909-31. *Cong. Record*, 65 Cong., 3 sess., 1526-27 (January 16, 1919). *New York Tribune*, February 9, 1919. Lodge was now satisfied the rift had been healed and that the G.O.P. would organize the new Senate without difficulty. Lodge to Beveridge, February 7, 1919, Lodge Papers.

December, 1919. It seemed likely that Wilson would call an extraordinary special session of the Sixty-sixth Congress whenever the peace treaty was completed, but when that would be nobody knew. The President did not have to call a special session. He might prefer not to have a Republican-controlled Senate begin at once to dissect the peace treaty; he might choose, instead, to let Congress remain idle while he generated support for the treaty among the people. Denying his opponents their Senate forum for as long as possible might be his best strategy. If he chanced to have read the postelection article by Illinois' senior bitter-ender, Lawrence Sherman, entitled "The Aims of the Republican Congress," he may justifiably have been worried about the prospect of a Republican Congress any sooner than necessary. Concerning the President's proposal for a league, Sherman declared: "We shall see, and since we have a Republican Congress, we shall see well before we sign. There will be no dim light hanging over the legislative halls when the Peace Treaty reaches us for final ratification. We shall have our spectacles on, we shall look for every dot on the i, for every comma and we shall put the periods in ourselves."[24]

The President's power to determine when the new Congress would assemble and therefore when the Senate would begin formal debate on the treaty, was not as absolute as it seemed. There was another consideration besides the treaty which could affect the calling of a special session. If the Sixty-fifth Congress failed to pass certain legislation which was needed to enable the government to function in the period before the Sixty-sixth Congress was regularly scheduled to begin, Wilson might be forced to call a special session.

For the moment there were other events which demanded more immediate attention, especially from Wilson and the Democratic senators; but Republicans had already begun to discuss ways they might insure a special session.[25] The clash would come at the close

24. Lawrence Y. Sherman, "The Aims of the Republican Congress," *The Forum* 60 (December 1918): 738-44.

25. As early as November 16, 1918, Lodge was privately expressing confidence he could force a special session. Lodge to James Bucklin Bishop, November 16, 1918, Lodge Papers, as cited in James Oliver Robertson, "The Progressives in National Republican Politics, 1916 to 1921" (Ph.D. diss., Harvard University, 1964), 145. By late January he was writing similarly to senators. See Lodge to Borah, January 23, 1919, Borah Papers (Library of Congress, Washington, D.C.), Box 195, and Lodge to Sherman, January 23, 1919, Sherman Papers (in possession of his daughter, Mrs. Marion Graham, Daytona Beach, Florida). Wilson was not completely neglecting the issue. Colonel House recorded in his diary of January 1, 1919, that he had advised the President not to call a special session and that Wilson "already had it in mind not

of the Sixty-fifth Congress, with the irreconcilables at its center.

The election results were still front page news when headlines proclaimed Germany's signing of armistice terms on November 11. The armistice was an event everyone could celebrate and the irreconcilables joined in the relief and rejoicing. Henceforth questions could be directed solely toward postwar problems.

One such question was answered shortly when the President announced his plans to attend the peace conference and conduct the negotiations in person. His reasons for this unprecedented procedure—previous Presidents had never left the country for more than a few days—were expected to be given in his annual message to Congress on December 2, and therefore most senators withheld comment until that time. An ominous Republican party statement, however, declared that "Congress should assert and exercise its normal and constitutional functions, including legislation necessary for reconstruction."[26]

In a second announcement, to which reaction was sharper, Wilson named the men who would comprise the Peace Commission and accompany him to Paris. The men chosen were: Robert Lansing, the Secretary of State; Henry White, a career diplomat; General Tasker Bliss, an expert on military matters; and Edward House, the President's alter ego and adviser. White was the only Republican. Not many complaints were voiced about the ability of this group; the major objection of Republicans was that men equally able and more representative of the G.O.P. could have been found. Elihu Root, the leading elder statesman of the Republicans, was the most frequently mentioned possibility. Wilson had, indeed, considered Root only to reject him and other less obvious Republicans who had been suggested.[27] Instead he selected White, a Republican without strong party ties, of little national prominence, and who, some Republicans felt, would not take an independent position, much less one that represented the opposition party. Hiram Johnson's com-

to do so." Edward M. House Diary (Yale University Library, New Haven, Conn.). Senate Democrats, however, apparently had not been told this, for they believed an extra session was almost inevitable. *Washington Post*, November 10, 1918, January 27, 1919.

26. *New York Tribune*, November 20, 1918. Charles Thomas recalled that in the cloakrooms Democrats were critical of Wilson's decision, feeling it would prove to be a grave blunder. Charles Thomas's unpublished autobiography, Charles Thomas Papers (State Historical Society of Colorado, Denver). Thomas probably exaggerated the extent of Democratic disaffection. See W. Stull Holt, *Treaties Defeated by the Senate* (Baltimore, Md., 1933), 255.

27. Tumulty, *Woodrow Wilson*, 337-38. Phillip C. Jessup, *Elihu Root* (New York, 1936), 2:379.

ment on the Commission: "There is no God but God, and Mo-
hammed is his prophet. In selecting himself as the head of the five
American delegates to the Peace Conference, President Wilson has
named himself five times," was only slightly more acidic than
others.[28] George Harvey, a former supporter of Wilson turned
vitriolic foe, cleverly made the same point in his magazine, *Harvey's
Weekly*, in this convenient boxscore.[29]

NAME	OCCUPATION	REPRESENTING
Woodrow Wilson	President	Himself
Robert Lansing	Sec. of State	The Executive
Henry White	None	Nobody
Edward M. House	Scout	The Executive
Tasker H. Bliss	Soldier	The Commander-in-Chief

Harvey's editorial appeared on December 7. Two days later he
received a letter from Lodge gently chiding him for having been too
harsh on White. Lodge explained that White had consulted
Roosevelt, Root, and himself before accepting the appointment, and
also had asked to see the Republican members of the Foreign Relations Committee. Knox, a member of the Committee, arranged for
him to meet with Borah, Brandegee, and Porter McCumber, the
only Republican members who were in Washington in the period
between the second and third sessions of Congress. All these men
expressed complete satisfaction with White's "attitude."[30] Ironically,
White's "attitude" was later to cause the irreconcilables some concern, while Lansing, who had been attacked as a rubber stamp, was
to give testimony to the Committee revealing his sharp differences
with Wilson and, indirectly, his support of certain irreconcilable
criticisms of the Treaty.

One other source of discontent regarding the Commission was
Wilson's failure to name a senator. Democrats as well as Republicans
thought the President erred in not taking along at least one member of the body to which he must eventually submit the treaty.[31]
Knox seemed a good choice to many Republicans, but the most
interesting recommendation came from Key Pittman, a Nevada

28. *New York Tribune*, December 1, 1918.

29. *The North American Reviews War Weekly* 1 (December 7, 1918). The
name of the magazine was soon changed to *Harvey's Weekly*.

30. Lodge to Harvey, December 9, 1918, Henry Cabot Lodge Papers
(Massachusetts Historical Society, Boston). McCumber was the most ardent
Republican supporter of the League of Nations.

31. *Louisville Courier-Journal*, December 2, 1918. G. F. Sparks, ed., *A
Many-Colored Toga: The Diary of Henry Fountain Ashurst* (Tucson, Ariz.,
1962), 90. Ashurst commented in his diary on December 1: "Two months ago
W. W. was the foremost character in the world. Today I doubt if he has
twenty friends in Congress." Also see Thomas's autobiography, Thomas Papers.

Democrat who was on the Foreign Relations Committee. Pittman, in a letter to the President which was composed but never sent, said he was "convinced that a majority of the Foreign Relations Committee" believed the Senate should be represented and that this was the consensus of the whole Senate. Pittman suggested Claude Swanson and Atlee Pomerene as suitable Democrats and Borah as an excellent Republican choice. The Idaho senator was "independent, fearless, and able," and "in complete accord with the principles pronounced by you." Moreover, his selection would be good strategy. He was "a powerful debater" and never feared using "his talents even against the leaders of his own party."[32]

Wilson's professed reason for not taking senators was that, "looking into the precedents," he had found serious objections to appointing men who would have to vote on a treaty they themselves had helped to write.[33] While this explanation was not convincing—as recently as 1898 McKinley had appointed senators on the commission to negotiate the peace treaty with Spain—Borah probably would have refused to serve even had he been asked. The important thing, however, was not whether he would have declined the invitation, for other senators surely would have accepted; nor that Pittman was misguided in his assessment of Borah's views. What mattered was that Wilson failed to offer any senator an opportunity to refuse a place on the Commission.

On December 2 the President appeared before a joint session of Congress to deliver his keenly anticipated annual message. Unfortunately, felt many irreconcilables, only a small portion of it was devoted to foreign affairs. His decision to go to the peace conference, Wilson said, rested upon two compelling factors: he had enunciated the Fourteen Points which the Allies had accepted as a basis for peace and which they now expected would be interpreted by him personally at the conference; and he also had the responsibility to see that American soldiers who had fought for the ideals he had tried to express during the war had not fought in vain. Wilson assured Congress that although he would be away he would "not be inaccessible," and in turn he asked for their "encouragement" and "united support."[34]

32. Pittman to Wilson, November 27, 1918 (never sent), Key Pittman Papers (Library of Congress, Washington, D.C.), Box 68.
33. Wilson to R. L. Williams, Governor of Oklahoma, November 26, 1918, in answer to Williams's letter of November 19 suggesting Senator Robert Owen of Oklahoma as a delegate on the Commission. Woodrow Wilson Papers (Library of Congress, Washington, D. C.), Series 6, Box 263.
34. Ray Stannard Baker and William E. Dodd, eds., *War and Peace: Presidential Messages, Addresses, and Public Papers, 1917-1921* (New York, 1927), 1:308-24.

As Wilson surely expected, he got neither of his wishes in full measure. Within minutes after the address was completed, Johnson and Reed told reporters that the President had unduly neglected issues of foreign policy. Reed further accused him of gross falsification for saying the Allies had fully accepted the Fourteen Points and that American soldiers had given their lives fighting for the President's personal beliefs.[35] A Boston newspaper, whose editor, James Williams, was a close friend of many irreconcilables, charged that Wilson had slighted the Senate again by mentioning it once and then only to censure it mildly for delaying ratification of a treaty with Colombia.[36] However senators themselves may have felt about this, it was clear from their speeches and resolutions in the next few days that they did not intend to let the President think he could ignore them with impunity.

On the day after Wilson's address, Sherman introduced a resolution that would have divested the President of all his Constitutional powers immediately upon his leaving the continent and have transferred these powers to the Vice President until a new election was held. With pressing domestic troubles such as unemployment, labor strikes, and race riots facing the country, the President's absence, Sherman stated, would "constitute an inability to discharge the powers and duties" of his office. Moreover, by leaving American soil Wilson was violating a longstanding tradition. Continuing in a mood half in irony, half in earnest, the Illinois senator declared that it was the intention of the Founding Fathers: "to guard the President against the insidious influences and flattery incident to the servile adulation and absurd pomp of the kings and council chambers of the Old World. . . . A courtier's smile and the bending knee of a sycophant have often in history entangled a nation in fatal alliances. A kiss of a sensuous woman has changed the course of empire. We ought not to put him [Wilson] in temptation."[37] Few could rival Sherman in the use of invective; but his remarks had little noticeable effect, other than to produce heated retorts from several Democrats and a few Republicans. The issue of Presidential disability, however, would be heard from again after Wilson's collapse on his speaking trip in September, 1919.

More important at this stage in the debates was Borah's resolution to permit the Senate to hold open sessions on the peace treaty—i.e., allow the public to come into the galleries to hear the debates and

35. *New York Times,* December 3, 1918.
36. *Boston Evening Transcript,* December 2, 1918.
37. *Cong. Record,* 65 Cong., 3 sess., 23-28 (December 3, 1918).

have the debates printed in full in the *Congressional Record*. Open sessions had been held before only infrequently.[38] Borah's resolution, like Sherman's, was not immediately acted upon, but he would eventually have his way. Moreover, the Foreign Relations Committee would conduct unprecedented public hearings on the Versailles Treaty. Open sessions and public hearings aided the irreconcilables immeasurably in their effort to foment opposition to the League, but they also appealed to Borah, Johnson, the peace progressives, and a few other bitter-enders as a means of activating the first of Wilson's Fourteen Points, namely, open diplomacy, openly arrived at.

When Wilson's supporters asserted that all the resolutions and critical remarks on the eve of the President's departure for the peace conference were designed to embarrass and weaken him in the eyes of other world leaders, the irreconcilables had only to quote the President's own writings to justify their concern about his future conduct. Since the former historian and political scientist had written extensively on the subject of treaty making and the relation between the Chief Executive and the Senate, it was not difficult to find a quotation to suit the purpose. La Follette, for example, cited Wilson's *Constitutional Government in the United States* in which he had said that the President's control over foreign relations was "very absolute," and that while the Chief Executive could not conclude a treaty without the Senate's consent, he could guide every step of diplomacy so as almost to insure the Senate's adherence to his wishes. "He need disclose no step of negotiation until it is complete, and when in any critical matter it is completed the Government is virtually committed. Whatever its disinclination, the Senate may feel itself committed also."[39] Yet in the same book Wilson had written that the Senate had "shown itself particularly stiff and jealous" in dealing with foreign affairs, and that a wise President would placate those senatorial jealousies.[40] Whether Wilson the President would follow the advice of Wilson the professor remained to be seen; he had already missed a big opportunity by not naming a senator to the peace commission. One thing was not in doubt: many senators were disinclined toward the President's peace proposals and a few would feel no desire to consent to whatever the majority might advise.

38. Ibid., 71 (December 4, 1918). Holt, *Treaties Defeated by the Senate*, 144, 282.
39. *Cong. Record*, 65 Cong., 3 sess., 724 (December 21, 1918).
40. Woodrow Wilson, *Constitutional Government in the United States* (New York, 1908), 139-40.

During Wilson's absence from the United States—from December 4, 1918, until February 23, 1919—senators constantly debated the issues surrounding peacemaking. While the idea of a league absorbed most attention, another matter was deemed of more immediate importance by a few irreconcilables, and that was the Allied military intervention in Russia. In the summer of 1918, several months after the Bolsheviks had come to power and had made peace with Germany, the leaders of England, France, and the United States ordered troops sent into northern Russia and Siberia. The purposes of the Allied expedition were chiefly, it seems, military: to prevent Germany from seizing military supplies and equipment within Russia and to open another front against her on Russian soil. Wilson denied any intention of using American soldiers to fight the Bolsheviks, even though a civil war was then raging in Russia and his sympathies clearly lay with the enemies of Lenin and Trotsky. He also hoped the troops could be withdrawn quickly. Nevertheless, when he sailed for Paris in December, American troops were not only still in Russia but were being used against the Bolshevik government.[41]

The irreconcilables characteristically did not agree on the American intervention. One group, of which Johnson and Borah were the most articulate, attacked the policy as inconsistent with the promises Wilson had made in his Fourteen Points address. At that time—January, 1918—he had warned that the treatment of Russia by the other nations would be "the acid test of their good will, of their comprehension of her needs as distinguished from their own interests, and of their intelligent and unselfish sympathy." Russia, he emphasized, must have "institutions of her own choosing." Now, Johnson charged, instead of aiding Russia or allowing her to determine her own destiny, American soldiers were shooting Russian peasants and being shot in return. The President had neither asked Congress for a declaration of war nor clearly explained the reasons for the intervention. Whatever the motives for sending the troops, Johnson wanted American boys immediately withdrawn.[42]

Other irreconcilables took an entirely different position, advocating open and vigorous opposition to the Bolsheviks. Poindexter spoke for those of this persuasion. To him, Bolshevism was on the same plane as a league of nations; each was an insidious threat

41. Cf. William A. Williams, *The Tragedy of American Diplomacy* (New York, 1962), 111-12.
42. *Cong. Record,* 65 Cong., 3 sess., 342-46 (December 12, 1918); Johnson to Hiram Johnson, Jr., December 7, 1918, Johnson Papers; Borah to James E. Babb, February 4, 1919, Borah Papers, Box 552.

based on messianic internationalism; each would lead to "imperial despotism."[43] Johnson and Borah agreed with Poindexter that Bolshevism was a pernicious doctrine, but they saw the Allies' intervention as the harbinger of how a league would function: the status quo powers suppressing weaker nations, putting down revolutions, waging wars without consulting their own elected representatives. Still another point of view was expressed by Joseph France, who condemned intervention but who was far more positive than Johnson and Borah in suggesting specific ways the United States could aid Russia.[44]

While the bitter-enders often found in either Bolshevism or the Allied intervention what they believed to be lessons militating against acceptance of a league, one can exaggerate the importance of those lessons in their final decision to reject the League of Nations, much less the total Treaty of Versailles. Many of the irreconcilables paid comparatively little attention to the Bolshevik revolutions—whether in Russia, elsewhere in Europe, or potentially in the United States—and even less attention to the Allied intervention. But even those irreconcilables who studied these events carefully and drew lessons from them had other and better reasons for voting against the Treaty. What one can discern in their attitudes toward revolution and counterrevolution are similar ideological splits which had marked their earlier conflicts over the issues of neutrality and preparedness and would also characterize their later disagreements over the Treaty of Versailles. Their differences respecting the idea of a league of nations, in particular, were becoming more obvious in December, 1918, at the time Wilson left for the peace conference.

The two months which Wilson spent in Paris drafting a constitution for a league of nations and getting the Allied leaders to accept it saw the senators principally engaged in analyzing the league proposal. About half of the irreconcilables delivered extensive speeches during this two-month period. In the main they took a negative attitude, attacking Wilson's ideas, sometimes emotionally, sometimes with cool rationality, depending on the individual. But there were also irreconcilables who offered alternatives other than the simple return to previous policies. The bitter-enders, however, usually were chary of formulating elaborate systems, in part because such activity detracted from what they considered their more immediate task of defeating the Treaty.

43. *New York Times,* February 1, 1919; *New York Tribune,* February 13, 1919.
44. *Cong. Record,* 66 Cong., 2 sess., 3554 (February 27, 1920).

As more of the irreconcilables spoke out, some shifting in the wartime divisions occurred. The peace progressives—La Follette, Norris, and Gronna—were joined by France. These four remained the most sympathetic to a "peace without victory" and concomitant international reforms of a sweeping and democratic character. The erstwhile advocates of preparedness, in contrast, began to divide on the basis of their alternatives into two loosely defined groups. The first, composed of Borah, Johnson, and Reed, was extremely negative, espousing traditional isolationist-nationalist policies. The second group, which included Knox, Poindexter, Brandegee, Moses, McCormick, Sherman, Fall, Fernald, and Thomas, was also nationalist-minded, but not isolationist; on the contrary, these nine bitter-enders were willing to accept limited obligations to America's wartime allies.

Borah, Reed, and Johnson were the most active irreconcilables during the entire League fight. They spoke frequently in the Senate, took to the stump again and again, usually had immediate comments on the latest-breaking news stories, and were active in considerations of strategy. They were especially effective orators, highly skilled in give-and-take debate, and were colorful personalities; they also had long careers in politics: Reed left the Senate in 1929, Borah and Johnson remained until 1940 and 1945 respectively. For these reasons they have overshadowed the other irreconcilables; but these three did not always deliver the most telling criticisms of the Treaty of Versailles, they were not the most skilled parliamentarians among the battalion of death, and their alternatives to the League of Nations were decidedly not the most constructive.

At this time Reed carried the heaviest speaking burden. As early as November 21 the Missouri bitter-ender presented a wide-ranging attack on the entire concept of a league. He began with a quotation from Washington's Farewell Address warning against "permanent alliance with any portion of the foreign world," and he concluded with his own observation that the United States had proudly stood alone since Washington's day, "independent, powerful, great, peaceful and prosperous," and time had not altered the wisdom of that policy. Those who wanted to replace it with a league of nations were seized with millennial notions, with visions of the lion and lamb lying down together; and they had not answered fundamental questions about any world organization, such as: what would the membership and voting procedures be? Should the United States, for example, be given a vote equal only to, say, Liberia? Or should it have a greater voice? If so, what became of the principle of equality? Again, would a league have the power to quash revolutions against tyrannical governments? Most importantly, who would control the league? What worried Reed, or so at least he claimed, was that the league would be dominated by European nations bound together by similar monarchial forms of government, blood relationships, and intermarriages. The United States would be an outsider, conspired against, and used for selfish purposes. Reed said he was averse neither to agreements among nations that sought to codify international law, nor to having the United States engage in other undertakings whose implementation rested upon mutual good will and honor. But he could accept no system which established reciprocal obligations to protect the territorial integrity of member nations. If American statesmen wanted to experiment in international diplomacy, why not look toward Latin America? That was an area, he said, where through "ties of commerce and of love" the United States could assist other peoples while simultaneously extending its influence and strengthening the Monroe Doctrine.[45]

Borah's message was similar. In a resolution on December 5, he asked the Senate to reaffirm its faith in the policies of Washington, Jefferson, and Monroe, and "seek in all matters coming before it touching the interests or affairs of foreign countries to conform its acts to these time-honored principles." The United States, he admitted, was closer in time to the European nations than when Washington lived, and perhaps it enjoyed better relations with Great Britain and France, but Europe's primary interests still were distinct from America's.[46] Commercial intercourse with foreign nations was acceptable, even desirable, as Washington said, but the United States must shun political-military entanglements. In analyzing the idea of a league, Borah sometimes distinguished between the League to Enforce Peace organization and those proposals which contemplated no coercive power. Any league that employed force was anathema: "God pity the ideals of this Republic," Borah remarked, "if they shall have no defenders save the gathered scum of the nations organized into a conglomerate international police force." Not only would such a league destroy the Monroe Doctrine; it would also lead to peacetime conscription, a

45. Ibid., 65 Cong., 2 sess., 11622-25 (November 21, 1918); 3 sess., 87-88 (December 4, 1918).
46. To his friend James Babb, Borah wrote: "I feel that while we have greater responsibilities and a wider range of influence as a nation that we can meet every obligation and discharge our entire duty to the world and remain perfectly true to the two great underlying fundamental principles of our foreign policy, no entangling alliances and the Monroe doctrine." Borah to Babb, December 2, 1918, James E. Babb Papers (Yale University Library, New Haven, Conn.).

giant navy, high taxes, and foreign standards for American labor. Furthermore, it would remove from Congress its Constitutional power to declare war. On occasion Borah implied he was not opposed to a league resting only on moral force, by which he meant the power of public opinion. But he had no confidence that such a league would be effective, and he feared that even this form of a league would be unhealthy. "It will finally lead us into all kinds of entangling obligations and conditions with European affairs. If we sit in the council chamber with nothing more than our moral influence and our moral suasion and exercising our intellectual powers, we are still dealing with European affairs and creating corresponding obligations upon our part, against which the Father of his Country declared."[47]

Borah, like Reed, prided himself on being a realist on the subject of human nature. The league proposal was too idealistic, it asked too much of man. "There is no such thing as friendship between nations as we speak of friendship between individuals. Any plan based upon such a theory is built upon shifting sands." Nor would economic sanctions prove effective; nations would trade where their interests dictated. Self-interest, race rivalries, nationalism, and patriotism moved nations as well as individuals.[48]

Hiram Johnson never displayed quite as much interest in foreign affairs as did Reed and Borah. Equally nationalistic but temperamentally more negative than Borah, he preached essentially an America-first doctrine. "It is time for an American policy," he declared in January, 1919. "Bring home American soldiers. Rescue our own democracy. Restore its free expression. Get American business into its normal channels. Let American life, social and economic, be American again." He stated at this time that he favored a league which did not relinquish American sovereignty and which would prevent future wars, but when Reed asked him immediately afterward how there could be such a league that did not decrease sovereignty, he replied that he would answer that question later.[49] He never did. Instead, he became increasingly critical of Wilson's

47. *Cong. Record,* 65 Cong., 3 sess., 124 (December 5, 1918), 195 (December 6, 1918), 1386-87 (January 14, 1919), 2425 (January 31, 1919).
48. Ibid., 196 (December 6, 1918).
49. Ibid., 1585 (January 17, 1919), 2261-62 (January 29, 1919); Johnson to Theodore Roosevelt, December 27, 1918, Johnson Papers. Johnson wrote as late as February 24, 1919, to his close friend C. K. McClatchy that he was still "waiting, and really hoping, to be convinced" he should support the League; "and I'm not like the individual who made this remark, and then added, that he would like to see the fellow who could convince him." However, Johnson in the same letter said the League "apparently justifies Borah's exclamation that it is the greatest triumph of all history for English diplomacy." Johnson to McClatchy, February 24, 1919, ibid.

ideas as the months passed and the Presidential election of 1920 neared.

By far the most significant remarks at this time were those of Knox. After introducing a resolution calling for the limitation of American aims at the peace conference to "restitution, reparation, and guaranties against the German menace," and asking for the postponement of any project for a general league of nations until some future date when all nations, not only the victorious belligerents, would participate, Knox explained his position.[50] By "restitution" he meant the return of Alsace-Lorraine to France and the evacuation of territory invaded by Germany. "Reparation" was "a matter of arithmetic, of law, and of equitable justice." Excessive indemnities should be avoided. The difficult problem was "guaranties." He warned that those who counseled against close association between the United States and other nations because of what George Washington said were as dogmatic as those who wanted to rush headlong into any world organization. "The questions we are considering," Knox declared, "will have to be decided by the application of present wisdom to present conditions, not by the easy misapplication of old wisdom to entirely new conditions."

Knox sketched a policy which he thought would prevent or at least mitigate future crises. First, Germany should continue to be subjugated (for how long he did not specify), her colonies confiscated and divided among or administered jointly by the Allies. Next, there should be created "new free states as a cordon to cut off for the future the 'Mittle Europa' and Near Eastern" ambitions of Germany. Effectuating this latter move would probably require periodic protection of these new states from external pressures and internal crises. Whenever their insecurity or instability threatened to upset the peace of Europe, the United States would become involved; but minor disputes within or between these states would be the primary responsibility of the European powers. Expressing his interpretation of the momentous events of the war years, Knox continued: "Here is the road we have travelled. The United States of America slowly, but in the end very clearly, perceived that a menace of Europe by the dominion of aggressive military power . . . was a menace also to the safety of this Nation. America manifested this perception by throwing its entire power into the scales to join in the suppression of that menace of Europe by military imperialism." Should there not emerge from these facts, he asked, a new policy, "a new American Doctrine," which would

50. *Cong. Record*, 65 Cong., 3 sess., 23 (December 3, 1918).

stand alongside the Monroe Doctrine? "I will state this great new doctrine in these words: If a situation should arise in which any power or combination of powers should, directly or indirectly, menace the freedom and peace of Europe, the United States would regard such [a] situation with grave concern as a menace to its own freedom and peace and would consult with other powers affected with a view to concerted action for the removal of such menace." Such a plan, Knox said, was based on the belief that nations normally did not undertake great obligations unless their vital interests were at stake. His plan also assumed that it was better for the United States to rely, not upon the judgment of a "world league" in making crucial commitments, but upon its own judgment in conjunction with that of other nations whose interests paralleled its own, in this case America's allies during the war. A "practicable league" rested upon the "principle of the creation of community of interest, of self-interest in peace and welfare." "If we perfect our diplomacy," he believed that "with due practical regard to" and "the gradual extension of . . . this common-sense principle, we shall enable it . . . to render great service to the world at large."[51]

Knox's resolution and accompanying speech received wider press coverage than any development in the Senate up to that time. They also won extensive support; but those who praised his policy suggestions did not always accept his call for postponing discussion of a league. The *New York Times,* for example, lauded as eminently realistic his proposal for separate European and American spheres of influence with concerted action in times of general disturbances. Knox and Wilson, the paper declared, were virtually agreed on what the nature of a league should be.[52] This surely was letting the wish be the father of the thought. Knox had not proposed that the European powers assist the United States when disturbances arose in the Western Hemisphere; and while his recognition of changed world conditions and appreciation of Europe's importance to American security placed him closer to the President than many senators, there was still a considerable gap between the two men. Wilson's concept of collective security was designed not to create but to eliminate spheres of influence, limited ententes, and alliances.

For those who were opposed to a league or were undecided, in contrast, that part of the Pennsylvanian's resolution which advocated immediate consideration of general peace terms and postponement of a league had appeal. For the out-and-out opponents, postponement offered the possibility that a league might

51. Ibid., 603-606 (December 18, 1918).
52. *New York Times,* December 20, 1918.

never be established, much less approved by the United States. Those senators who had not yet determined which way to vote on a league welcomed the opportunity for further deliberation. Postponement even appealed to certain senators who favored a league in some form but did not want it tied to a treaty which they feared would be unjust and which a league would help perpetuate. It also appealed to those who favored the imposition of harsh terms on Germany but did not desire a league.[53]

The resolution was never reported out of the Foreign Relations Committee. Wilson adamantly opposed any move to separate the League from the Treaty, and Democratic members of the Committee respected the President's wishes.[54] The Republicans were divided on the resolution. Borah and Johnson, both of whom liked the separation proposal, could not accept the resolution as long as it contained Knox's "new American doctrine." A few pro-League Republicans rejected both the separation proposal and the "new American doctrine." Taft, representing the latter senators, threatened to undertake a nationwide speaking tour against the resolution. Lodge, although in favor of the resolution, was concerned with party unity, and therefore he did not try to report it out.[55] Knox, however, would later reintroduce it, only to have it fail again largely due to the opposition of Borah and Johnson.

While Knox was the most articulate of those irreconcilables who submitted nonisolationist alternatives, there were other bitter-enders in those early months who at least expressed approval of his suggestion for continued close relations with America's recent allies. Charles Thomas made his views known in an able speech on January 3, 1919. Unlike other irreconcilables, Thomas criticized the Senate's Constitutional role in the treaty-making process. While many pro-League Democrats joined in this criticism after it became evident the Versailles Treaty was going down to defeat, Thomas was one of the few who from the beginning questioned the wisdom of the system itself. The Founding Fathers, he believed, had erred in dividing executive authority in this realm. The Senate, or at least one-third of its members, had too often been irresponsible. He admitted that a politically sagacious President should consult with senators in advance of making a treaty, for "Senators, like humbler

53. *Washington Post,* December 16, 1918; *New York Times,* December 17, 1918; *Boston Evening Transcript,* December 18, 1918.
54. *Washington Post,* December 19, 1918. Joseph Tumulty wired Wilson on December 21: "This country unanimous for League of Nations and not anxious for details. Lodge and Knox playing into our hands." Tumulty to Wilson, December 21, 1918, Wilson Papers, Series 6 A, Box 4.
55. *New York Times,* December 17, 1918.

men, are human, and therefore appreciate due recognition by the Executive of their official attributes." Thomas also disapproved of the demand for open diplomacy at the peace conference. Full publication of treaties was desirable, but the diplomats must not be forced to negotiate in public view. Unlimited publicity would cause dissension, provoke controversy, embarrass delegations, and lead to protests and confusion.

Thomas wished the President well at the peace table. He sympathized with his proposal for tariff reduction, though he was skeptical of its being effected, given nationalistic prejudices. He agreed there should be international codification of laws regarding freedom of the seas; but he thought more attention in the future should be given to the regulation and control of air power. Above all, he had doubts about any league of nations that must ultimately depend upon moral force to be effective. "Morality is a static element in human affairs, . . . its quality is essentially unchangeable." Because he thought it true "that man advances and his social condition improves with his extending grasp and domination of material things, and that his happiness and comfort are the outgrowth of the same forces which breed strife and conflict," then "it must be true that their peaceful adjustment can not depend with safety upon the possible concentration of static elements upon them." Man was a "fighting animal," life was a contest, conflicts would continue. Transferring battles "from the field to the forum" did not change the nature of man, only his methods of doing battle. Therefore, while morality was "an invaluable ally of peace and of war when its precepts [were] duly observed by all, . . . if depended upon as a controlling influence in international affairs, it is apt, like a poorly tempered sword, to break in the hands at the moment of its greatest need."

What was Thomas's answer, then, to the problems of peace-keeping? He thought the most that could be done immediately was to continue the allied coalition that had defeated Germany. "Because an alliance actually exists, there is groundwork for its growth into a league. And I think in the nature of things a league must be a growth."[56]

56. *Cong. Record*, 65 Cong., 3 sess., 994-99 (January 3, 1919). The *Washington Post*, January 4, 1919, called Thomas's speech "an unexpected development," and "a direct confutation of the charge" that only Republicans opposed Wilson's proposals. Other criticisms that he was making can be found in his article "The Evils in Our Democracy: Weak Spots in Our National Life That Must Be Remedied," *The Forum* 61 (January 1919): 44-52. Thomas's opinion of open diplomacy was not subsequently altered by the results of the peace conference. See *Cong. Record*, 66 Cong., 2 sess., 6910 (May 12, 1920).

Poindexter and Sherman agreed that maintaining close relations with England and France was preferable to joining a league of heterogeneous nations with diverse interests. Toward her recent allies, Poindexter stated, the United States must cultivate "good will—nay, more, affection." "We ought to cherish not a league but an entente," and to say to the allies: " 'We will follow your leadership in European affairs'; and then they will follow ours in American affairs."[57] Sherman declared that "Senator Knox announced the doctrine that I believe in." Peace should first be made; then the United States could "safely enter into a league that will continue the present defensive alliance between our associated nations in Europe and ourselves, with such other friendly nations as desire to join."[58]

In contrast to these suggestions were the remarks of La Follette and France. La Follette was deeply distrustful of the Allies' purposes at the conference table. If they were as interested in an enduring peace as they professed to be, he said, they would have done with diplomatic evasion and "rhetorical flim-flam." If they wanted an effective league of nations, they would get at the real causes of war: "Exact from each contracting nation binding covenants with proper guarantees to: First: Abolish enforced military service. Second: Declare, or make no war, except to repel actual invasion of territory, without first submitting the question of war, or no war, to a vote of the qualified electors of the country. Once the matter of making war is put under popular control the people will speedily realize the folly of maintaining instruments for wars in which they have determined never to engage."[59] France's proposals were set forth in a resolution requesting the President to convene a conference of Western Hemispheric nations to consider "plans for the closer cooperation of these Governments in promoting justice, progress, and friendship" among the conferees. Then, the President should invite all the world's nations to meet to consider

---

57. *Cong. Record,* 65 Cong., 3 sess., 1801-1803 (January 21, 1919); Poindexter to W. H. Cowles, publisher of the *Spokane Spokesman Review,* January 10, 28, 1919, Poindexter Papers, Series 4, files 50, 51.

58. Sherman to C. W. Baldridge and to Ruth F. Bonsall, January 6, 1919, Sherman Papers. Illinois' other irreconcilable, Medill McCormick, wrote that he would "very readily vote for a League which does not threaten the peace and security which is ours through our geographic isolation," or that was not a superstate. McCormick to J. S. Dickerson, February 7, 1919, copy in Salmon O. Levinson Papers (Harper Library, University of Chicago). McCormick later announced he would support a modified Treaty of Guarantee, to aid France for a limited period. McCormick to William Jennings Bryan, November 22, 1919, William Jennings Bryan Papers (Library of Congress).

59. *La Follette's Magazine* 10 (December 1918), 1.

such things as population congestion and sparsity; exploitation of natural resources; self-determination; economic and educational assistance to backward nations; "the ultimate establishment of a league of nations or world federation of republics for the purpose of promoting the cause of progress and of peace throughout the earth." Before attempting the latter, however, the President should conclude a peace settlement with Germany.[60]

Although the irreconcilables dominated the debates in this early stage of the fight, they were challenged frequently by both Democrats and Republicans. A not uncommon rebuttal to those bitter-enders who maintained that a league resting on moral force would fail was to ridicule them for having no faith in mankind, or to accuse them of not knowing the Scriptures. "Jesus Christ dreamt it. David, the sweet singer of Israel, dreamt it," affirmed John Sharp Williams, Democrat from Mississippi. On another occasion, when responding to Borah, Williams read verse to make his point:

Behold! the dreams that prophets dreamed are now upon the way—
A league of nations may be formed to match the dawning day,
A bond of human brotherhood, a true God-welded bond,
To hold mankind together, with cohesion far beyond
The strength that comes from weapons and from armaments of might,
Nations allied to nations by everlasting right.
This potent league of nations will need no gun nor sword,
Its order is the law of the Everliving Lord—[61]

When Key Pittman heard Knox's proposals, he immediately pronounced them "as cold as the North Pole" and "as barren of hope as Hades."[62]

In answering one of the irreconcilables' contentions—that a league ran counter to the advice of George Washington—pro-League senators sometimes fervently reverted to the eloquent reconstruction of American history. James Hamilton Lewis, Democrat from Illinois, argued that Washington had warned the American people not to take sides between the European nations, unless the United States was threatened by attack. Since the League, Lewis instructed, was to include all nations, the United States would not choose one nation over another but would be a beneficent neutral. She would "sit in the court of nations as mediator of their differences and arbiter of their grievances, . . . vanquishing force by scorning its use. In her brow glows the star of justice that

60. *Cong. Record*, 65 Cong., 3 sess., 1383 (January 14, 1919).
61. Ibid., 84-85 (December 4, 1918), 1388 (January 14, 1919).
62. Ibid., 606-8 (December 18, 1918).

will illumine where war has blackened. About her heart is the shield of honor, in her hands neither spear of power nor the scepter of authority. She will but sway her wand of love, and beneath this will arise the genii of trust and faith to lead the nations of the world to justice, liberty, and peace—the mission of America is to mankind."[63] These were the words of the party whip. Gilbert Hitchcock, who would be Democratic minority leader in 1919-1920, also denied the irreconcilables' appeal to the Founding Fathers. If Washington were on the scene today, Hitchcock contended, he would "punch a button, summon a stenographer, and dictate to the people of the United States an urgent recommendation that they join this League."

More frequently, the bitter-enders were charged with distortion and exaggeration, with setting up straw men in their attempts to discredit the League. No sane person, Wilson's defenders said, would support a league with the power as the irreconcilables alleged it would have, to destroy a nation's sovereignty. "What I am here reprehending and condemning," Hitchcock angrily declared, "is the idea that the President's efforts can be belittled and nullified by attacking something which he is not seeking to bring about." This led Knox to ask Hitchcock if he would "be good enough to tell us what the President's league is? . . . The difficulty is we do not know; and if the Senator from Nebraska does know what he is so enthusiastically supporting, will he not take us into his confidence?" Hitchcock said he did not know what it was; he knew only what it was not. It was not a Frankenstein; the League would "not require armies or navies. . . . The power of public opinion in the United States and the power of public opinion through the civilized world will be the supreme power, the moral power, which will naturally bring compliance with any agreement duly made."[64]

Borah was very unhappy with the League's proponents and asked them to get their arguments straight. When questioned about what powers and authority the League should possess, they had sometimes vaguely suggested an international military police force, at other times insisted that no force but public opinion would be necessary, and frequently sidestepped the issue completely. Yet these same senators called those who questioned Wilson's ideas insincere, even soulless and depraved. Either the proposed league would have control over a nation's vital interests, and in such case

63. Ibid., 189 (December 6, 1918).
64. Ibid., 4417 (February 27, 1919), 74 (December 4, 1918), 2656-57 (February 4, 1919).

would reduce a nation's sovereignty, or it would not have such control, and consequently would amount to "nothing more than an old lady's international quilting society."

Thomas J. Walsh, Montana's able Democratic senator, tried hard to blunt Borah's reasoning. Did Borah really want the United States, Walsh asked, to retain the liberty and freedom—hence sovereignty—to conquer another country in the future as it had conquered part of Mexico in 1846? Borah immediately answered that he did; he trusted the American people to make the right decision, whereas he had serious doubts about any international organization. Temporarily thwarted, Walsh replied that Borah might be right with respect to the United States, but what about other countries? Was it not this freedom of action for Germany that led to World War I? Would not a league prevent a similar tragedy? Borah, of course, said no. It would merely offer more temptation to a scheming Metternich or Bismarck or Kaiser Wilhelm. The Idaho irreconcilable then became the interrogator. Did Walsh want American affairs controlled "by the 57 varieties" of European nations? Did he desire to have an international organization dictate the military strength of the United States? Walsh replied negatively. In that case, said Borah, the few great powers would simply rule the world, much as the Holy Alliance had done. Walsh had no reply.[65]

The irreconcilables more than held their own in these running debates, in part because they were skillful debaters. But it was also true at this time that Wilson's followers labored under a serious disadvantage. Not knowing what form a league would take, they had to defend general concepts subject to any number of interpretations. This situation would soon be changed. In Paris Wilson had succeeded in persuading the Allied powers to accept what was largely his version of a league. On February 14, 1919, he appeared before a full session of the Peace Conference to read the completed draft of the League of Nations Constitution, or Covenant as it was called. "A living thing is born," he declared. Now he faced the task of getting the child adopted by two-thirds of the United States Senate.

On February 15 Wilson's ship left Brest harbor to bring him back to the United States. He wished the senators to view the Covenant at firsthand, in his presence. He was confident that, given this opportunity, they would appreciate what he had accomplished. Events of the past few months should have prepared him for the worst.

65. Ibid., 190-92 (December 6, 1918).

3 CONFRONTATION WITH WILSON

IF PRESIDENT WILSON believed, as did some American representatives at the Peace Conference, that the publication of the League Covenant would seriously handicap his opponents at home, he was to be sadly disappointed.[1] While it was true that the irreconcilables now were forced to address themselves to a specific document, it did not follow that their arguments would be fewer or more sympathetic. The "facts" of the Covenant did not speak for themselves. On the contrary, the Covenant raised many new questions without answering all the old ones. Wilson's troubles were only beginning and the next few weeks would sorely test his mettle. He would stay only a short time in the United States—from February 23 to March 5—just long enough to explain the Covenant to the Senate, before returning to Paris to complete the negotiations. But he spent sufficient time at home to sense the hostile mood among many senators, and before he departed he had received two direct challenges to his leadership; by then the lines of the struggle had begun to harden.

The Covenant which had been fashioned at the Peace Conference consisted of a preamble and twenty-six articles. Its heart, as Wilson frequently said, was Article ten, which pledged the signatories "to respect and preserve as against external aggression the territorial integrity and existing political independence of all States members of the League." In case of actual or threatened aggression the Executive Council was to "advise upon the means by which this obligation shall be fulfilled." Most irreconcilables agreed, among themselves and with Wilson, that Article ten was crucial. But they felt that other articles needed scrutiny also.

Not so much at this time but increasingly as the debates progressed, for example, Article seven became a source of controversy.

It provided for admission to the League of all "fully self-governing countries including Dominions and Colonies" which had manifested their intention to abide by international obligations. The controversy involved the six votes of the British Empire—England and her five "satellites," in contrast to the one vote of the forty-eight United States. Other important articles were: eight, calling for the reduction of national armaments; eleven, making "any war or threat of war . . . a matter of concern" to the League; twelve, proposing arbitration or submission to the Executive Council of disputes between members not settled by ordinary diplomatic procedures; sixteen, declaring that any member violating the twelfth article by resorting to war would "ipso facto be deemed to have committed an act of war against all other members," with immediate economic sanctions and consideration of additional military and naval action against the guilty member; eighteen, entrusting the League with supervision of the arms trade when such supervision seemed necessary for the common interest; and nineteen, establishing a mandate system over formerly German and Turkish colonies.[2] Omissions in the Covenant also were significant to the irreconcilables; there was no statement, for example, exempting the Monroe Doctrine from League jurisdiction, and no provision for withdrawal from the League. The Covenant would later be revised to correct these omissions, though still not to the satisfaction of many senators and not until the irreconcilables had fully exploited Wilson's original failure to include statements concerning these subjects.

In his speech to the delegates at Paris on February 14, Wilson had elaborated on the essence of the League. Its effectiveness, he said, would depend "primarily and chiefly upon one great force, and that is the moral force of the public opinion of the world." Armed force would be employed only if moral force proved inadequate. The League had a dual nature: it was practical in the machinery it created for the settlement of disputes; and it was humane both in its promise to uplift the world's laboring classes (Article twenty) and in the willingness of the great powers to assume obligations in the form of mandates over backward areas. But even more important than specific practical or humane aims was the spirit of cooperation which the Covenant breathed: "People that were suspicious of one another can now live as friends and comrades in a single family, and desire to do so. The miasma of distrust, of

1. *New York Tribune*, February 17, 1919.
2. Ray Stannard Baker and William E. Dodd, eds., *War and Peace: Presidential Messages, Addresses, and Public Papers, 1917-1924* (New York, 1927), 1:413-23.

intrigue, is cleared away. Men are looking eye to eye and saying, 'We are brothers and have a common purpose. We did not realize it before, but now we do realize it, and this is our covenant of fraternity and of friendship.' "[3]

The President may have expressed in these words the sentiments of millions of the world's peoples, but there were senators who remained suspicious, who were convinced that distrust and intrigue had not vanished, who felt no desire to live as brothers in one big happy family. A few of the irreconcilables—notably France and the peace progressives—shared Wilson's feeling about human brotherhood (without necessarily subscribing to all the League's articles), but most were negative and critical. The President would find his most difficult problem was not to persuade millions, but to induce sixty-four senators to accept his program.

On the day that Wilson presented the League Covenant in Paris, he sent cablegrams to all members of the Senate Foreign Relations Committee and House Foreign Affairs Committee requesting a meeting in the White House when he returned to the United States. He wanted to explain the Covenant "article by article" before it was formally debated in Congress.[4] He hoped that Knox and Lodge, in particular, would remain silent until he had spoken to them.[5]

Knox and Lodge, like most senators, respected the President's wish, but others refused to withhold comment, perhaps justifiably, given the announcement on February 15 that Wilson, upon landing in Boston, would deliver a speech there on the League.[6] Massachusetts was Lodge's home state. It appeared that the President intended to make a frontal assault on the Republican minority leader and ranking Republican on the Foreign Relations Committee. This latest announcement, coming as it did on the heels of the President's request for silence, seemed grossly partisan to some Republicans. "It rather takes the edge off the White House dinner," as one senator remarked.[7]

3. Ibid., 423-29.
4. Ibid., 412.
5. *New York Tribune,* February 17, 1919.
6. Knox and Lodge expressed their feelings in separate letters to Albert Beveridge. Knox wrote: "All present indications are that the new constitution of the universe will be properly attended to in the Senate and if men will vote as they talk there will be small chance for it." Knox to Beveridge, February 18, 1919, Beveridge Papers, Box 215. Lodge, more concerned with public opinion, advised Beveridge that it would not "be wise for us at this stage to make it a party issue, nor to confront it with a blank negative." Lodge to Beveridge, February 18, 1919, ibid., Box 216.
7. *New York Times,* February 16, 1919.

Poindexter, Borah, and Sherman issued statements on February 16. Poindexter denounced Articles eight, twelve, eighteen, and nineteen as contrary to American traditions and destructive of the nation's sovereignty. Borah similarly attacked these four articles as well as Article ten and also noted the absence of any reference to the Monroe Doctrine; the League, he asserted, would obliterate "all distinction between European and American affairs." Sherman emphasized the League's weakness. Its enforcement sanctions appeared innocuous to him; they resembled the Hague Convention with one addition, namely, economic pressures. But at the same time he reaffirmed his opposition to any league which delimited American sovereignty.[8] Thus the familiar double-edged argument.

On February 19 Poindexter further disregarded the President's request for silence by discussing the League in the Senate. Lodge and Knox had apparently wanted him to wait until Wilson had spoken in Boston, believing that "the only way to pin him [Wilson] down is to let him lay all his cards on the table." But Poindexter did not wait.[9] He said he had no qualms about speaking out. The President's request was patently unfair. Why should senators who questioned the wisdom of the League's proposals remain mute while champions of the League such as Taft's League to Enforce Peace organization continued to propagandize in its favor? How could the President expect silence when he himself made ready to speak before conferring with the Congress? If the League had merit, debate would so indicate; if it lacked merit, that, too, would come out.

In the characteristic irreconcilable way, Poindexter prefaced his criticism of specific articles by ridiculing or denouncing some general aspect of United States policy. The tactic was effective, if done well, since it made the subsequent criticisms appear to be, as they in fact often were, grounded on a solid analysis of Wilson's larger ideological purposes. In this instance Poindexter challenged Wilson's wartime references to the United States as an associate rather than an ally of England and France. The United States was for all practical purposes an ally and the alliance still offered, as the Washington irreconcilable had previously insisted, the best hope of preserving peace. But—and he now led into his main points—if this

8. Ibid.; *Brooklyn Daily Eagle*, February 16, 1919.
9. Charles M. Thompson (editor of the *Boston Advertiser*) to Poindexter, February 17, 18, 1919 (telegrams); Poindexter to Thompson, February 19, 1919, Poindexter Papers, Series 4, file 51. Poindexter told Thompson that he had not received the request from Lodge and Knox, which Thompson relayed, in time; but he may simply have decided to ignore it. Thompson's telegrams should have arrived prior to the senator's speech.

alliance "has been so diverted from its purposes and so preoccupied in seeking for a permanent and universal league for the establishment of future peace, that it has not been able to restore present peace, or set up orderly government in central Europe and Russia, can we expect the proposed future league to accomplish more?"

Everyone longed for universal peace, he continued, but nobody wanted to sacrifice his nation's vital interests. Vital interests might seem well protected in peacetime situations, but there were always underlying threats. When these threats became serious, it was often imperative for a nation to forestall danger early and quickly, "by war, if necessary, as a last resort—rather than to allow the menace to develop to such proportion as will call for greater sacrifices in the end." The League's machinery, Poindexter believed, would either be too cumbersome for such purposes or it would impede a nation's meeting such threats by its own resources. While the League's supporters gave assurances that the organization would not encroach on a member nation's freedom to act, there would always be moral pressure on a nation not to act, perhaps to wait too long. If the United States did not follow the League's general prohibitions and specific recommendations, it would appear to the world as untrustworthy and deceitful. There could be no doubt it would sometime appear that way, for the mere fact of being in the League would not deter the United States from acting as it saw fit in vital emergencies, as it had always done. Why, then, Poindexter asked, was there no provision for withdrawal from the League? A dissatisfied member should have the right to withdraw, after observing the legal steps, without obloquy. Such a withdrawal might be required by certain vital issues of national interest.[10]

At one point, when the Washington bitter-ender was questioning the constitutionality of the Covenant, he was challenged by Norris, who thought it incorrect to say the League was less Constitutional than any previous treaty the United States had made. The Supreme Court had held acts of Congress to be on an equal Constitutional footing with treaties, and Congress could, if it desired, overrule the League. Poindexter responded that the League would involve the United States in countless difficulties, which was not an answer to Norris. Norris replied that "the history of the world has shown that we have gotten into a good deal of trouble by staying out [of a league]." Brandegee then intervened to ask Norris if Wilson's League was not quite different from an ordinary treaty. Norris

10. *Cong. Record,* 65 Cong., 3 sess., 3746–56 (February 19, 1919).

answered affirmatively, but said that that was not his point. There the exchange ended. While Norris was unwilling to commit himself in favor of Wilson's League, neither was he at this time decided against it.[11] Like La Follette, he would wait until the rest of the peace terms were known before making a major speech on the Covenant.

Within three days of Poindexter's speech, Sherman, Borah, and Reed each took the floor. Sherman introduced a resolution asking the President to make no public address until he had met with the Foreign Relations and Foreign Affairs Committees. To speak in Boston would be "unwise, undiplomatic, and calculated to promote discord and misunderstanding" between the two branches of government. The President must not forget the Senate's "equal rank and dignity" in treaty making.[12]

On that same day, February 21, Borah delivered what his colleagues considered one of his most effective speeches of the League fight. While he expounded at length about the conflict between the League and the Monroe Doctrine, his sharpest points were made against Article seven, admitting self-governing dominions and colonies to the League. Under this article, he asserted, the British Empire would control the League, for Britain's dominions would surely do her bidding. Moreover, she had neither relinquished her position as the greatest naval power nor complied with Wilson's demand for freedom of the seas. In contrast, the United States was being asked to surrender its historic policies, to take the first step toward sterilizing nationalism. Reaching his peroration, the Idaho bitter-ender fervently proclaimed the proper course for Americans to follow: "What we want is . . . a free, untrammeled Nation, imbued anew and inspired again with the national spirit; not isolation but freedom to do as our own people think wise and just; not isolation but simply the unembarrassed and unentangled freedom of a great Nation to determine for itself and in its own way where duty lies and where wisdom calls."[13] As Borah took his seat, both Democrats and Republicans rushed to shake his hand. Anti-League senators were "in ecstacies" about the speech.[14] Wilson's personal secretary, Joseph Tumulty, was suf-

11. Ibid., 3749-51. A few days later Norris contradicted Lodge's interpretation of Articles twelve and thirteen of the Covenant. Ibid., 4525 (February 28, 1919).

12. Ibid., 3909 (February 21, 1919).

13. Ibid., 3913-15 (February 21, 1919).

14. *New York Times,* February 22, 1919; *Philadelphia Public Ledger,* February 24, 1919; Gus Karger to William Howard Taft, February 22, 1919, William Howard Taft Papers (Library of Congress), Box 451.

ficiently concerned to ask Key Pittman how much of an impression
Borah had made. Pittman felt "compelled to admit" that it was
a "powerful and effective" performance and that Borah's arguments
had converted some Republican senators and weakened the convictions of some Democratic members.[15] While Pittman may have
overstated the effect of the speech—he was inclined to overstate-
ment—there is little reason to doubt that the Idaho irreconcilable
had aroused the emotions of his listeners as had no one heretofore.

But the next day, Borah's performance was equaled, at least in
effect if not in quality, by James Reed's oration. It was February 22,
Washington's birthday, "a day devoted to Americanism at the
Capitol." The Senate galleries were packed, as they had been for
the past several days; discharged soldiers, many of them "clinging
to crutches or swinging empty sleeves," looked down on the proceedings, while almost all the senators and more than fifty representatives were present.[16] Reed started slowly, like Borah, criticizing Article seven, which would give Great Britain undue influence; charging that Article ten would freeze the status quo, much
as the Holy Alliance had done; finding the "fangs" of Bolshevism—
"that monster"—embedded in the spirit of the Covenant. Americans
had to understand, Reed shouted, that control of the League of
Nations would mean control of the world. "I want to burn it into the
brain and heart of the American people, that every nation entering
the League yields to its arbitrament and decision all controversies
with other countries, even though they involve the national honor
or the national interest."[17] For five minutes the galleries applauded,
drowning out Vice President Marshall's gavel. As after Borah's
speech, senators of both parties came to congratulate Reed. Lodge,
in particular, had many kind words for both Borah and Reed.[18]

15. Pittman to Tumulty, February 21, 1919, Pittman Papers, Box 68, AC.,
10, 355. Not all Democrats were discouraged. Thomas Walsh wrote on the
twenty-first: "It looks as if the republican brethren are about to align
themselves against the League of Nations in the hope of discrediting the
President. In my judgment, we should encourage them to take that course.
I am satisfied that the country is overwhelmingly in favor of the plan. They
[the Republicans] have all sorts of troubles before them, being obliged to
depend upon the vote of Senator La Follette to organize the upper branch of
Congress and to carry any measures which they desire to pass." Walsh to
Thomas Arthur, February 21, 1919, Walsh Papers, Box 284. For a similar ex-
pression by another Democratic politician, see the March 21 diary entry in the
Breckenridge Long Diary (Library of Congress, Washington, D.C.).
16. *Washington Post,* February 20, 23, 1919. Shortly before Reed's address,
Joseph Frelinghuysen, a New Jersey Republican, read aloud Washington's
Farewell Address.
17. *Cong. Record,* 65 Cong., 3 sess., 4027-33 (February 22, 1919).
18. Denna Frank Fleming, *The United States and the League of Nations,*

Clearly the irreconcilables were accelerating their attack on the eve of Wilson's return.

On February 23 Wilson landed in Boston and on the next day delivered his address, already controversial before he said a word. Colonel House, from Paris, had cabled the President on the twentieth disagreeing with his decision to speak before meeting the committees. Under the circumstances, House advised, he should confine his remarks to generalities.[19] Wilson in the beginning did just that, not discussing the articles of the Covenant, but stressing the great idealism of American policy. "Speaking with perfect frankness," he said, "in the name of the people of the United States I have uttered as the objects of this great war ideals, and nothing but ideals, and the war has been won by that inspiration." Such idealism had inspired among the world's peoples trust in American purposes. It was that trust which created the burden the United States must carry; but it was a burden "any nation ought to be proud to carry," and he had no doubt it would be gladly borne. At the close of his address, Wilson disregarded House's advice and turned on his Senate foes. He realized, he said, there had been a few critics of his ideals. There would always be naysayers, but these individuals would be crushed. "Any man who resists the present tides that run in the world will find himself thrown upon a shore so high and barren that it will seem as if he had been separated from his human kind forever." These men had a perverted vision of the mission of the United States. In explaining this mission, Wilson expressed virtually the same view as had Joseph France in the summer of 1918. "We set this Nation up to make men free and we did not confine our conception and purpose to America, and now we will make men free. If we did not do that all the fame of America would be gone and all her power would be dissipated. She would then have to keep her power for those narrow, selfish, provincial purposes which seem so dear to some minds that have no sweep beyond the nearest horizon." Wilson flung down the gauntlet: "I have fighting blood in me and it is sometimes a delight to let it have scope, but if it is challenged on this occasion it will be an indulgence."[20]

1918-1920 (New York, 1932), 124. *Philadelphia Public Ledger*, February 24, 1919; *Washington Post*, February 23, 1919.

19. House to Wilson, February 20, 1919, Wilson Papers, Series 8 A, Box 21. On the same day Wilson wrote to L. S. Rowe, Assistant Secretary of the Treasury: "I sometimes get the impression that all that is being said in America is critical and very little of it approving." Wilson to Rowe, February 20, 1919, ibid. Wilson soon showed he was in no conciliatory mood.

20. Baker and Dodd, eds., *War and Peace*, 1:432-40.

The irreconcilables said little publicly about the speech, but pro- and anti-League senators alike believed the President had made a direct move to arouse public opinion in his favor.[21] As if to confirm his offensive stance, Wilson on the twenty-fifth told Democratic Senator Thomas Martin of Virginia that he would not call a special session of Congress before he returned from Paris the second time with the completed Treaty; any delay in passing bills in this session would be attributable to Republicans.[22]

Events were moving rapidly. February 26 was the day of the President's meeting with the Foreign Relations and Foreign Affairs Committees. Two senators—both irreconcilables—would not be attending. Borah announced that "the differences between the President and myself on this question are fundamental," and he did not want to receive information which undoubtedly he would be obliged to regard as confidential but which he might obtain from other sources. Albert Fall similarly preferred to remain free of any restrictions and suggested that Wilson's proper course would have been to address a joint session of Congress. Some thought Fall's reasons for declining the invitation may have been influenced by the President's open opposition to his reelection the previous November.[23]

The meeting was held in the evening at the White House, preceded by a dinner at which Lodge sat next to Mrs. Wilson. After the dinner, which Brandegee described as "uncomfortable and uncongenial," Wilson led the senators and representatives into the East Room, "gathered them in a semi-circle in front of him, like a school class, and announced that, of course, he had no statement to make, but if anybody wanted to ask any questions that they were at liberty to do so."[24] No reporters were present at any time during the evening and the accounts by participants about what took place differ. As nearly as can be determined, the questions which arose most frequently concerned the Monroe Doctrine, withdrawal, and Article ten, especially its meaning for Ireland in her

21. *Louisville Courier-Journal,* February 25, 26, 1919.
22. *New York Times,* February 26, 1919; *Washington Post,* February 26, 1919.
23. *New York Tribune,* February 19, 22, 1919; *New York Times,* February 21, 1919; *Hartford* (Conn.) *Daily Courant,* February 21, 1919.
24. Brandegee related the story to Chandler D. Anderson, an international lawyer who had served as a counsel for Knox when the latter was Secretary of State. See Anderson's diary entry of March 13, 1919, in the Chandler D. Anderson Papers (Library of Congress), Box 4. Charles Thomas gave a quite different account of the dinner. He said the affair was very pleasant and that Wilson entertained the guests with great charm. Thomas autobiography.

struggle for independence from England. All those present recalled that Brandegee was the most persistent inquisitor.[25]

According to the *New York Sun,* a paper whose publisher, Frank Munsey, had excellent contacts with the bitter-enders, Brandegee elicited from Wilson the statement that there had been four proposed drafts of the Covenant and that the final draft closely resembled the one submitted by England. Anglophobic senators felt this information confirmed their opinion that the League would be dominated by England. Discussion then turned to the Monroe Doctrine. When Wilson stated that the League would not destroy the Monroe Doctrine but extend it to the entire world, Brandegee resumed his questioning. What would happen, he asked, if at some future time a European country decided to reestablish its former position of influence and power in Latin America? "Would the United States still have the authority to prevent an extension of European authority in this hemisphere?" Wilson thought Brandegee's hypothetical situation "inconceivable," but if it did, "it would be very distressing." "Most distressing," Brandegee dryly agreed.[26]

The question of what the League proposed to do about Ireland provoked the sharpest reaction from both Wilson and the irreconcilables. The White House subsequently issued a statement branding as "a deliberate falsehood" press reports that the President had said the question "was a matter between Ireland and England."[27] No further explanation about the substance of statements at the meeting was given. The subject came up for debate in the Senate on the twenty-eighth, however, which gave the bitter-enders a chance to cross-examine the Democratic members of the Foreign Relations Committee. Borah, whose fame as a frontier lawyer preceded him to Washington, did most of the interrogating. He was especially persistent in his questioning of Hitchcock. The Democratic minority leader was in the process of chastising Republicans for having given out inaccurate reports of what had happened at the meeting with the President. According to Hitchcock, one Republican representative had quoted Wilson as having said, in effect, "Ireland is to be left to the mercies of England." Nothing even resembling that statement had been made, Hitchcock asserted. Borah interrupted:

25. Henry Cabot Lodge, *The Senate and the League of Nations* (New York, 1925), 100; *New York Tribune,* February 28, 1919; *New York Post,* February 27, 1919; *New York Sun,* February 28, 1919. The *Sun* has the fullest newspaper account of the conference.

26. *New York Sun,* February 28, 1919.

27. *New York Times,* March 1, 1919.

"Would it be permissible for the Senator to state what the President did say with reference to Ireland?"

"The President practically stated nothing with reference to Ireland. The Irish question was not under consideration," Hitchcock replied.

"But there were questions asked?"

"There was a question asked which was greeted with laughter, and there was nothing more said about it. It was not an issue in the conversation and had nothing to do with it. We were not discussing internal questions but international questions."

"Does the Senator say the President made no response to the question which was presented to him with reference to the independence of Ireland?"

"It was not a serious question presented; it was not presented in a serious way."

"Pardon me. Does the Senator say the President made no response to it?"

"I do. However, the Senator from Mississippi [Mr. Williams] corrects me. He says the President stated that the League had nothing to do with domestic and internal questions. He did state that; he stated it several times during the evening. . . ."

"Then, if I understand the Senator correctly, what the President said with reference to the question, since he has raised the question himself with reference to Ireland, was that the League had nothing to do with it."

"The Senator from Mississippi recollected that."

"And that was a matter, therefore, with which the League had nothing to do, but which must necessarily be settled by Ireland and England?"

"The Senator can draw his own conclusion," Hitchcock said, and then tried to shift his ground by maintaining that his quarrel was not with the senators who had made public comments about the meeting, but with the newspapers which had printed them. Borah, however, would not let his foe go free. It surely appeared, he said, as if Hitchcock was at least indirectly attacking those who questioned Wilson, even if he stated otherwise. In any case, Borah said, "If the Senator from Mississippi and the Senator from Nebraska are at a difference as to what the President said upon that important matter, other Senators might have understood it in a different way." Borah took his seat and Hitchcock started to turn to another subject. Before he could finish a sentence Poindexter was asking for recognition and demanding that Hitchcock reconcile the President's statement that the League would exercise no control over a nation's immigration policies, with the provisions in Article twelve of the Covenant giving the League power to arbitrate disputes between nations.[28]

The White House meeting, in short, probably had little effect on senators' opinions. Its importance lay in the misunderstandings and recriminations that followed. Such comments as that which Brandegee made after the meeting: "I feel as if I had been wandering with 'Alice in Wonderland' and had had tea with the mad hatter," could only add to Wilson's growing wrath.[29] Democratic senators were reportedly worried lest the President's attitude become too inflexible on the League.[30]

That Wilson was incensed by the reception he and the League were receiving was made vividly apparent at a private luncheon given for members of the Democratic National Committee on February 28. In the course of his speech to the Committee members he scathingly castigated his detractors. They were "blind and little, provincial people," who reminded him "of a man with a head that is not a head but is just a knot providentially put there to keep him from ravelling out." These men went against the whole impulse of modern times. "They are going to have the most conspicuously contemptible names in history. The gibbets that they are going to be executed on by future historians will scrape the heavens, they will be so high. They won't be turned in the direction of heaven at all."[31] Wilson's speech was to have remained confidential, but inevitably such sensational remarks as these reached the press. The irreconcilables seized upon them. Here was further evidence, they charged, of the President's egoism, vanity, and vindictiveness. It

28. *Cong. Record*, 65 Cong., 3 sess., 4528-30 (February 28, 1919).

29. *New York Sun*, February 28, 1919. Wilson, according to House, "spoke with considerable bitterness" of the way Republican senators had treated him. House Diary, March 14, 1919, House Papers.

30. *New York Times*, February 28, 1919. On the twenty-fifth Thomas Walsh, less sanguine than a few days before, wrote to the President that "the recent discussions in the Senate and the study which individual members have made of the draft of the . . . League . . . has disclosed not a little in the language employed that is obscure and more, the wisdom of which is seriously questioned by the earnest friends of the project." Walsh asked the President to meet with six senators and six congressmen (he suggested only Democrats) "to go at the draft as one of our committees is accustomed to do with important bills . . . subjecting the draft to real constructive criticism." Wilson acknowledged that there were "many parts of the proposed Covenant . . . which could with advantage be clarified and rewritten," but he did not have time to hold "deliberate conferences" with the group. Walsh to Wilson, February 25, 1919, and Wilson to Walsh, February 26, 1919, Wilson Papers, Series 8 A, Box 21.

31. Joseph Tumulty, *Woodrow Wilson As I Know Him* (Garden City, N. Y., 1921), 377-79. Cf. Arthur Walworth, *Woodrow Wilson*, 2d ed., rev. (Boston, 1965), 2:273-74.

was truly regettable, Sherman said very solemnly, for a President of the United States who had written a history of his country as well as a study of American political institutions, to descend to the "raw vernacular" in discussing members of the Senate. As for the President's assertion that those who opposed the League had pygmy minds and were against the stream of history, Sherman said he was reminded of visiting a mental institution in which all the patients swore that they were sane and everyone outside was demented.[32] The irreconcilables were not to be outdone in the art of vituperation.

Surely one reason for Wilson's angry outbursts in late February was his dawning realization that the Sixty-fifth Congress might adjourn on March 4 before passing several important pieces of legislation; indeed, it appeared there might even be a filibuster to forestall congressional action and thereby force the President to call a special session of the new Sixty-sixth Congress months before it was regularly scheduled to meet. Such a special session would, of course, allow the Republicans—victorious at the last election—to take control of the legislative branch. The irreconcilables naturally looked forward to this prospect, not only because most of the group were Republicans, but mainly because the Senate was by far the best forum in which to publicize their views.

In his statement of February 25 insisting he would not call a special session of Congress until he again returned from Paris, the President had cited such measures as the army and navy appropriation bills, the water power act, and the oil and coal leasing bill, among others that were long overdue for congressional action. In making this announcement, he obviously hoped to prod the lawmakers into quickening their pace. But by taking such an inflexible stance, Wilson left himself vulnerable. For while he had the Constitutional authority not to call an extraordinary session of Congress, in fact Congress could, by refusing to enact necessary legislation, almost compel him to take such action. The power of a small minority to block legislation at the close of a congressional session was notorious. Even if Wilson's influence over the Senate had been greater and even if there had existed a crisis atmosphere which seemed to compel legislative action, his threat not to call a special session still would have been a questionable tactic. Given his recent actions, it had almost no chance of success. It was, indeed, one of his more notable mistakes of the League fight, one curiously neglected or underemphasized in accounts of the Treaty fight,

32. *Cong. Record,* 65 Cong., 3 sess., 4977-80 (March 4, 1919).

perhaps because the filibuster which killed the legislation and insured the special session has been overshadowed by the more dramatic Round Robin which occurred at the same time.

Speculation about an extra session had started after the Republican victory in the congressional elections the previous November. By late January, 1919, Republicans were declaring and some Democrats conceding that a special session was inevitable. Bills had piled up even more than usual, chiefly because of the great interest in the peace treaty. Speeches by senators of both parties had been frequent and lengthy. Moreover, Democratic leadership in the Senate was not functioning as smoothly as it might have. Pittman complained in a letter to Wilson's private secretary that the Democrats had been unable even to keep a quorum and that they had not caucused nearly often enough. Committees which should have reported out months earlier had waited until the last minute when a filibuster could tie up the proceedings. He predicted that an extra session was unavoidable.[33] Pittman's letter was written on February 21, four days before Wilson lambasted Republicans for delaying legislation, tactics which he asserted would not cause him to call a special session.

Republican motives for desiring a special session were mixed. Lodge, whose part in bringing about the special session has not been properly stressed, in contrast to the treatment of his role in the Round Robin, for which he sometimes is given undue credit, was mainly interested, as were most Republicans, in having the Senate in session to watch critically over the developments relating to the peace treaty. For several months he had been writing letters to this effect. La Follette, who was to be the actual leader of the filibuster, also wanted the Senate in session, so as to keep the American peace commissioners informed of the Senate's attitude, but the Wisconsin progressive's first concern was to prevent the passage of certain bills that he felt would despoil America's natural resources.[34]

La Follette had been aware of Lodge's desires for some time before Lodge approached him in early February and said, "There *must* be an extra session." When La Follette asked why nothing had been said about it recently, Lodge answered that he had been busy

33. Pittman to Tumulty, February 21, 1919, Pittman Papers, Box 68. Tumulty wired Wilson on the nineteenth: "Hitchcock and friends embarrassed to know what their attitude should be toward answering Borah and other leaders of opposition." Tumulty to Wilson, February 19, 1919, Wilson Papers, Series 8 A, Box 21.

34. Belle Case La Follette and Fola La Follette, *Robert M. La Follette* (New York, 1953), 2:932-48.

but now intended to devote more attention to the question and "might welcome anything that took up the time." La Follette had little confidence that Lodge and his conservative followers would work openly with him in a filibuster, especially if it appeared there might be pressures against it, but he did expect to receive covert support. Therefore he went ahead and on February 23 telephoned Sherman—a conservative, to be sure, but intensely anti-Wilson as well as anti-League, and with none of Lodge's concern for public reaction and its effect on the party—to ask if he would assist him. Sherman readily agreed; on the same day France and Gronna consented to join them.[35]

At this time there were occasional newspaper reports discussing the possibility of a filibuster, but La Follette and his cohorts effectively kept their precise intentions concealed. Democratic senators continued to make speeches on the League, even after Wilson's announcement, thus consuming valuable time. On March 1, however, the filibusterers were pressed into action. Pittman, as conference manager, gave the Senate report on the coal and oil bill. He admitted that it could be killed by means of a filibuster since only a few hours remained before the $7 billion victory bond bill was scheduled for consideration, and once the bond bill was taken up the leasing bill would be lost for this session. Two speeches on the League by Knox and Thomas Hardwick, an anti-Wilson Democrat whose term was ending, occupied about three hours. La Follette then got the floor and, frankly avowing his determination to talk the leasing bill to death, spoke until the Senate recessed at 5 P.M. to permit a Republican caucus to decide if the party would support a filibuster of the bond bill.[36]

The caucus was extremely acrimonious. Several senators, in-

35. Ibid., 941, 944. Gronna was not feeling well at this time and could do nothing more than ask opportune questions of the other active filibusterers in order to give them occasional rests. Norris opposed a filibuster, though he blamed Wilson as well as the Senate for not expediting legislation. See Norris to Walter Locke, March 18, 1919, Norris Papers, Box 10.

36. *Cong. Record*, 65 Cong., 3 sess., 4682-94 (March 1, 1919). *New York Tribune*, March 2, 1919. Knox attacked the League on several counts: that it did not abolish war; that it violated the Constitution, encroached on American sovereignty, and threatened American independence. At the same time he suggested different alternatives, including the outlawing of war. Salmon Levinson, the Chicago lawyer whose unrelenting activity in behalf of outlawry helped lay the groundwork for the Kellogg-Briand Pact of 1928, conferred with Knox for three days before Knox's speech and thereafter did so regularly. Levinson to William E. Borah, December 8, 1921, and Levinson to Medill McCormick, January 24, 1922, Levinson Papers, Boxes 5 and 58. The outlawry proposal was never promoted too vigorously by Knox, who was always more interested in his "new American doctrine."

cluding Norris and La Follette, did not attend; the latter had already made up his mind and would not be halted by a party edict. France introduced the motion to filibuster against the bond bill. Heated debate followed. The chief opposition to the motion came from Lodge and Knox, both of whom said that the party could not risk the responsibility for defeating such an important bill. Obstruction, Lodge argued, would be construed as partisan, and the bill's failure "might cause serious unrest in financial circles." Lodge probably had concluded that La Follette and his colleagues were determined to filibuster regardless of the caucus vote; therefore he would oppose the motion so as to appear responsible, knowing that a special session would be likely anyway as the result of the filibuster. Leading the support for a filibuster were France, Sherman, Brandegee, and Boies Penrose. They argued that the Democrats had been lax in reporting the various bills and now were attempting to push them through too hastily. Furthermore, the press was saying that if the bond bill passed it would be a great partisan victory for the Democrats. The vote was finally taken; it was 15 to 14 against a filibuster. Sherman, Brandegee, and Penrose stalked out of the meeting, Sherman declaring loudly to reporters that if his colleagues had no "backbone" and would not "call the President's bluff," he saw no reason to serve in the Senate any longer as a mere pawn. He might as well stay in Illinois after Congress adjourned and not return when the Republicans organized the Sixty-sixth Congress. Sherman, who was well aware that the party needed every member present to organize the new Senate, warned Republican leaders: "You fellows might need a vote later, when you won't get it."[37] His threat was not as idle as it might seem. Suffering acutely from a failing sense of hearing, he had already decided to retire from politics when his term expired in 1920; for several months he had been despondently confiding to close friends that his inability to hear what was said on the floor rendered him almost useless.[38] The caucus vote clearly would not restrain the filibusterers.

The Senate reconvened at 7 o'clock. Army blankets and extra

37. *New York Times*, March 2, 1919; *Brooklyn Daily Eagle*, March 2, 1919; *New York Sun*, March 2, 1919. La Follette and La Follette, *La Follette*, 2:945. The latter two sources state that the caucus vote was 13-12 and 14-11 respectively. Although France did not make any threatening statement, La Follette wrote that he was as furious as Sherman. Both were ready "to quit the party and go in for a new deal" (*La Follette*, 2:945).

38. Sherman to Noah C. Bainum, December 9, 1918, saying he had made his decision not to run for reelection in 1920 as early as June, 1916. See also Sherman to Charles Dawes, December 10, 1918, Sherman Papers.

chairs had been brought in by the sergeant-at-arms so that senators who stayed the night could get some rest.[39] La Follette resumed his speech and for the next several hours debate continued. According to the *New York Times,* Lodge seemed worried, pacing "up and down the Senate chamber, his hands clasped behind his back, apparently without definite knowledge" of the plans of the filibusterers. Sherman was the only Republican willing to join La Follette in filibustering against the bond bill, although Reed spoke for a few hours, undoubtedly with the intention of helping force an extra session. At 6:40 A.M. on March 2, La Follette and Sherman gave up and let the bond bill pass. Thereupon the Senate adjourned until the morning of March 3. The most important legislation yet to be considered was the general deficiency bill, carrying $840 million in appropriations for expenses already incurred by the government, including a sizable sum to finance government operation of the railroads. Democratic leaders still had hope for the bill's passage.[40] La Follette, however, had other ideas. Fearing that if the general deficiency bill passed, the leasing bill might also go through, he resolved to continue the filibuster. Sherman and France agreed to spell him during the final hours.[41]

The final twenty-six hours of the session began at 10 A.M. on March 3. A spirited exchange between Irvine Lenroot, Republican from Wisconsin, and Thomas Martin, Virginia Democrat, highlighted the afternoon hours. Martin charged that the defeat of the general deficiency bill would bring financial panic to the country. Lenroot asked if its defeat would impel the President to call a special session. Martin replied that "in two conversations, in the plainest possible English, [the President said] that he had made up his mind, and it was final, that no extra session of Congress will be called under any circumstances until his return from France."[42]

As the hours dragged by, La Follette, Sherman, and France bided their time, willing to let others occupy the floor. Only when it appeared a vote might be taken on the general deficiency bill did they begin to filibuster. At 1 A.M. on March 4 Sherman started speaking. After an hour he was relieved by La Follette who spoke for the next four hours. He decried the attempt "to coerce Senators into playing the shameful part of automatons and blindly voting

---

39. *Buffalo Courier,* March 2, 1919; *Pittsburgh Gazette - Times,* March 5, 1919.

40. *New York Times,* March 2, 3, 1919. The *New York Tribune* reported that the passage of the bond bill removed any chance of an immediate extra session after March 4. *New York Tribune,* March 4, 1919.

41. La Follette and La Follette, *La Follette,* 2:946.

42. *New York Times,* March 4, 1919.

measures through." Attacking the leasing and water power bills, he charged that selfish private interests were behind the measures. Similarly, big bankers had been responsible for pressing Republican senators into opposing a filibuster of the victory bond bill. A minor part of his speech stressed the need of the Senate to be in session while Wilson was in Paris, but La Follette did not align himself squarely against the League. Throughout his filibuster he was given support by a half-dozen irreconcilables asking sympathetic questions and making comments.[43]

France took the floor at 6 A.M. Most of his remarks concerned international affairs. He concurred in Knox's advice about making peace first and then attending to a world organization, but it was clear he did not share Knox's view of what a league should be. Any organization that sought mainly to preserve the status quo, France said, was doomed to failure. A successful league must destroy the balance of power and devote itself to promoting "world progress and human justice." It should assume "constructive and humanitarian" responsibility for assisting other nations, especially in Africa. As the most powerful and prosperous nation, the United States had a particular obligation in this area. France also recommended a more liberal policy toward Russia. American troops should be withdrawn and in their place plows and other farm equipment should be sent. It was imperative that friendly relations be established with Russia if a lasting peace were to be effected.[44]

At 8 o'clock it was Sherman's turn. He had earlier indicated that his purpose would largely be to ridicule Wilson and denounce the League. The most effective way of doing this, he said, was to defeat the appropriation bills and force an extra session. Unlike La Follette, Sherman saw no "grave questions involved" in these bills that were up for passage. Since nothing serious was at stake, senators could sit back and enjoy the proceedings. He would play the court jester to King Woodrow, for only a king would use language such as gibbeting his enemies. "Let us be the King's fool a while, because while the King has certainly come home again, his stay is brief, and, indeed . . . we make holiday tonight 'to see Caesar and rejoice in his triumph.'" Sherman taunted Wilson by

43. *Cong. Record*, 65 Cong., 3 sess., 4980-90 (March 4, 1919). Thomas criticized the filibuster, although by doing so on several occasions he also contributed to it. Ibid., 4980, 4985, 5007.

44. Ibid., 4999-5006. "Rarely have the halls of the Senate resounded with such an eloquent plea in behalf of the African nations as in this filibuster by a Southerner, a Republican from Maryland, [and] an irreconcilable." Rayford Logan, *The Senate and the Versailles Mandate System* (Washington, D. C., 1945), 37-38.

referring to his Boston speech: "I challenge the President . . . that we may combat with him in an open forum and on equal terms. If he is not a political and governmental coward, he will give us that right. An honorable antagonist would do no less, and if he has the fighting blood he boasts, he will do even more."[45] No one excelled Sherman in the art of invective. Vice President Marshall, who had once taken pride in his mastery of words "that would wound," admitted he was "a mere kindergarten pupil" in comparison to the Illinois bitter-ender.[46]

On the morning of March 4 Wilson came to the Capitol so that he could hurriedly sign any bills that were passed before Congress adjourned at noon. Huge crowds of spectators thronged the corridors. As Sherman continued speaking, Democratic senators tried unsuccessfully to take him off the floor. Lodge and Knox privately made last-minute pleas to allow the general deficiency bill to pass, probably pointing out that enough other legislation had been defeated to insure an extra session.[47] But not until 11:30 did Sherman take his seat, assured there was inadequate time left to accomplish anything. Thirty minutes later Vice President Marshall rapped his gavel and declared the Senate adjourned *"sine Deo,"* a bitter pun on the customary *"sine die."*[48] The Sixty-fifth Congress, which had begun in 1917 as a special session called to declare war on Germany—after a filibuster had ended the Sixty-fourth Congress—closed two years later with a filibuster designed to force a special session of the Sixty-sixth Congress to consider the peace settlement.

Of all the important bills that had awaited action, only the bond bill and a wheat appropriation measure were passed. The leasing bill, the water power act, the army and navy appropriation bills, and the general deficiency bill went down to defeat. The filibusterers had carried through their plan. The next move was the President's.

The other major confrontation with Wilson was the Round Robin. In contrast to the filibuster, it required only a few minutes to execute. But it was not, as usually pictured, either in content or in the manner of its implementation an almost accidental or spon-

---

45. *Cong. Record,* 65 Cong., 3 sess., 4867 (March 3, 1919), 4977 (March 4, 1919).

46. Thomas R. Marshall, *Recollections* (Indianapolis, Ind., 1925), 290.

47. *New York Times,* March 5, 1919; *Washington Post,* March 4, 5, 1919. The *New York Post,* March 4, 1919, said that the killing of the army and navy appropriation bills alone would have been sufficient to force an extra session. Lodge admitted that he "gave some personal attention" to killing the naval appropriation bill. Lodge to William Sturgis Bigelow, March 4, 1919, Lodge Papers.

48. *Washington Post,* March 5, 1919.

taneous strategem. Its content had been suggested as early as October, 1918, when Knox had called for the postponement of discussion over a league until general peace terms had been negotiated with Germany. Since that advice had been disregarded and since the Covenant that Wilson brought back from Paris was unacceptable to many senators, there remained the question of how to register this sentiment in a more formal way. Was the Senate powerless before the President's initiative, as Wilson had said in his *Constitutional Government?* Must it wait until the treaty had officially been presented to it for approval? Senate leaders thought they saw a way to exert a prior influence. As early as January 10 the *Washington Post* reported that several senators, including Lodge, were considering a suggestion that would have thirty-three members of the next Senate pledge themselves not to vote for any peace treaty containing a league. If thirty-three members of the forthcoming Sixty-sixth Senate went on record in this manner, there would be the necessary one-third plus one needed to defeat the treaty. A canvass at that time showed that at least forty-one senators were agreeable to such a resolution, but Lodge was not ready to act until it became clearer what kind of a league would emerge from Paris.[49] The events since February 14, especially Wilson's threat not to call a special session while the peace conference continued to meet, created the need for such a statement.

The final impetus came rather suddenly. Early on Sunday morning, March 2, after the Senate had passed the victory bond bill following the all-night filibuster, Brandegee went to his office to pick up his mail. There he found a letter from some man he did not know who suggested "in a vigorous way the thought which had been floating through" Brandegee's own mind, namely, that unless the Senate passed a resolution or made a public declaration opposing the League in its present form, the President could return to Paris saying he had discussed the League with the Senate and House foreign affairs experts, had answered their questions, and was authorized to speak for the American people.[50]

After reading the letter Brandegee went directly to Lodge's house—he did not telephone because he believed the administration had tapped his wires—to discuss the proposal. Lodge, according to Brandegee, agreed it was a fine idea but said it would be impossible to pass a resolution and he did not know what else could be done. Brandegee replied that if Lodge would draft a resolution he would undertake to get at least thirty-three senators to sign it; if that

49. Ibid., January 10, 1919.
50. Chandler P. Anderson Diary, March 13, 1919, Anderson Papers.

proved impossible the resolution could be put in the *Congressional Record.*[51]

During the day Lodge wrote a rough draft of the resolution and that evening went to Brandegee's house where, joined by Knox, they put the resolution in final form. The following morning, March 3, Brandegee took it to the Republican cloakroom and showed it to Albert Cummins, an Iowa Republican, who suggested a few slight changes. It was understood that the resolution would not be used or its existence disclosed if fewer than thirty-three senators could be induced to sign it. At first there was some difficulty, but as Brandegee enlisted the aid of others who circulated the resolution, it soon had thirty-seven names on it (two more subsequently signed). All were Republicans, and all would be members of the new Senate.[52]

Shortly before midnight, March 3, Lodge arose in the Senate to present the resolution. This was the moment of crisis, he believed, the only possible weak spot in the plan. If the Democrats, some of whom knew what was happening, permitted the resolution to be voted upon, a big majority might possibly be rolled up against it. Even if more than one-third of the Senate voted for it, Democrats would be able to discount the votes of Republicans who would be leaving the Senate after March, and so the "psychological effect . . . against it would have been enormous."[53] Lodge counted upon at least one Democrat objecting to anything he presented, especially since it would be out of order in the condition of existing business. After being recognized by the chair, Lodge began reading the resolution: "That it is the sense of the Senate that . . . the constitution of the league of nations in the form now proposed to the

51. Ibid. Cf. Mark Sullivan, *Our Times* (New York, 1933), 5:548, based on an interview Brandegee gave to Sullivan on October 21, 1921. Lodge's story of the event was that he was "struck by Brandegee's proposition" and he soon became convinced of its "essential and even vital importance." Lodge, *The Senate and the League of Nations,* 118. Knox later told Chandler Anderson that he had received a letter on the same day as had Brandegee, making almost the identical suggestion. Anderson Diary, December 16, 1920, Anderson Papers. Another who tried to take credit for the Round Robin was James Beck, a lawyer from Philadelphia and later to be Harding's solicitor general. Beck wrote to Lodge on March 2, 1919, suggesting something similar to what became the Round Robin. Beck's letter, Lodge said, had come after "the decision had been made," but it had strengthened them in their resolve. Beck to Lodge, March 2, 1919, Lodge Papers; Beck to Lodge, March 19, 26, 1919, and Lodge to Beck, March 24, 27, 1919, James Beck Papers (Princeton University Library).

52. McCormick, Lodge, Knox, and Harry New, an Indiana Republican, were reportedly the most active in soliciting signatures. See *Syracuse Journal,* March 4, 1919, and New to Beveridge, March 8, 1919, Beveridge Papers.

53. *New York Sun,* March 4, 1919.

peace conference should not be accepted by the United States";
and that the United States delegates should immediately begin "the
urgent business of negotiating peace terms with Germany . . . and
that the proposal for a league of nations to insure the permanent
peace of the world should be then taken up for careful consideration." Lodge then asked unanimous consent for the immediate consideration of the resolution; such consent, if given, would have
brought it to a vote. Claude Swanson, Democrat from Virginia,
objected. Lodge quickly replied, "Objection being made, of course,
I recognize the objection. I merely wish to add, by way of explanation, the following." He then proceeded to read the names of
the signers who, "if they had had the opportunity . . . would have
voted for the [resolution]."[54]

Eleven irreconcilables signed the Round Robin and on the
following day Albert Fall wired his acceptance, making twelve in
all. Norris, La Follette, Reed, and Thomas did not sign. Norris
later wrote that he had not been invited to sign because he "was
still very much under the displeasure of the Lodge group" for his
vote against the war resolution and his party irregularity.[55] Gronna,
however, was one of the signers and he had voted against war; La
Follette also was apparently asked to sign and refused.[56] If indeed
Norris was not asked, it was probably because at the time he was
thought to be one of the few Republicans not hostile to Wilson's
League.[57] No support was solicited from Democratic senators.
Various explanations were advanced for this. Lodge claimed that
"we did not wish to involve or embarrass them and we also were
able to exercise a greater freedom in taking this position than was
possible for them." Johnson's explanation was even less candid:
"We concluded, because of the vindictive treatment of certain
Democrats who had opposed issues they were commanded to
espouse, that in justice to them they ought not to be asked to
sign." Brandegee, in defending himself against charges that the
Round Robin was a partisan move, stated that Democrats were
not asked because they "did not care to commit themselves
openly upon the matter at this time."[58] Obviously, however, there
were Democrats willing to commit themselves. Reed undoubtedly

54. *Cong. Record*, 65 Cong., 3 sess., 4974 (March 4, 1919).
55. George Norris, *Fighting Liberal* (New York, 1945), 203.
56. La Follette and La Follette, *La Follette*, 2:948.
57. *Harvey's Weekly* 1 (March 15, 1919): 2; *New York Times*, March 5,
1919; *Syracuse Journal*, March 4, 1919.
58. Lodge, *The Senate and the League of Nations*, 118; Johnson to A. B.
Boynton, March 12, 1919, Johnson Papers; Brandegee to the faculty of
Wesleyan College, *Hartford Daily Courant*, March 25, 1919.

would have signed, and while Thomas criticized its form as openly partisan, he could not have quarreled with its substance. There were, in fact, several Democrats and a few more Republicans who might have signed under other circumstances, and the Republicans who did sign were not slow to point this out.[59]

The significance of the Round Robin lay mainly in its demonstration that the Republican senators, while of many minds on the League Covenant, were able to cooperate in a maneuver designed to challenge the President. The Round Robin was so worded as to satisfy many viewpoints. By stating that the League was unacceptable "in the form now proposed," it called for changes without specifying what was desired, thus permitting certain irreconcilables who wanted to reject any kind of a league to join with those Republicans who supported the present Covenant but demanded minor modifications.[60] Signing the resolution constituted a very limited commitment at best; if even the slightest changes were made in the Covenant, a signer could justify supporting the revised version. Furthermore, it should be noted, the resolution did not require separation of the League from the general peace treaty for senators to support the League. Similarly, because of the language, irreconcilables could refuse to support any revised League on the grounds that it did not contain the changes they envisioned.

The Round Robin was clearly a blow to Wilson. In his cablegram to the members of the Foreign Relations and Foreign Affairs Committees, he had said there was "a good and sufficient reason for the phraseology and substance of each article" of the Covenant. Now, more than a third of the new Senate had denied his contention, and these senators would, it surely seemed, be coming together in an extra session of the Sixty-sixth Congress long before it was officially supposed to begin. For the irreconcilables, many of whom had played crucial roles in the events of the past several weeks, the future looked much brighter than before.

Wilson's reaction to the filibuster and Round Robin was immediate and hostile. On the morning when he sat in the Capitol, almost within earshot of the filibuster, he appeared unruffled and even managed a confident smile.[61] This seemingly placid demeanor changed drastically after Sherman's final words had been spoken. A statement issued that same day from the White House began as

59. *New York Tribune,* March 5, 1919; *New York Times,* March 4, 1919. *Cong. Record,* 66 Cong., 1 sess., 1372 (June 19, 1919).
60. Lodge considered the Round Robin to be the "foundation of our entire resistance to the League." Lodge to Harry New, October 6, 1920, Harry New Papers (Indiana State Library, Indianapolis).
61. *New York Times,* March 5, 1919.

follows: "A group of men in the Senate have deliberately chosen to embarrass the administration." Wilson went on to explain that his choice lay between attending the peace conference and being present during a session of Congress. The former was more important and, in addition, he did not think it was "in the interest of the right conduct of public affairs" that a special session should be called before his return. The final paragraph grimly pointed the finger at the filibusterers: "I take it for granted that the men who have obstructed and prevented the passage of necessary legislation have taken all of this into consideration and are willing to assume the responsibility of the impaired efficiency of the government and the embarrassed finances of the country during the time of my enforced absence."[62] Sherman's reply was typically blunt: "We are willing to take that responsibility. If the constitution of the league of nations is the result of his attendance at the Paris conference and his administration of the railroads of the United States is the result of his constant attendance upon Congress, both Paris and Congress can do better without him. He is a superfluous luxury anyway."[63] Lodge, disclaiming any party responsibility for the filibuster, maintained that three-fourths of the Republican senators had wanted to pass the general deficiency bill, but Sherman, France, and La Follette were "beyond control."[64] While possibly true, this was not the whole story by any means. As Sherman wrote privately, "There were more Senators than really appeared on the surface" working for a special session.[65] No great dismay was evidenced by Lodge, nor did the squabble that erupted over the caucus vote against a filibuster have lasting repercussions.[66]

The President's reaction to the Round Robin was as vigorous and challenging as his condemnation of the filibusterers. To a large audience at the Metropolitan Opera House on the evening of March 4, he pledged his determination not to return from the peace conference "until it's over, over there." As for the proposal that the League be separated from the rest of the Treaty, the President said: "When that treaty comes back gentlemen on this side will find the Covenant not only in it, but so many threads of the treaty tied to the covenant that you cannot dissect the covenant from the treaty without destroying the whole vital structure."

62. Baker and Dodd, eds., *War and Peace*, 1:456. Senators were quick to note the similarity of Wilson's words to his characterization of the armed-ships bill filibusterers of 1917. *New York Tribune*, March 5, 1919.

63. *Chicago Tribune*, March 5, 1919.

64. *New York Times*, March 5, 1919.

65. Sherman to C. E. Chiperfield, March 10, 1919, Sherman Papers.

66. *New York Times*, March 5, 1919.

The opponents of the League were again portrayed as outside the mainstream of humanity. Most Americans, unlike these few dissidents, were "ready to make the supreme sacrifice [for the League], the supreme sacrifice of throwing in our fortunes with the fortunes of men everywhere." Deeply convinced of this, he was returning to Paris "with renewed vigor."[67]

Instead of tempering his outlook, the filibuster and Round Robin seemed to have the opposite effect, at least on his rhetoric. The danger, as some friends of the League were perceiving, was that Wilson would become too vigorous in defending the League to recognize the shadings of opinion in the Senate. The chief beneficiaries of that lack of recognition would be the irreconcilables.

67. Baker and Dodd, eds., *War and Peace*, 1:444-55.

4 THE FIGHT OUTSIDE THE SENATE

THE FILIBUSTER and Round Robin sounded a fittingly partisan end to six years of Democratic control of Congress and the beginning of at least two years, and as it turned out fourteen, of Republican hegemony on Capitol Hill. When the special session, and therefore the new reign, would commence was as yet unknown. Consequently, beginning in March, 1919, there occurred an indefinite hiatus in the parliamentary struggle. To this point the irreconcilables, or those whose opinions were in varying degrees already formed, could feel satisfied that they had accomplished as much as could reasonably be expected. They had seized the initiative in debating the idea of a league, dominated the debates on the proposed League Covenant, led the inquisition of Wilson at the White House meeting, and, with Lodge's assistance, engineered the filibuster and Round Robin. But they were far from the day when they could begin to think of ultimate victory. Ahead lay many problems, the solutions to which were as yet unclear; and for an extended period they would be forced to perform without the forum where their previous successes had been won.

Public attention would now shift to Wilson's labors at the peace conference. Probably none of the bitter-enders believed the President would return with a League that was fully satisfactory; and still to be revealed was the rest of the peace settlement which, if Wilson had his way, would have to be considered not on its own merits but in one treaty with the League included. Yet at this stage only a few of those who eventually voted as irreconcilables had committed themselves so uncompromisingly as to leave no doubt about their future actions. Borah and Reed seemed certain to reject the League, regardless of the public support it enjoyed, the reservations or amendments which the Senate attached to it, or the number of votes it received. Sherman and Poindexter may also have been committed. Sherman had consistently and vehemently attacked Wilson, his ideas, and his methods; furthermore, his decision to retire in 1920 made him impervious to any appeal for moderation based upon political considerations. Poindexter, if not so acerbic as Sherman, had been equally sweeping in his criticism; and while he harbored Presidential ambitions that might cause him to modify his views, thus far he had given no indication that he would. These four had been by far the most hostile and resolute opponents. Others, to be sure, had expressed strong disagreement with the League, were rabidly partisan, or disliked Wilson intensely; but they had not gone on record so unmistakably as the four described above. In the period before the Sixty-sixth Congress assembled, many of them would make their positions clearer.

Of the major concerns of the irreconcilables the most immediate was the need for some kind of organizational and financial assistance to aid them in continuing their efforts while the Senate was out of session. A concerted series of actions to publicize the dangers of the League must be taken, they felt, for without further discussion the people might accept whatever Wilson brought back. Borah in particular placed great faith in the power of public opinion to resolve the parliamentary deadlock that was in the making. "Only by organizing public opinion can we succeed," he wrote. "The machinery here is geared up against us."[1] Months earlier Poindexter had lamented that the anti-League forces had no propaganda organization comparable to the League to Enforce Peace. What was needed to arouse the people was "a league for the preservation of the independece of the United States."[2]

In late February and early March, 1919, several irreconcilables began corresponding or meeting individually with private citizens to make plans for such an anti-League organization.[3] The leading promoter was Henry Wise Wood, an exuberant New York inventor, aeronautical engineer, and sometime poet. On March 7 Wood an-

1. Borah to Charles L. French, March 1, 1919, Borah Papers, Box 552.
2. Poindexter to T. J. Murray, November 25, 1918, Poindexter Papers, Series 4, file 50.
3. *New York Times*, March 7, 1919. Borah was exchanging letters with Henry Wise Wood and William Randolph Hearst on the need for an organization. Jack Kendrick, "The Republican Senate and the League of Nations, 1918-1921" (Ph.D. diss., University of North Carolina, 1952), 116-18. See also James E. Clark to Borah, March 3, 1919, Borah Papers, Box 550. Clark was Secretary of the Conference Committee on National Preparedness, Inc., of which Wood was chairman. See also Frank Munsey to Albert Beveridge, March 8, 1919, Beveridge Papers, Box 216.

nounced the formation of the League for the Preservation of American Independence, having as its goal: "to defend from impairment the fundamentals of American policy as expressed in the Declaration of Independence, the Constitution of the United States, the Monroe Doctrine, and Washington's Farewell Address." The organization, Wood said, was not opposed to a league of nations which did not infringe on American sovereignty, threaten the Monroe Doctrine, or possess the authority to send American boys into foreign wars without congressional consent; but the League that Wilson had presented was inadequate on all those counts.[4] A few days later the papers reported that five Republican senators had joined the advisory council of the new organization. Included were three irreconcilables—Poindexter, Moses, and France—in addition to Harry New of Indiana and Howard Sutherland of West Virginia. Borah and Reed agreed to cooperate with Wood; Knox and Lodge expressed approval of the organization's purposes.[5] Shortly thereafter George Wharton Pepper, a Philadelphia lawyer and legal scholar of some standing, was named director. Pepper became the organization's guiding spirit. Henry Watterson, Democratic editor of the *Louisville Courier-Journal,* was designated as president.[6] Appointment of the seventy-nine-year-old Watterson was obviously an effort to make the Independence League appear nonpartisan, over the objections of some Republicans who wanted to exclude all Democrats.[7] Watterson's duties were largely ceremonial. Although another Democrat, ex-Senator Thomas Hardwick of

4. *New York Times,* March 7, 1919; *New York Tribune,* March 8, 1919.

5. *New York Sun,* March 10, 1919; *New York Times,* March 10, 1919; telegram from Wood to Henry Watterson, March 21, 1919, Henry Watterson Papers (Library of Congress), Vol. 30.

6. *Chicago Tribune,* March 14, 1919; *New York Times,* March 14, 1919; *Philadelphia Public Ledger,* March 14, 1919. The press reported that the organization was being formed on the thirteenth. Wood did not participate in this organizational meeting, which was held in Reed's office. Borah, Poindexter, and Pepper were the others present. Apparently these four men wanted to take credit for founding the Independence League, and they also may not have desired Wood's leadership. The decision to name Watterson as president was reached by the above men, excluding Wood, in addition to Lodge and Moses. See William A. De Ford to Pepper, March 11, 1919, George Wharton Pepper Papers (University of Pennsylvania library), Box 18.

7. Munsey was a proponent of an exclusively Republican organization. Munsey to Beveridge, March 8, 1919, Munsey to Will Hays, March 15, 1919, Beveridge Papers, Box 216. Reed was one of those who insisted on a bipartisan organization, and Pepper shared his views. See Reed to Lodge, March 14, 1919, Pepper to Lodge, March 14, 15, 1919, Lodge Papers. Some Republican senators opposed any connection between William Randolph Hearst and the organization. Ibid. Sherman tried to get Illinois Democrats to join him in the League. Sherman to B. F. Harris, March 11, 1919, Sherman Papers.

Georgia, served on the Board of Directors, and Reed, who had been instrumental in its founding, continued to work closely with the Republican leaders, the organization by the summer of 1920 would be distributing literature celebrating the defeat of the League of Nations as a triumph for the Republican party.[8]

Subdivided into eight district units with many state and city chapters, the Independence League functioned as a nationwide publicity organ for the opponents of the League of Nations.[9] According to Pepper, it was intended to accommodate not only those sympathetic to some kind of international organization but also those who believed that any league of nations was impracticable.[10] Its chief importance to the irreconcilables was in helping finance their speaking tours,[11] arranging for newspaper advertisements, renting halls, and in general preparing the scene for effective performances. Speeches and articles were also reprinted and mailed out by the tens of thousands, form letters were written so that local citizens could petition their senators, and phonograph records were even made of some of the senators' speeches so that they could be replayed in outlying hamlets which were denied the presence of the orators themselves.[12] Pepper also wrote a considerable amount of literature, some of it in the form of "Primers" which posed leading questions and gave simplistic answers. At the local level many anti-League of Nations meetings were held under the

8. See a League Primer written by Pepper, n.d., referring to the 1920 Democratic Presidential candidate, James Cox. To the question: "Is the United States . . . required to insure all the European tinder-boxes?" Pepper replied, "It would be if it were not for the Republican Party." Pepper Papers, Box 3. A letter from W. M. Cain, Secretary of the Nebraska League, to Sherman, October 21, 1919, Sherman Papers, indicates that the League may have been more bipartisan at the local level.

9. *Boston Evening Transcript*, March 31, 1919.

10. Pepper to Mary B. Palmer, November 10, 1921, Pepper Papers, Box 54.

11. James Reed in August, 1919, said he had expended "approximately $1000" of his own money in traveling, sending telegrams, etc., and had received "about $126" from the League in helping meet his expenses. Reed to A. M. Carpenter, August 18, 1919, original in Taft Papers, Box 466.

12. Anti-League of Nations speeches outside the Senate would be inserted in the *Congressional Record* and mailed out under the senators' franking privileges. Interview with Lee Meriwether, the Independence League's Publicity Director, March 14, 1961; Meriwether's autobiography, *My First Ninety-Eight Years, 1862-1960* (Columbia, Mo., 1960), 102. At other times the League bore the cost of reprinting and distributing the speeches and articles of private citizens who opposed the League of Nations. Ten thousand copies each of two articles by David Jayne Hill were ordered. Aubrey L. Parkman, "David Jayne Hill" (Ph.D. diss., University of Rochester, 1961), 522. As an example of a form letter see one prepared by the Massachusetts branch, in the Collection of Independence League materials in the Widener Library, Harvard University, Cambridge, Mass. The *New York Sun*, June 29, 1919, has the story of the phonograph records.

auspices of the organization; in Georgia alone forty-three such meetings were sponsored.[13]

In its early stages the organization had great difficulty in finding enough money to carry on operations.[14] No membership fees were required and sole dependence was placed on subscriptions. These were solicited in amounts from $1 to $10,000; at least a few donations of $5,000 were received.[15] Considering the size of these contributions, Lee Meriwether's claim that the organization collected a total of only $125,000 may be doubted.[16]

The financial worries of the irreconcilables, if not of the Independence League, were finally ended in May, 1919. Several of the group had gathered at Brandegee's home to discuss ways to raise more money. After various plans were proposed and discarded, and with everyone pessimistic and gloomy, Knox proposed that a personal appeal be made to Henry Clay Frick and Andrew Mellon, multimillionaire industrialists whom Knox had once served as legal counsel. George Harvey, a New York magazine editor, said that he would see Frick the following evening and would present the irreconcilables' case. After hearing Harvey's arguments—which stressed the point that the United States would be controlled by its debtors within the League—Frick consented to "go along." When Knox learned of Harvey's success, he wrote to Mellon "and obtained the same amount" as Frick had pledged. Medill McCormick, when informed of the good news, declared that he could now go to Chicago and "raise about twenty."[17] One source states that Frick and Mellon agreed to contribute $10,000 each,[18] but Harvey's account, without mentioning a specific figure, would suggest it might have been more, at least if needed. "The desired

13. Lee Meriwether, *Jim Reed "Senatorial Immortal"* (Webster Groves, Mo., 1948), 67-80.

14. Pepper wanted to disband the League in April if $50,000 could not be raised. Pepper to Reed, April 21, 1919, copy in Borah Papers, Box 194.

15. See copy of article by J. J. Hill, "The President's Challenge to the Senate," reprinted by the Independence League, Sherman Papers; letter from Salmon Levinson, Jules S. Baches, and Geoffrey Payne to Reed, November 12, 1919, pledging $5,000, Levinson Papers, Box 74; Louis A. Coolidge, President of the Massachusetts Branch, to Lodge, September 5, 1919, mentioning a $5,000 contribution of Colonel Robert M. Thompson and James Beck, Lodge Papers; Pepper to Lodge, April 10, 1919, asking Lodge to sign a pledge of support for the League in connection with a contribution of $10,000 by a Thomas H. Powers. Lodge did not sign, but praised the League to Powers (Lodge to Powers, April 7, 1919, Lodge Papers). There is no evidence to indicate whether Powers gave Pepper the $10,000 or a lesser amount.

16. Meriwether, *Jim Reed*, 72.

17. George Harvey, *Henry Clay Frick* (New York, 1928), 325-29.

18. Allan Nevins, "Andrew Mellon," in *Dictionary of American Biography* (New York, 1958), vol. 22, Supplement Two, 446-52.

reservoir had been found and it was both deep and full," Harvey wrote. "All anxiety respecting sinews of war was dispelled. Rejoicing pervaded the camp of the Irreconcilables, efforts were redoubled all along the line and the redoubtable little band pushed on."[19]

Long before the resolution of these organizational and financial problems, many irreconcilables had embarked upon extensive speaking tours. Borah, Poindexter, and Reed spoke most frequently, although Sherman, McCormick, Johnson, Thomas, and several others were also busy. In fact, on the stump as in the Senate the bitter-enders carried the battle to the League's proponents; not only were they superior orators but they also worked harder at their task. Borah, for example, had already delivered twenty-one public addresses before Congress adjourned.[20] In the period from March 6 through April 10 he gave sixteen major speeches in seven widely scattered states,[21] and he often spoke more than once on the same day. Poindexter's itinerary was equally ambitious, extending from Washington, D. C., to Cincinnati to the West Coast and back to New York. Sometimes the bitter-enders appeared on the same stage, as when Borah, Reed, and Thomas addressed the Society of Liberal Arts and Sciences in New York City on March 6. Their audiences were diverse. McCormick addressed the Swedish-American Club in Chicago and the Friendly Sons of St. Patrick in Philadelphia. Moses spoke to the Republican members of the Massachusetts legislature. Fall informed the Albuquerque Chamber of Commerce of the League's shortcomings. Sherman met with a Springfield Methodist Church group. They spoke to anyone willing to listen. As Borah put it, "All I want is people and a lot of them; I don't care who they are or what they represent."[22]

Their speeches embodied substantially the same arguments they had made in the Senate. The League would abrogate the Monroe Doctrine, control immigration policies, dictate a nation's armaments, order American soldiers to distant shores, and in many other ways destroy American sovereignty; the League was unconstitutional, immoral, and contrary to self-interest; it would increase the power of the British Empire and force the United States to help England suppress the Irish whenever they sought their freedom. "The League of Nations," Borah declared in Ft. Wayne, "makes it

19. Harvey, *Frick*, 329.
20. Borah to James E. Babb, April 22, 1919, Borah Papers, Box 522.
21. Waldo Braden, "William E. Borah's Senate Speeches on the League of Nations, 1918-1920," *Speech Monographs* 10 (1943): 60, n. 231. Braden omits Borah's New York speech.
22. *Boston Evening Transcript*, March 13, 1919.

necessary for America to give back to George V what it took away from George III."[23] Article ten was attacked repeatedly. Reed anticipated the later controversy over whether the League imposed legal or moral obligations upon its members. It would be disastrous, he said, if the League could legally compel a nation to act contrary to its self-interest, and this explained why the League's proponents maintained that the obligations were only moral. Yet moral obligations would be even more binding and catastrophic for a nation like the United States which fulfilled its commitments so faithfully. Nations less scrupulous in their international behavior would mercilessly exploit America's trust and good will.[24]

The receptions accorded the irreconcilables were usually favorable and sometimes enthusiastic, but there were exceptions. McCormick was hissed and booed in Philadelphia. Thomas had been invited by Colorado Republicans to speak to the state legislature, but pro-League Democrats blocked his appearance. Reed suffered the most embarrassing experience. In the midst of his harangue to the Missouri legislature, sixteen Democrats walked out and on the following day fifty of the sixty-seven Democratic legislators signed a resolution asking him to resign and run for reelection on an anti-League platform. Reed countered by daring them to resign, whereupon all fifty agreed to do so if he would. Nothing, however, came of the bluffing, and Reed continued his trip around the state.[25]

When not out in the country speaking, the irreconcilables were engaged in writing articles, sending letters to editors of newspapers, raising money, and privately encouraging their Senate colleagues to take a stronger stand. Several bitter-enders who had said little in the Senate before March now began to clarify their positions. Brandegee sent a letter to the New York Sun which left little doubt about his future course. The Connecticut senator bluntly stated: "If the President submits the proposed League of Nations plan in anything like its present form, so linked with any treaty that the two cannot be separated by amendment in the Senate, then I shall unhesitatingly vote to reject both treaties. I shall never be imposed upon by such an apparent trick. I shall never be intimidated by such an outrageous attempt at coercion."[26] McCormick wrote an open letter to the president of the City Club of Chicago, the contents of which a distinguished contemporary his-

23. New York Times, March 20, 1919.
24. Ibid., March 19, 1920.
25. Philadelphia North American, March 18, 1919; New York Times, March 20-22, 26, 1919.
26. Quoted in Harvey's Weekly, March 22, 1919.

torian, George Burton Adams, described as "the most extreme appeal yet made to prejudice and ignorance." According to McCormick, the League was designed as a superstate; it would result in "efficient and economical Japanese operating our street railways . . . Hindoo janitors in our offices and apartments . . . Chinese craftsmen driving rivets, joining timbers, laying bricks in the construction of our buildings."[27] Hiram Johnson told close friends that he was becoming "more and more set" against the League.[28]

The peace progressives also began to express themselves. Gronna, who had made no set speech on the League before the adjournment of Congress, responded instantly to Wilson's denunciation of the filibuster and Round Robin. "I for one will die," the North Dakota senator remarked, "before I will vote for the League of Nations in its present form."[29] La Follette became increasingly apprehensive about the peace negotiations. It appeared to him that "a cold blooded, sordid 'peace' treaty [was being] dressed up in a maze of rhetorical flim flam." Self-determination, open diplomacy, and impartial settlement of colonial claims had all been flouted; and there could be no League strong enough to enforce a peace that embodied such egregious wrongs.[30] Norris was somewhat more sympathetic to the President's labors. In an article for the *Nebraska State Journal*, he revealed a mind still undecided. Several of his objections to the League were familiar. He agreed with other bitter-enders who criticized the mandate system. He believed that the British Empire was given excessive voting power and that domestic affairs should be free from League authority. But he disagreed with those irreconcilables who condemned the League for its control over a nation's armaments. What was needed, Norris said, was not less but more control. Nor did he accept the argument that the League should be rejected because it encroached upon American sovereignty. Some loss of sovereignty was "true of every agreement in civilization, whether individual, state, or national." Absolute freedom of action was impossible and the attempt to practice it led to anarchy. Similarly, those who feared that the League would destroy the Monroe Doctrine were taking much too provincial a viewpoint. The League would destroy the Monroe Doctrine, but this would be all to the good if the League also abolished the right of conquest and insured disarmament. His discussion of entangling

27. *New York Times,* March 6, 1919.
28. Johnson to C. K. McClatchy, March 27, 1919, Johnson Papers.
29. *New York Times,* March 6, 1919.
30. Belle Case La Follette and Fola La Follette, *Robert M. La Follette* (New York, 1953), 2:953-54.

alliances might have been written by Wilson himself. "If it were possible for us to keep out of European alliances, it would of course be desirable," he admitted. "But we are only now emerging from an European war, that demonstrates that, try as we may, we cannot keep out of world entanglements." One of the purposes of the League was "to prevent entanglements and thus save not only our nation but all nations from getting into them." Norris did not, however, accept Wilson's belief that the League should enforce its decisions by military might if moral pressure was ineffective. He granted that economic reprisals would perhaps be necessary to check an aggressor, but if there were disarmament, open diplomacy, arbitration tribunals, and no declaration of war until the people had so voted in a referendum, international relations would proceed with little difficulty. In spite of his many questions about specific articles of the League, Norris thought "we ought to construe every doubt in favor of its adoption."[31]

How much of an effect did the irreconcilables produce by their scores of speeches and writings? While impossible to measure with any high degree of accuracy, public opinion, though still strongly pro-League, seemed to be shifting from what had once been a largely uncritical acceptance of the idea of a league to a more skeptical attitude toward the actual League Covenant.[32] The irreconcilables had probably converted relatively few people to outright rejection—indeed that was not the purpose of many of them at this time—but they had begun to plant doubts. Pro-League Democrats evinced concern in their letters to Wilson.[33] Even Tumulty acknowledged the growing opposition, though he blithely informed the President that its extreme nature would react against itself.[34] Such was not to be, however, and the bitter-enders were pleased with the effect they had had.

31. *Nebraska State Journal,* March 30, 1919, copy in Norris Papers, Box 10, Tray 75. See also "extract" of letter from Norris to Walter L. Locke, March 18, 1919, ibid.
32. See the nationwide press poll in *The Literary Digest* 61 (April 5, 1919): 13-16, 120-28; *Philadelphia Public Ledger,* March 31, April 2, 1919; *New York Times,* March 25, 1919; *Chicago Tribune,* March 22, 1919; *Washington Post,* March 16, 1919; John A. Aman, "Views of Three Iowa Newspapers on the League of Nations, 1919-1920," *Iowa Journal of History and Politics* 39 (July 1941): 235, 243; Forrest Carlisle Pogue, Jr., "The Monroe Doctrine and the League of Nations" (Ph.D. diss., Clark University, 1939), 145-47.
33. Joint letter to Wilson from Key Pittman, Thomas Walsh, David Walsh, Peter Gerry, and John Kendrick, April 17, 1919, copy in Pittman Papers, Box 91.
34. Tumulty wire to Wilson, March 16, 1919, Wilson Papers, Series 8 A, Box 24.

If the irreconcilables' publicity campaign did nothing else it helped to stimulate a widespread demand in March and April that Wilson make some modifications of the League Covenant. Friends of the League who urged changes mainly to pacify dissident senators were joined by those who believed a thorough revision of the Covenant was necessary. No one raising his voice at this time had more impact than Elihu Root, a respected international lawyer who had served as McKinley's Secretary of War and as Roosevelt's Secretary of State. On March 29 Root proposed that Wilson secure six amendments to the Covenant before concluding the peace negotiations.

Root's entry into the League fight was due at least in part to the urging of irreconcilables. On March 12 Lodge had received a request from Peace Commissioner Henry White asking for specific changes that would insure the Senate's approval of the League.[35] Uncertain as to how to respond, Lodge telephoned Brandegee and Knox for advice. Brandegee, highly suspicious by nature, feared a trap had been set by Wilson, which "Lodge would fall into . . . unless [he] was stiffened up." Therefore he went to see Chandler Anderson, a respected international lawyer who had served as a special counsel to Root when the latter was Secretary of State. Brandegee asked Anderson to go to New York and persuade Root to impress upon Lodge the danger of making any precise commitment. Also, Brandegee believed that in his reply to White, Lodge should take the opportunity to suggest that the Senate be convened in extraordinary session to advise the President.[36] Anderson saw Root, who agreed to write to Lodge urging him to do substantially what Brandegee had outlined. Lodge's cable to White followed Root's advice.[37] Thus when Root on the twenty-ninth made public his suggested amendments—disclosed in an open letter to Will Hays, the Republican National Chairman, and drawn up after consultation with Hays, George Harvey, and Henry Stimson —he made the first of what were to be many contributions to Republican Senate leaders, particularly Lodge.[38]

35. John A. Garraty, *Henry Cabot Lodge: A Biography* (New York, 1953), 357-58.

36. Anderson Diary entry of March 13, 1919, Chandler Anderson Papers (Library of Congress), Box 4.

37. Ibid.; see also the memo for Lodge prepared by Brandegee, March 12, 1919, and Elihu Root to Lodge, March 13, 1919, Lodge Papers. Knox wired Lodge on the seventeenth from Florida also advising against making specific suggestions; ibid.

38. Stimson Diary entry of March 29, 1919, Henry Stimson Papers (Yale University Library, New Haven, Conn.).

In his letter Root proposed changes that would protect the Monroe Doctrine from League jurisdiction; reserve to the United States the sole right to deal with its own domestic questions such as immigration; make obligatory the arbitration of "justiciable questions," which should be carefully defined; initiate steps to codify international law; give to the permanent disarmament commission powers of inspection to insure compliance with the commission's decisions; and limit Article ten to a trial period of five years.[39] These suggestions were not significantly different from those of others, but they got a far more enthusiastic reception, chiefly because of Root's reputation as a statesman and a moderate. Almost all Republicans and several Democrats endorsed them. American delegates at the peace conference were reported as sympathetic toward them. There were predictions in Washington that the League would be speedily passed by the Senate if the Covenant was revised in accordance with Root's letter.[40]

The irreconcilables who praised Root's letter did so without altering their opinion that his proposals still did not meet all their objections to the Covenant. The bitter-enders presumably reasoned that they could not afford to dismiss Root's efforts as only another attempt to bring about the League's ratification. It still seemed likely the League would eventually be approved, and if this occurred it was desirable that the United States be protected as much as possible. If his amendments were not accepted by Wilson, Root undoubtedly would become less sympathetic to the League and take a larger role in opposing it. They could not, of course, foresee all that would happen, but Root's "subtle brain and cunning hand"— the words were those of Frank Munsey—in addition to his vast prestige, would prove vital to their cause.[41] If Root himself could have foreseen the way in which his proposals would be used by the irreconcilables, he might have adopted a different course of action.

While the irreconcilables were appealing to public opinion at home, Wilson was struggling in Paris to secure changes in the League that would immobilize his Senate critics. By making certain concessions to his European adversaries—acceding to France's demand, for example, for a limited military occupation of the Rhineland—Wilson finally succeeded on April 28 in getting the revised Covenant accepted. The changes included a clause permitting a nation to withdraw from the League after giving two years notice,

39. Richard W. Leopold, *Elihu Root and the Conservative Tradition* (Boston, 1954), 136.
40. *New York Times,* April 1, 2, 1919; *Harvey's Weekly,* April 5, 1919.
41. Munsey to Beveridge, April 7, 1919, Beveridge Papers, Box 216.

providing it had fulfilled its obligations under the Covenant; ex-
clusion of domestic matters from League supervision; modification
of Article twenty-one to read that "treaties of arbitration or
regional understandings like the Monroe Doctrine" were inviolable;
and making the acceptance of mandatories dependent on a nation's
explicit willingness to accept them. Articles ten and sixteen, two
of the most controversial, were left intact.[42]

The irreconcilables had immediate comments. Though a few
admitted that the Covenant had been slightly improved, the general
reaction was highly unfavorable. Borah stated that since Article
ten had not been changed, the Covenant was totally unacceptable.
He also criticized the wording of the clause exempting the Monroe
Doctrine, which he said was not a regional understanding, as the
revised Covenant read, but rather a unilateral declaration of
policy.[43] Reed, who was in Kansas City on a speaking engagement,
telegraphed Borah in Washington asking for advice on the correct
procedure to follow in responding. Borah answered: "The new
league . . . is just as vicious as the old. Let's keep up the fight."
Reed then proclaimed the revised Covenant worse than the original.
He thought the voting system, as he told reporters publicly, was
still inadequate.[44] Privately he revealed his prejudices. "Think of
submitting questions involving the very life of the United States,"
he wrote to a Missouri political ally, "to a tribunal on which a
nigger from Liberia, a nigger from Honduras, a nigger from India,
or an unlettered gentleman from Siam, each have votes equal to
that of the great United States of America."[45] Sherman charged
that the League was still a superstate. He also believed the mandate
system was too vague and, in some respects, should be extended.
France and Great Britain, for example, should "accept the manda-
tory to put the Turk out of Europe," and the United States should
"clean up Mexico."[46] McCormick saw the Covenant as a "guaranty
of empire" and a "triumph for Mr. Lloyd George," England's
Prime Minister. "The 'phrase-maker of the King' is a better negoti-
ator than the 'King of phrase-makers.' "[47] Brandegee claimed that
none of Root's suggested amendments had been incorporated into

42. Ray Stannard Baker and William E. Dodd, eds., *War and Peace:
Presidential Messages, Addresses, and Public Papers, 1917-1924* (New York,
1927), 1:469-73.
43. *New York Times,* April 28, May 3, 1919.
44. Reed to Borah, April 28, 1919, Borah to Reed, April 29, 1919, Borah
Papers, Box 550. *New York Times,* April 28, 1919.
45. Reed to Isaac H. Lionberger, May 5, 1919, Isaac H. Lionberger Papers
(Missouri Historical Society, St. Louis).
46. *New York Tribune,* April 29, 1919; *Chicago Tribune,* April 29, 1919.
47. *Boston Evening Transcript,* May 2, 1919.

the revised Covenant and he therefore would not accept it.[48] Moses found the new Covenant no better than the original. Article fifteen, he maintained, did not adequately reserve a nation's right to be the judge of its immigration policies; he envisioned Japan protesting to the League about any American legislation that discriminated against Orientals. Gronna voiced his opposition to the revision without giving his reasons. That changes had been made by Wilson, he said, was proof that those who had argued the need for such changes were right all along.[49] Johnson announced he would release a statement after giving the document additional scrutiny. "I am studying the League of Nations as an American, a selfish, provincial, little American, if you please but with my whole thought for my country. I am only an American, for America first." His correspondence left no doubt that he was opposed to the revision.[50]

Several polls measured senatorial opinion on the revised Covenant. One, made by Republicans themselves, revealed thirty-four G.O.P. senators against the modified version unless further amendments were made. Included were twelve of the irreconcilables. Five Republican senators were classified as "in favor of the covenant beyond hope of conversion." Norris was placed in this group. The remaining ten senators were listed as "doubtful," and La Follette was considered to be one of these.[51] The poll of the League to Enforce Peace was made public at the same time. Contrary to the above figures, it had sixty-four senators as definitely in favor of the revised League, twelve against it, and twenty described as doubtful. Only seven future bitter-enders—Borah, Sherman, Reed, Moses, Fall, Knox, and Poindexter—were included in the anti-League forces, while Johnson, Brandegee, McCormick, Fernald, France, and La Follette were called "doubtful." Norris and Gronna, according to this poll, would support the League wholeheartedly.[52] Two weeks later a *Chicago Tribune* poll found that all forty-nine Republicans and six Democrats would support Senate amendments to the Covenant. Seven Democrats were termed doubtful and thirty-four were behind it as it stood.[53] As events would demonstrate, the Republican and *Tribune* polls were more accurate than that of the League to Enforce Peace.

48. *New York Times*, May 6, 1919.
49. Ibid., April 29, May 2, 1919.
50. *New York Tribune*, April 29, 1919; *New York Times*, April 29, 1919; Johnson to Meyer Lissner, May 8, 1919, copy in Chester Rowell Papers (Bancroft Library, University of California, Berkeley).
51. *Boston Evening Transcript*, May 1, 1919.
52. Ibid.
53. *Chicago Tribune*, May 16, 1919.

Publication of the revised League Covenant on April 28 coincided with growing rumors that Wilson would soon have to call a special session of the new Sixty-sixth Congress. Several departments of government simply could not continue to function without the appropriation of operating funds. The prospect of a special session, which the Republicans would organize, made urgent the problem of party unity on the League; and it was to this problem that Republican leaders turned in the immediate aftermath of the publication of the revised Covenant.

The man primarily responsible for Republican unity was Henry Cabot Lodge, the upcoming majority leader. His major concern was the irreconcilables. On April 28 Lodge spoke to Brandegee and Pepper and also telephoned Root.[54] The next day he conferred with a group including Brandegee, Pepper, Borah, Johnson, Moses, and McCormick, along with two other Republican senators, Harry New and Joseph Frelinghuysen, both of whom strongly opposed the League although not quite to the point of irreconcilability. They all agreed that the League for the Preservation of American Independence definitely would "be recognized as an ally of the Senate group" opposing the League. It was further decided that Brandegee and Pepper should go to New York to consult Root.[55] At this meeting Root approved of Pepper's Independence League waging an educational campaign against the revised Covenant, which Root believed had not incorporated his earlier suggestions. He therefore favored Senate amendments to the Covenant.[56]

On April 29 Lodge also met privately with Borah.[57] The Idaho bitter-ender was the most outspoken opponent of the League, but more important to Lodge were Borah's increasingly sharp attacks on the Republican party for its failure to take a stand against the League. If Borah were to break from the party leadership, he might draw other bitter-enders with him, some of whom had already made gestures in that direction. As majority leader, Lodge's primary objective was party unity.[58] Republican harmony was especially urgent on the eve of the organization of the new Senate. Some understanding with Borah, therefore, must be reached that would keep him and other irreconcilables in line. Lodge's attitude toward the League itself was mixed. Like other senators, he had once sup-

54. Leopold, *Root*, 137.
55. George Wharton Pepper, *Philadelphia Lawyer: An Autobiography* (Philadelphia, 1944), 125.
56. Pepper to Henry Stimson, May 3, 1919, Stimson Papers, Box 88.
57. *New York Times*, April 30, 1919.
58. Garraty, *Lodge*, 362-63. Lodge to Beveridge, March 21, 1919, Beveridge Papers, Box 216.

ported the idea of a league, but he was not happy with the actual Covenant that Wilson had written. His general outlook on foreign affairs closely resembled Theodore Roosevelt's and, for that matter, the outlook of certain irreconcilables such as Knox. Lodge was not willing, however, to pose a flat negative to the entire treaty containing the League.

To Borah defeat of the League came first, party unity only afterward. Lodge would keep his party together even if it meant accepting the League in some form. Borah would defeat the League even if it required bolting the party. As much as Lodge needed Borah's cooperation, Borah was at least equally dependent on Lodge. Despite his protestations that public opinion was shifting toward an anti-League position, Borah realized that most Americans still wanted the League approved. Moreover, the final outcome would rest with the senators themselves, of whom only a handful shared his attitude. It seemed improbable that thirty-two senators would join him to vote to reject the League outright; but if that remote possibility were to materialize, it was imperative that there be time to continue the fight and prevent any immediate vote. Borah recognized the value of delay. Since early March he had been promoting the idea of a national referendum on the League, "not only as a matter of right but as a matter of tactics." "If we can force a popular vote," he wrote to Munsey, "it will give us more time."[59] A referendum, however, was impossible unless the Constitution was changed. Time could be won primarily in the Senate. Since an extended filibuster by only a few irreconcilables, even if possible, surely would not convince senators to reject the League, some other method must be found. Lodge was committed to a full discussion of the treaty, however he might vote on it. For the full discussion to be effected, the Republicans must organize the new Senate. Especially vital was their control of the Foreign Relations Committee to which the treaty containing the League would be referred. If the Republicans split prior to Senate organization, the Democrats might gain control. They would then be in position to bring the League to a vote at an earlier date. Thus, any break in the party prior to the opening of the Sixty-sixth Congress would jeopardize the irreconcilables' hope of gaining time. Borah may have been influenced by a letter he received from Albert Beveridge on April 27. The former senator from Indiana and militant foe of the League wrote: "My confidence in Lodge grows all the time. . . . I think it would have been better strategy if he had frankly assailed the entire plan. Still, I realize that he has been and will be in a

59. Borah to Munsey, March 9, 1919, Borah Papers, Box 550.

rather delicate position until the Senate is safely organized by the Republicans. That, of course, is the most important practical and immediate consideration. I have begun to feel that, if this is accomplished, Lodge will lead the assault as strongly and directly as even you and I could wish."[60]

Given their different goals, then, Lodge and Borah reached the only understanding that was feasible. Borah conceded that Republicans would not be in favor of total opposition to the League at this juncture and that senatorial amendments should be supported.[61] Consideration of amendments would take up time. More importantly, if they were adopted they might cause Wilson to reject the League. The distinction that later arose between amendments and reservations was not made at this time; both simply referred to further Senate changes in the League. Lodge possibly implied he would vote against the League if amendments were not adopted, though it is more likely he refused to commit himself in view of his position as a party mediator. He agreed that Borah could break with the party and vote against the League even if amendments were adopted, and he apparently thought that Borah would cooperate in organizing the Senate.[62]

The agreement clearly was provisional; if a strategy other than that of amendments subsequently offered a better chance of defeating the League, Borah would take it. Borah also must have insisted that he would continue to do everything he could to commit the party to a stand of total rejection. He believed, correctly, that the hesitancy of some Republicans to attack the League was due to political expediency. Openly contemptuous of expedient men, he hoped that as public opinion grew stronger, "the courage and foresight and statesmanship of some of our leaders will grow dependable."[63] He would try to hurry that process in any way he could. An open letter to the editor of the *Boston Evening Transcript,* dated May 7, illustrates his tactics. It would be better, Borah stated, that the Republican party declare its absolute faith in the League than "to go skulking through such a fight without views or convictions or even an attitude." "I would not ask my party to agree with me, but I would ask it to state its position and I will

60. Beveridge to Borah, April 27, 1919, ibid.

61. Henry Cabot Lodge, *The Senate and the League of Nations* (New York, 1925), 147.

62. Ibid. On April 30 Lodge wrote to Beveridge: "My desire is to get together, assure the Republican organization of the Senate, then take up amendments; with this course Borah is in full sympathy, and our conversation was in every way most satisfactory." Beveridge Papers, Box 216.

63. Borah to Pepper, April 23, 1919, Borah Papers, Box 194.

soon determine my course." The League was a "matter about which only cowards and political pimps could have no convictions." Under such circumstances, "can a Republican go feeling and smelling around as the white livered satellite of base expediency? It would be a thousand times better to stand forth even if defeated with certainty."[64] The day before he wrote this open letter, he informed a friend in Idaho that "it is not a breach of confidence to say that I am satisfied Senator Lodge is just as much opposed to it [the League] now as I am."[65]

Borah's faith in the Republican majority leader would wax and wane during the League fight. Neither man really trusted the other. Lodge saw in Borah and several other irreconcilables certain traits that characterized Wilson: a stubborn commitment to principle, self-righteousness, and ignorance of practical tactics. The Idaho senator, on the other hand, disliked Lodge's political maneuvering on an issue of such vital importance; in contrast, he appreciated and respected Wilson's commitment to principle. The important fact, however, was that Borah, in spite of his differences with Lodge, ultimately did compromise and cooperate with the majority leader. There was no conspiracy or secret agreement between the two, but they came to recognize each other's importance to their respective objectives.

Despite the assertions of his open letter, however, Borah had no intention of allowing the Republican party to take a stand in favor of the League, as he demonstrated on April 29. On that day one of Lodge's many visitors was Senator Charles Curtis, the party whip. From their meeting a telegram was drafted and sent to all Republican senators, asking them to "reserve final expressions of opinion respecting the amended League covenant until the latest draft has been carefully studied and until there has been an opportunity for conference."[66] Already, of course, several Republican irreconcilables had issued statements on the League, and the irreconcilables in general resented the telegram. Borah immediately protested against any conference to determine the party's position. "This is a matter no political party can bind me on unless it agrees with my views," he stated. His sentiments were reiterated by Johnson and other bitter-enders.[67]

The irreconcilables were not the only ones who disapproved of

64. *Boston Evening Transcript,* May 9, 1919; the letter is dated May 7.
65. Borah to E. H. Dewey, May 6, 1919, Borah Papers, Box 550.
66. *New York Times,* April 30, 1919.
67. *Boston Evening Transcript,* May 1, 2, 1919; *New York Tribune,* May 1, 1919; *New York Times,* May 2, 1919.

the telegram. Several Republican senators who favored the League also objected to what they considered an attempt to control them. They were as concerned that Lodge might try to turn the party against the League as the irreconcilables were that he would not oppose it with sufficient firmness. Like the irreconcilables, the pro-League Republicans understood Lodge's political motivations and were scornful but also, paradoxically, somewhat comforted in the knowledge that he would modify his views on the League to meet changing pressures.

There was another reason why both the irreconcilables and the senators sympathetic to the League criticized Lodge's call for a party conference, criticism which indirectly questioned his leadership. Lodge was a strong conservative on domestic issues, whereas about half of the irreconcilables and many of the pro-League Republicans were, by comparison, more reform-minded. The press referred to all these reform Republicans as "progressives," although they represented a wide spectrum of views. Among the irreconcilables, for example, they included not only the peace progressives —La Follette, Norris, and Gronna—but Borah, Johnson, McCormick, and one or two others who were less outspoken. A fight was looming between the two wings of the party over the organization of the Sixty-sixth Congress. Lodge's call for a conference was regarded by his critics as an attempt in advance of Congress's opening to commit the party to his way of thinking not only on the League but on domestic issues as well.

Thus, for all his maneuvering in the two or three day period following publication of the revised Covenant, Lodge had not unified the Republican senators. On the contrary, his efforts seemed only to have exacerbated the disunity. The irreconcilables, aware of Lodge's objective, were prepared to exploit his difficulties to forward their own purposes. Their opportunity came when Wilson, on May 7, announced from Paris that an extraordinary special session of the Sixty-sixth Congres would open on May 19.[68]

The Republican intraparty struggle over the organization of the

68. *New York Times,* May 8, 1919. Wilson said in his public announcement that the requirements of "public interests" had forced him to call the special session. The pressure had come from various sources, but Wilson had finally yielded at the insistence of Cabinet officers whose departments were without funds. The Wilson Papers, Series 6, Box 54, contain letters from businessmen's groups asking for a special session. See also Secretary of the Treasury Carter Glass to Wilson, March 8, 18, 1919, Series 8 A, Box 23; Secretary of the Navy Josephus Daniels to Wilson, March 27, 1919, Series 8 A, Box 29; Secretary of Labor W. B. Wilson to Wilson, March 5, 1919, Series 8 A, Box 221; Woodrow Wilson to Tumulty, May 6, 1919, Series 8 A, Box 45, Wilson Papers.

new Senate had roots that went deep into the party's history and was fraught with implications for the future. As recently as 1912 the rivalry between the conservative and progressive wings had resulted in the birth of a third party under Roosevelt's guidance. Roosevelt soon returned to the Republican fold and became something of a mediator between the conflicting factions, though he certainly leaned toward the progressives (except those who voted against war). His death in January, 1919, removed a major block to conservative ascendancy in the party.

Lodge, as one of the staunchest conservatives, had no intention of allowing the progressives to take control of the Senate. To maintain conservative domination, he had to prevent the progressive Republicans and the Democrats from combining to put through liberal reconstruction legislation and at the same time keep the leadership of the League fight in his hands. No doubt, as a recent study argues, this dual purpose was one reason he favored delay on the League, for as long as that remained undecided, domestic issues would necessarily be deferred.[69] Lodge was fortunate in that his progressive critics were divided between the friends and the enemies of the League. He also benefited from Wilson's failure to promote an alliance of the progressive Republicans who favored the League with his own Democratic followers. By classifying as a bitter enemy almost any Republican who questioned his peace plans, the President helped Lodge more than he knew. Lodge was shrewd enough in his own right to make certain concessions to the progressives, such as his move to drop the wartime disloyalty charges against La Follette.

In spite of their disadvantages, the progressive Republicans were not ready to yield unprotestingly to Lodge's rule; and as the time came to organize the Senate, pro- and anti-League progressives tried to find common ground in a stand against conservative domination of the committees. The key committees were Finance and Appropriations (though Foreign Relations also was to become involved in the controversy). According to the seniority rule, the chairmanships of both the Finance and Appropriations Committees would pass to conservatives: Finance to Boies Penrose and Appropriations to Francis Warren. Penrose had long been the bane of

---

69. James Oliver Robertson, "The Progressives in National Republican Politics, 1916 to 1921" (Ph.D. diss., Harvard University, 1964), 127, 168-69. Robertson's interpretation is more persuasive when applied to the Old Guard than to the progressives. To claim, as Robertson does, that Hiram Johnson saw the League primarily as an issue to break the power of the conservatives in 1920 unduly neglects Johnson's ideological reasons for opposing the League.

progressives and it was he more than Warren whom the progressives wanted to replace with a man of liberal views. Shortly after Wilson announced the special session, eight of the progressives—Borah, Johnson, McCormick, Norris, Charles McNary, Wesley Jones, Albert Cummins, and William Kenyon—began holding conferences. Borah was the acknowledged leader.[70] La Follette and Gronna did not attend the conferences and were said to be in favor of "a harmony program."[71] Lodge, genuinely alarmed that the attack on Penrose might be carried to the Senate floor and thereby endanger Republican organization prospects, quickly acted to head off the incipient revolt.[72] He first delegated Moses to approach the progressives and offer a *modus vivendi*, probably certain desirable committee assignments in return for the progressives calling off their campaign.[73] Whatever Moses said, it seemed to be effective, for after he had met with them most progressives were reported as being unwilling to take their fight to the floor. Borah, however, and to a lesser degree Johnson, remained adamant. To pacify Johnson, the Old Guard offered the ceremonial post of president pro tempore of the Senate. But Johnson would not be bought off so cheaply, and when he rejected the offer, Cummins was given the position. The progressives then agreed to nominate Kenyon and Jones for positions on the Committee on Committees, which was charged with naming the members of the major committees.[74]

As Congress prepared to open on May 19, the chairmanship question was still unresolved. Lodge moved to break the deadlock by appointing Borah and Johnson to the Committee on Committees, notwithstanding that Borah personally had informed him that Kenyon and Jones were the progressives' nominees.[75] By putting

70. *Philadelphia Public Ledger,* May 13, 1919; *New York Times,* May 13, 1919.

71. *New York Times,* May 13, 1919. In their biography, Belle and Fola La Follette confusingly state that Senator La Follette did not join in the fight against Penrose because he thought the progressives should fight all the conservative committee chairmen and also that they shoud unite to gain control of one important committee. La Follette and La Follette, *La Follette,* 2:961. But the latter was essentially what the progressives were doing. Lodge's earlier efforts to exonerate La Follette from disloyalty charges may have had some bearing on the senator's abstention.

72. Lodge to James T. Williams, editor of the *Boston Evening Transcript,* May 13, 1919, Lodge Papers.

73. *New York Times,* May 13, 1919.

74. *New York Tribune,* May 15, 1919. Johnson to C. K. McClatchey, May 20, 1919, Johnson Papers; Lodge to J. T. Williams, May 13, 1919, Lodge Papers. *New York Times,* May 20, 1919.

75. *Washington Post,* May 20, 1919; *Philadelphia Public Ledger,* May 20, 1919; *New York Times,* May 20, 1919.

Borah and Johnson on the Committee on Committees, Lodge hoped to contain their opposition to that Committee, and, in addition, give the two prominent bitter-enders a voice in naming the members of the Foreign Relations Committee. Borah and Johnson, however, declined the assignments and wrote open letters insisting that Kenyon and Jones be appointed. Kenyon and Jones caused Lodge further embarrassment by refusing to be second choices, whereupon Lodge named Gronna and McNary.[76] At this point the struggle over the Finance and Appropriations Committees became intertwined with the appointment of the members of the Foreign Relations Committee.

There were four new Republican positions to be filled on this premier committee. Lodge, who would succeed to the chairmanship, wanted to appoint men who were at least as much opposed to the revised Covenant as he was and, if possible, conservative. The names of Kenyon, Frank Kellogg, McCormick, Johnson, Moses, and Irvine Lenroot were frequently mentioned as possible new members.[77] Kellogg was anxious to be on the committee and he was conservative enough, but he had not signed the Round Robin and he was sympathetic to the League. Lodge offered him a position on the condition that he follow his leadership. When Kellogg refused, Lodge named Moses.[78] That left three vacancies, two of which were filled by the appointment of Warren Harding and Harry New, both of whom were conservative, loyal party followers, and hostile to the League. One opening remained. Lodge probably would have liked to name a man whose views were not so obviously anti-League, to balance off Moses, New, and Harding, especially since there were already four irreconcilables—Borah, Brandegee, Knox, and Fall—on the committee. Only one holdover, Porter McCumber, was pro-League, so that if Lodge appointed another, the lineup would still be 8 to 2 against the League. If he did this, however, and if all seven Democrats on the Committee voted with the two Republicans, Lodge would lose control. But to appoint another anti-League man might cause the pro-League progressives to go their own way, alienate public opinion, and disrupt the party's future

76. Ibid. Johnson to Lodge, May 19, 1919, Lodge Papers. *New York Times,* May 21, 1919.

77. *New York Times,* May 8, 1919.

78. David Bryn-Jones, *Frank B. Kellogg: A Biography* (New York, 1937), 113-14. Lodge wrote to Root that Kellogg "was not put on the Foreign Relations Committee and, justly perhaps, has no warm affection for us on that account." Lodge to Root, August 15, 1919, Elihu Root Papers (Library of Congress), Box 231. Kellogg to Lodge, May 27, 1919, enclosing letter of Kellogg to Brandegee, May 27, 1919, Lodge Papers.

political chances. The progressive Kenyon now appeared to have the best chance of getting the last seat, even though he had not signed the Round Robin.[79] Still to be heard from, however, was Borah. As the leader of the progressive revolt and the most militant irreconcilable, he was in a position to pressure Lodge into naming the irreconcilable Johnson as a *quid pro quo* for not continuing the fight against Penrose and Warren. Borah claimed in later years that this was what happened.[80] At the same time Borah was prepared to sacrifice an important committee chairmanship of his own in return for Johnson's appointment. On May 25 Borah went before the Committee on Committees and relinquished his post as chairman of the Labor and Education Committee so that Kenyon could be named chairman and Johnson could have the Foreign Relations position.[81] Another story had Hitchcock, who would become Democratic minority leader, approaching Lodge with a proposition whereby the Democrats would not assist the progressives in blocking Republican organization of the Senate in return for one more Democratic seat on the Foreign Relations Committee.[82] If such an offer were made, Lodge did not accept it. Instead, he named Johnson, making a total of six bitter-enders on the Committee. Democrats, including Thomas, charged that Lodge had brazenly "stacked" the Committee against the League. McCormick answered by saying that the Republicans were only taking a page from the President's book. He had taught them the lesson by "stacking" the Peace Commission.[83]

The progressives made one final gesture. At a Republican conference on May 27, they introduced a motion to strike Penrose's name from the chairmanship of the Finance Committee. The vote was 34 to 8 against the motion.[84] Vice President Marshall then ruled that until the new committees were organized, the old, Democratic-controlled ones would continue in existence. This ruling, thought some observers, was another reason for Borah to cooperate with Lodge.[85] When the Senate on May 28 voted on the committee as-

79. *Boston Evening Transcript*, May 22, 1919; *Washington Post*, May 25, 1919.

80. Borah to his biographer, Claudius Johnson, December 11, 1935, cited in James Hewes, "William E. Borah and the Image of Isolationism" (Ph.D. diss., Yale University, 1959), 224.

81. *Washington Post*, May 25, 1919. Two weeks later Kenyon declared that Hiram Johnson was the Republicans' strongest Presidential candidate. Ibid., June 11, 1919.

82. Hamilton Holt in *The Independent* 97 (June 1919): 387-88.

83. *Congressional Record*, 66 Cong., 1 sess., 1373 (June 19, 1919).

84. *New York Tribune*, May 28, 1919.

85. Ibid.; Gus Karger to Taft, May 27, 1919, Taft Papers, Box 460.

signments, Penrose and Warren were accepted as chairmen of the Finance and Appropriations Committees respectively without any opposition. It is impossible to say what Borah would have done had Lodge not appointed Johnson, but it seems doubtful he would have gone so far as to bolt Lodge's leadership and vote against the party choices. Lodge, however, could never be certain. It is also unlikely that Lodge would have appointed a Republican partial to the League even if Borah had been less obstructive, but he probably would have chosen someone other than Johnson. It was already known that the California progressive sought the Republican Presidential nomination, and Lodge, as his subsequent actions testify, did not want to aid Johnson by allowing him any unnecessary opportunities for public exposure.

Thus, as the Sixty-sixth Congress got underway the irreconcilables were much stronger than at the end of the Sixty-fifth in early March. In the interim they had formed a propaganda organization, secured funds to help finance it, and had begun to wage an intensive campaign among the people. Elihu Root had been brought into the fight in favor of changing the Covenant if not for outright rejection. From the struggle over organizing the new Senate they had emerged with six of the ten Republican seats on the Foreign Relations Committee. With that kind of representation they could influence Lodge's handling of the Treaty. By delaying its consideration and by calling hostile witnesses, they could foment further opposition. Knox saw the possibilities when he wrote to his friend Salmon Levinson: "I think when you hear of the membership of the committee . . . you will be satisfied that the League of Nations is going to have the time of its life when we get hold of it officially."[86] They were to get their hands on it before much longer and Knox's prediction would become prophecy.

86. Knox to Salmon Levinson, May 23, 1919, Levinson Papers, Box 46.

5 RESERVATIONS: A STRATEGY FOR VICTORY

WITH THE OPENING of the Sixty-sixth Congress on May 19 the focus of the League fight swung directly to the Senate. The next three months would be difficult for the bitter-enders. No longer could they dominate the debates as they had in the Sixty-fifth Congress. Many more senators were speaking out, and recognizable divisions began to form. Newspapers now contrasted the mild reservationists to the strong reservationists and the Wilsonians to the irreconcilables. Frequent editorials appeared on the irreconcilables, usually in condemnation but occasionally laudatory. There seemed to be no halfway ground, which was the way most bitter-enders wanted it. Their basic strategy would remain the same: to delay proceedings so that public opinion might shift in their favor, and thereby enable them to convert enough of their colleagues to an irreconcilable position so that the League could be defeated on a straight-out vote. If the latter proved impossible, they would have to utilize indirect devices to accomplish their goal. That, indeed, was what became necessary, and the next three months would see much parliamentary maneuvering, primarily over the question of reservations.

There was one thing the bitter-enders could do that did not depend on their colleagues, and that was to continue attacking the League and, as the terms gradually become known, the rest of the Treaty. Reed, Borah, Sherman, and Johnson led the onslaught during the first month of the new session. Each made a special appeal to prejudice.

Reed's speech on May 26 was one of the more demagogic of the debates. His opening remarks summarized his argument: "It will come as a distinct shock . . . that this is a colored league of nations; that is to say, the majority of the nations composing the league do not belong to the white race of men. On the contrary they are a conglomerate of the black, yellow, brown, and red races, frequently so intermingled as to constitute an unclassifiable mongrel breed."[1] In November, 1918, he had claimed that the European monarchies would rule the League. Now, because of new information, he said, he had changed his mind. He "proved" his latest assertion with a set of statistics showing that seventeen of the thirty-two prospective members of the League contained a majority of dark-skinned peoples. In population these seventeen "dark" nations outnumbered the "white" by more than five hundred million, and these five hundred million came from such insignificant nations as Liberia, Haiti, and Nicaragua. Turning to the southern Democratic senators, he asked how they could face their constituents and at the same time endorse an organization in which Liberia and Haiti had votes equal to the United States. He also reminded them that *Crisis,* the magazine of the National Association for the Advancement of Colored People, had said a league was imperative for the "salvation" of Negroes. "Chew on that quid in your reflective moments, you men of the South!" Reed declared.[2]

Reed's harangue was the signal for Hitchcock, the Democratic minority leader, to make an ill-fated interruption, one of many he would make in the debates. It was nonsense, he said, to believe that countries like Liberia would have power in the League comparable to that of the United States. All important actions would be taken by the executive council, which required unanimous consent and in which the United States was a permanent member. Upon questioning by Reed, Hitchcock admitted that a dispute between two parties could be referred to the League assembly; but he pointed out that a unanimous vote was still necessary and nations like the United States could not be controlled. Reed, however, asked if this situation did not similarly make it impossible for the great powers to control the smaller nations. "Certainly," Hitchcock answered. Thus, concluded Reed, "you tie the hands of the United States by the vote of . . . Liberia; and where do you come out? All you have argued thus far is that your league is an innocuous thing because it is powerless, and yet you tell us it is to save the world!"[3] Laughter and then applause swept through the galleries at the Missourian's riposte.[4]

A few days later Reed was challenged by a southern Demo-

1. *Congressional Record,* 66 Cong., 1 sess., 236 (May 26, 1919).
2. Ibid., 236-46.
3. Ibid.
4. *Washington Post,* May 27, 1919.

crat, Joseph Robinson of Arkansas, to a contest in which each would immediately resign his seat and run for reelection on the sole issue of the League. When Reed evaded the challenge, Robinson called him, in effect, a coward, and asked him what alternatives he proposed to the United States joining the League. Reed replied that war was "a thing which can not be remedied." Only palliatives were possible, and of these he preferred the codification and clarification of international law and the establishment of an "international judicial tribunal" to hear justiciable disputes, but without any power to enforce its decisions.[5]

Reed's appeal to racial prejudice probably had little if any effect on the League's defeat. The effect of Borah's appeal, based on his claim that the British would dominate the League, was a different matter altogether. The Idaho senator aimed his remarks at the hyphenates, especially the Irish-Americans, and he helped foster massive protests against the League by the American-based Sinn Fein organizations. The Irish vote, always important in American politics, had added significance for the League fight. Ireland's bid for independence, stimulated by Wilson's wartime call for self-determination, reached its climax simultaneously with the League debates.[6] Until 1919 Irish-Americans were hopeful supporters of Wilson's peace proposals. But as 1919 wore on Borah began to replace Wilson as their recognized champion.[7] The bitter-enders, it will be recalled, had seized the issue early in the debates. Some of the anglophobes among them had been quick to point out the English influence in helping draft the League. Then, when the Covenant first was published, they had attacked Article seven, which "gave" the British Empire six votes, and Article ten which, they claimed, was even more onerous since it would perpetuate England's control over the Irish by requiring the United States to guarantee the status quo. American boys, including those of Irish descent, would be forced to shoot down blood brothers who tried to win their freedom.

Borah had been spreading the hyphenate message throughout the fight. On May 29 he introduced a resolution requesting the American delegates at Paris to obtain a hearing for representatives of Ireland. Reported favorably from the Foreign Relations Committee, the resolution passed the Senate by an overwhelming vote of 60 to 1, after an amendment had been added expressing the

5. *Cong. Record*, 66 Cong., 1 sess., 328-43 (May 28, 1919).
6. Selig Adler, *The Isolationist Impulse* (New York, 1957), 80-85.
7. Joseph Edward Cuddy, "Irish-America and National Isolation" (Ph.D. diss., State University of New York at Buffalo, 1965), 185.

Senate's sympathy for the cause of Irish independence.[8] The resolution failed to produce its desired result in Paris, but it did produce a flood of letters to senators in Washington. The Friends of Irish Freedom, for example, was instrumental in getting over thirty-five thousand postcards sent to Joseph Frelinghuysen, a New Jersey Republican, each card bearing the signature and address of a New Jersey voter.[9] While Frelinghuysen never became an irreconcilable, he assailed the League at every opportunity and he was later to assist the irreconcilables in preventing any compromise between Lodge and the Democrats.

The Irish issue did not, however, unite the foes of the League, as has sometimes been stated.[10] Borah received no sharper criticism for his resolution than from Charles Thomas. The Colorado bitter-ender, who said he would have voted against the resolution had he been present, pointedly asked Borah why he had not introduced a resolution to free the Korean people from Japan. Thomas supplied the answer himself: "Korea has no votes in America." He wondered what the senators would say if a member of the British House of Commons introduced a resolution in behalf of Puerto Rico or for the freedom, "if you please, of the colored people of the South."[11]

Borah, in replying, was candid enough "to admit that, of course, there is politics in the resolution." He was not unmindful of the "millions of people in the United States who sympathize with the cause of Ireland, and who through political machinery . . . express their desires from a political standpoint." But he maintained that the "deeper and profounder reason" for his resolution was to give Ireland a hearing to plead its case. Thomas was not convinced, but he sat down after warning Borah that his courting of the hyphenated Americans might lead to the kind of foreign entanglements which he and most Americans wanted to avoid.[12]

Whereas Reed foresaw the nonwhite races controlling the League and Borah feared the British Empire's predominance, Sherman, in a sensational address on June 20, affirmed that the Pope would rule the organization. Until this time the question of religion had received little attention. There had been some opposition among

8. *Cong. Record*, 66 Cong., 1 sess., 393 (May 29, 1919), 732 (June 6, 1919).

9. Charles C. Tansill, *America and the Fight for Irish Freedom* (New York, 1957), 335-36.

10. Adler, *The Isolationist Impulse*, 74-75.

11. *Cong. Record*, 66 Cong., 1 sess., 1374 (June 19, 1919), 1726-27 (June 25, 1919).

12. Ibid., 1728.

Protestant clergymen to Wilson's meeting with Pope Benedict XV in early 1919, but their protests seemed unimportant in view of the larger issues being discussed.[13] Borah, it is true, had announced he would oppose the League even if Jesus Christ should appear on earth to advocate it, but this was only a way of expressing his intransigence.[14] It remained for Sherman to inject the religious issue squarely into the debates. The main tenet of his address was that the Catholic nations would comprise a majority of the League members. While this in itself was of little consequence, he said, there was danger in the Papacy's doctrine of temporal as well as spiritual authority, and in the possibility that the Pope might someday be in a position to dictate policies to the Catholic nations. For that reason, "the Covenant of the League of Nations bears within its folds a reactionary power more fatal and insidious than a Prussian helmet, more dangerous than future war." Sherman claimed he had no prejudice against Catholicism as such. He would as readily denounce any Protestant sect which assumed such omnipotent authority as to menace civil government. Protestant as well as Catholic nations had been guilty of intolerance and persecution in the past. As for his personal religion, he believed in a God, though he belonged to no church. Many people would misunderstand his purpose in making the speech and malign him for it, he thought, but this did not disturb him; a man's character was often determined by the enemies he made.[15]

Sherman was right in assuming that his speech would provoke a reaction. Democrats, including Thomas, publicly denounced him, and even his fellow Republican irreconcilables declined to come to his defense. He also found himself widely condemned in the press. Catholic journals generally opposed the address, but the reaction was not as adverse in Illinois as elsewhere.[16] Many League supporters, while deploring the speech, probably were at the same time pleased because they believed it would have a reverse effect. Tumulty hurried off an optimistic report to the President. Sherman's remarks, Tumulty predicted, would make him "the Doctor Bur-

13. Arthur Walworth, *Woodrow Wilson*, 2d ed., rev. (Boston, 1965), 233.
14. Thomas A. Bailey, *Woodrow Wilson and the Great Betrayal* (New York, 1945), 65.
15. *Cong. Record*, 66 Cong., 1 sess., 1435-37 (June 20, 1919). Sherman to W. H. Hainline, July 5, 1919; Sherman to Will Colvin, March 13, 1919, Sherman Papers. Judged by his private remarks, Sherman appears to have been a deist.
16. Borah said he deeply regretted the speech and that many of Sherman's friends had tried to dissuade him from making it. Borah to Elmer Peterson, June 24, 1919, Borah Papers, Box 550. See *Literary Digest* 62 (July 19, 1919): 32-33, for press reaction.

chard of the Republicans in this country."[17] Sherman's correspondence, however, revealed quite the opposite response. He received at least twice as many favorable as unfavorable letters, with a large number of the former coming from Protestant ministers in the South. Noting this, the Illinois senator mailed out more than 27,000 copies of his speech, including a batch for James Reed's constituents, at the latter's request.[18]

While it seems clear that Sherman's primary motive in introducing the religious issue into the debates was to raise doubts and fears against the League, he also may have been sincere in claiming to have no particular prejudice against the Catholic Church. Both in his correspondence and on the Senate floor he frequently attacked Protestant clergymen who differed with him on the League. His concern for religious freedom and the separation of church and state was genuine, but it was qualified by his first duty of defeating the League. This was made more evident later in the debates when he introduced an amendment which would have inserted the word "God" in the Treaty. Berating the Treaty as the most materialistic document ever written, he observed that the delegates at Paris had not even offered prayers before commencing their labors. When several senators, including Borah and Lodge, spoke against the amendment, and a motion to table it carried by a large majority, Sherman let the religious argument die.[19]

Many of the irreconcilables' new criticisms concerned the general terms of the Versailles Treaty. At the time when the Treaty was first presented to Germany on May 7 for its study and objections, senators displayed relatively little interest. Everybody was still occupied with the revised League Covenant and the Treaty's terms were only fragmentary. Not surprisingly, La Follette found the Treaty excessively harsh on Germany.[20] While a few irreconcilables subsequently joined him in condemning the Treaty on these grounds, most of them had no serious quarrel with the treatment accorded the recent enemy. The section of the Treaty apart from the League which provoked the loudest outcry had nothing directly to do with Germany. Then, as later, the most widespread opposition centered on the provisions regarding Shantung, the formerly Chinese province that Germany had seized in 1898 and Japan in turn had conquered during the war. In addition to the right of

17. Tumulty to Wilson, June 20, 1919, Wilson Papers, Series 8 A, Box 64.
18. Sherman to Reed, October 11, 1919, Sherman Papers.
19. *Cong. Record*, 66 Cong., 1 sess., 7680-83 (October 29, 1919).
20. Belle Case La Follette and Fola La Follette, *Robert M. La Follette* (New York, 1953), 2:955.

conquest Japan had been promised certain rights in the province by Britain and France in accord with the terms of secret treaties made by these governments in 1917. At the Peace Conference Wilson had acceded to Japan's claims notwithstanding their violation of the principle of self-determination. China protested this decision, but Japan threatened to walk out of the Conference if her claims were not met. Rather than see this happen, which he believed would have meant the collapse of all negotiations, Wilson gave in. Actually, Japan had not asked for full control over Shantung but only for the German economic rights and possessions; in addition she promised to return the province to China and withdraw her troops, which she did in 1922. Wilson was aware that most Americans were very sympathetic to China and would take strong exception to his action. The Shantung settlement in fact was one of the few parts of the Treaty that nobody liked; and the irreconcilables, badly divided on many other questions, condemned it without exception.

One of the first and most persistent critics of this section of the Treaty was Johnson, many of whose California constituents were virulently anti-Japanese. "The blackest page in all" American history, "the rape of China," and similar phrases poured from Johnson's lips. Japan would not be satisfied with this enormous victory, he said. She would ask the League to rule on American immigration policies and on California's alien land law, and Johnson feared the worst from an organization composed of corrupt autocracies and blatant imperialists. But the worst feature of the Shantung "betrayal" was that, under Article ten, the United States would be forced to preserve Japan's conquest, as it also would the spoils of war acquired by England, France, and Italy. "How can any man of liberal views agree to Article Ten . . . ? The Section freezes the world into immutability."[21]

The argument that the League was reactionary and designed only to maintain the status quo was used by all the irreconcilables, but especially by Johnson, Borah, and the peace progressives. The argument was most effective in response to charges that they opposed the League because they had no conception of changed conditions in the world and clung to old and outworn traditions and institutions. The League's defenders pointed out that the provisions of the League were flexible: that, for example, Article nineteen of the Covenant provided that the League "may from time to time advise the reconsideration by members of the League of

21. *Cong. Record,* 66 Cong., 1 sess., 504-508 (June 2, 1919).

treaties which have become inapplicable," and that Article twenty-six further provided for amendment of the League after it had been established. But the irreconcilables replied that innumerable articles in the Treaty would be administered solely by the chief Allied powers, which also had permanent membership in the League's executive council. In practice, the League would defend the status quo.

The bitter-enders made their attacks chiefly from the floor of the Senate during this time. But they also journeyed outside Washington at every opportunity. The League for the Preservation of American Independence was now in a position to sponsor some of their tours, and with McCormick coordinating the speaking itineraries, things generally went smoothly. Johnson made the most successful tour. Swinging through New England in early July, he drew record-breaking crowds wherever he spoke; audiences cheered when he talked of old-time Americanism and hissed when he mentioned Wilson's name.[22] McCormick felt the bitter-enders were "in much better shape" by mid-July than they had ever been.[23] A pro-League newspaper editor, William Allen White, confirmed this opinion. After touring the Midwest in August under the auspices of the League to Enforce Peace, he found that the League of Nations was "in pretty bad with the folks."[24]

The irreconcilables' racial, ethnic, religious, and jingoistic appeals were certainly spreading seeds of doubt among the people, but the League's foes could not be unduly optimistic; for it was only in the Senate that they could win their victory; and the senators paid less attention to the speeches than they did to the parliamentary jockeying. The bitter-enders, however, did not neglect this facet of the struggle. On the contrary, they gave it their closest attention. From the moment the Sixty-sixth Congress opened on May 19, 1919, they demonstrated skill in using every available weapon to further their end.

At the outset of the new Congress, the irreconcilables found an excellent opportunity to make political capital. The Allied powers, upon completing the Treaty and presenting it to Germany for inspection, had agreed to keep the exact terms of the document a secret. If the Treaty was later to be modified to meet German objections, it obviously would be much easier if the Allied peoples did not know the original terms. To the irreconcilables, however,

22. *Boston Evening Transcript*, July 1, 8, 9, 15, 1919.
23. McCormick to Beveridge, July 15, 1919, Beveridge Papers, Box 215.
24. Walter Johnson, *William Allen White's America* (New York, 1947), 318.

this procedure smacked of secret diplomacy. Accordingly, Hiram Johnson offered a resolution on May 20 calling on the State Department to transmit the full text of the Treaty to the Senate.[25]

Before Johnson's resolution was acted upon, the bitter-enders had another issue. Germany was not bound by the nonpublication agreement, and copies of the Treaty were soon circulating widely in Europe. Inevitably some reached the United States. On June 3 Lodge announced that he had seen the Treaty and Borah charged that "special interests" in New York—international bankers and financiers—possessed copies. Johnson wrote Beveridge that he suspected "a receivership for the world" was being prepared.[26] Henceforth it was one of the bitter-enders' stock arguments, of conservatives as well as liberals, that Wall Street was engaged in a sinister plot to get the Treaty ratified. Borah and Johnson searched unceasingly but futilely for concrete evidence to support their conspiracy theory.[27]

The "Treaty leak," as the press referred to it, had other repercussions. Democrats joined in expressing criticism of the incident, and on June 6 Johnson's resolution passed the Senate, along with a resolution calling for an investigation of the "leak."[28] Wilson, meanwhile, had informed the Senate that he endorsed the investigation but could not in good faith break the pledge of secrecy he had made with the other powers.[29] Borah was not one to be restrained by such considerations. On June 9 he walked into the Senate chamber carrying a bulky package under his arm. After getting recognition from the chair he calmly stated that he had a copy of the Treaty, secured, he claimed, from the *Chicago Tribune's* foreign correspondent. When the Democrats objected to his request to have the Treaty printed, Borah began reading it aloud. After thirty-five minutes of this, the Democrats consented to let the question come to a vote; a motion to have the Treaty printed carried easily, and the irreconcilables had scored a minor triumph.[30] As La Follette re-

25. *Cong. Record,* 66 Cong., 1 sess., 63 (May 20, 1919).

26. Denna Frank Fleming, *The United States and the League of Nations, 1918-1920* (New York, 1932), 220. Johnson to Beveridge, June 3, 1919, Beveridge Papers, Box 215.

27. While there was no plot or conspiracy by American businessmen to get the Treaty ratified, there seems little doubt but that it received widespread support from business.

28. *Cong. Record,* 66 Cong., 1 sess., 735 (June 6, 1919).

29. Ray Stannard Baker and William E. Dodd, eds., *War and Peace: Presidential Messages, Addresses, and Public Papers, 1917-1921* (New York, 1927), 1:508.

30. *New York Times,* June 10, 1919.

marked, Borah had made good "Wilson's pledge of open Covenants openly arrived at."[31]

Simultaneously, various senators had considered subpoenaing prominent financial figures to explain to the Foreign Relations Committee what they knew about copies of the Treaty. Borah also wanted Root and Taft called to testify. Root, perhaps disturbed at the prospect of being dragged into the investigation, wrote to Brandegee, chiding the bitter-enders for belaboring such a trifling issue. "The country is looking for leadership by the Republican Senate. . . . The President gives affirmatives. Can the Senate give any policy to follow?"[32]

Brandegee was in no mood for a lecture, even from Root, and he fired back a blistering letter. The irreconcilables would not be intimidated by "you fellows over in N. Y.—with what you represent and control—in newspapers-banks-trust co.s et. al. et. al. et. al." Wilson and his League were going down to defeat and those who truckled to him would also fall. Nobody could presume to give advice who was far from the scene of battle and unwilling to get his hands dirty. "I am for *you*," Brandegee said, "but you ought to come out in the *open* with the rest of us." Some people, he continued, "apparently want to shield their carcases [*sic*] behind a camoflouge [*sic*] and let us take the bayonet thrusts, the poisonous gas and the cold blue steel, [while] *they* count their profits. I am getting a trifle *weary* of being the 'Goat.' *Do you get me?*"[33]

It appears that neither Brandegee nor Root knew precisely what the other's position was. Brandegee may have believed, incorrectly, that Root wanted the League defeated as much as he did. Root had consulted frequently with several bitter-enders; he had followed Brandegee's suggestions at the time of Henry White's letter to Lodge; and he seemingly had not been disturbed when some irreconcilables had praised his proposed amendments and at the same time had continued to insist on total defeat of the League. It is more likely, however, that Brandegee understood Root's indecision about what course to take, in which case Brandegee's hyperboles, added to Borah's request for Root to testify, might impel the New Yorker to assume a more hostile attitude. Root, for his part, obviously misunderstood the actions of certain irreconcilables; a few months later he wrote to Lodge in disgust that the bitter-enders had used devious means to defeat the League, viz., by sup-

31. La Follette and La Follette, *La Follette*, 2:965.
32. Root to Brandegee, June 8, 1919, Root Papers, Box 231.
33. Brandegee to Root, June 9, 1919, ibid.

porting his proposed changes in the hope that Wilson would not accept them, without themselves intending to vote for the Treaty under any conditions.[34] For whatever reasons Root was misled, his confusion benefited the irreconcilables' cause.

The furor over the Treaty "leak" quickly subsided afer Root voluntarily testified before the Foreign Relations Committee. He explained that the copy of the Treaty he had seen, and had shown to Lodge, belonged to Henry Davison, head of the League of Red Cross Societies, who had received the copy from Thomas Lamont, a financial adviser to the American delegation at the Peace Conference. When Borah pointed out that both Davison and Lamont were members of the firm of J. P. Morgan and Co., and asked Root if there was not an impropriety in these two men having secret information which could be used for private advantage, Root vigorously denied any wrongdoing by himself or Davison and Lamont. It was perfectly understandable, Root argued, that Davison and Lamont in their official positions should have had copies of the Treaty. When Davison left Paris, there was no restriction on personal possession or distribution of copies. The President's injunction against distribution came later. Moreover, Root said, the Treaty was public knowledge in Europe because of Germany's publication of it. Root's testimony was corroborated by Davison and J. P. Morgan, the latter denying Davison had shown him the Treaty. Borah nevertheless announced that he had been vindicated in his charge that "special interests" had possessed copies of the Treaty before the Senate learned of its terms; but he did not press the investigation any further, perhaps feeling that to do so would anger Lodge and Root at a time when the irreconcilables needed their cooperation. Nor were the Democrats anxious to continue the inquiry, even though Hitchcock had earlier declared that Lodge possessed "stolen goods." The fact that Lodge's copy originated with Lamont no doubt persuaded Hitchcock to drop the matter, for fear the whole issue might ultimately prove embarrassing to Wilson.[35]

Root's letter to Brandegee admonishing the Republican senators to take a more affirmative policy probably was shown to Knox, for on June 10, several days earlier than expected, the Pennsylvania irreconcilable presented a five-part resolution containing several positive suggestions.[36] Similar in form to his proposals of December,

34. Root to Lodge, May 14, 1920, Lodge Papers.
35. *New York Times,* June 10–12, 1919; *Philadelphia Public Ledger,* June 16, 1919.
36. *Washington Post,* June 11, 1919.

1918, the resolution called for the separation of the League and the Treaty, "to facilitate the early acceptance of the Treaty" and allow fuller discussion of the League. While this part of his resolution won the assent of most Republicans, not so the fifth section, which stated that it would be the government's "declared policy" to regard a threat to Europe's peace and stability by any power or combination of powers as "a menace to its own peace and freedom." When such a threat occurred the United States would "consult with other powers affected with a view to devising means for the removal of such menace, and [would], the necessity arising in the future, carry out the same complete accord and cooperation with our chief cobelligerents for the defense of civilization."[37]

Referred to the Foreign Relations Committee, the resolution was considered in a stormy two-hour session on June 12. Borah and Johnson strenuously objected to section five. While there is no record of what they said in committee and neither commented upon it later in the debates, section five obviously affirmed a commitment which they were not prepared for the United States to make. Narrower in scope yet more precise than Article ten of the League Covenant, Knox's plan was probably the more repugnant to these two irreconcilables, as well as to the peace progressives. Borah and Johnson told Lodge that if it were not removed, they would vote with the Democrats against the entire resolution.[38] Lodge got Knox's consent to strike the section out, which was done, all of the Republicans except Porter McCumber voting to remove it, all of the Democrats plus McCumber voting to retain it.[39] A few days later John Sharp Williams, one of the Democratic committee members, spoke of the politics behind the voting. The Democrats, he said, "voted to keep section five in so as to make them [Borah and Johnson] vote against you [the Republicans]. Politics; yes. You voted to take section five out to let them vote with you. Politics; yes."[40]

As amended, the resolution was favorably reported out of the Committee. Republican senators except for McCumber and four or five others who were undecided, immediately lined up behind the resolution while all Democrats but Reed and Gore opposed it. Thomas said that the "best part" of the resolution had been

37. *Cong. Record,* 66 Cong., 1 sess., 894 (June 10, 1919).
38. *Boston Evening Transcript,* June 12, 1919. La Follette also urged Knox to eliminate section five because it committed the United States in advance.
39. *Proceedings of the Committee on Foreign Relations, United States Senate, from the Sixty-Third Congress (Beginning April 1, 1913), to The Sixty-Seventh Congress (Ending March 3, 1923)* (Washington, D.C., 1923), 138-41.
40. *Cong. Record,* 66 Cong., 1 sess., 1373 (June 19, 1919).

section five; but the rest of it he denounced as partisan and unconstitutional. It was "a perfect illustration of the declaration of an
executive policy by a legislative body."[41] Pro-League senators reacted in noteworthy fashion to section five. McCumber declared
that he would be satisfied if this section, "without elimination or
addition, should be the only compact between the great nations of
the world." Senator J. C. W. Beckham, Kentucky Democrat, saw
no difference in principle between section five and Article ten of
the Covenant. Kenneth McKellar, Democrat from Tennessee, saw
a considerable difference. Section five, he declared, was more far-
reaching and dangerous. "If it were carried out . . ., we would become simply the chief of police of Europe . . . not with agreements
that war should not be made, but with an agreement that Europe
can stir up all the wars she wants and we will be the policeman and
we will stop the wars. Why . . . it would take 5,000,000 American
soldiers on guard in Europe all the time to preserve the peace."[42]
McKellar's remarks could have been substituted without change
for one of Borah's attacks on Article ten.

Knox took the floor on June 19 and delivered a strong speech in
behalf of his resolution, but he had nothing to say about the
deleted section. Instead he emphasized the League's shortcomings,
particularly its failure to allow a nation to withdraw until the League
itself had decided whether the nation had fulfilled its international
obligations to the other members. He also believed the Monroe
Doctrine was still inadequately protected. Contrary to the wording
of the Covenant, the Doctrine was not, he said, a "regional understanding." "The Monroe Doctrine is and . . . must continue to be
merely a policy. . . . Its precise character, the extent, method, and
time of its application, all are matters of our high and uncon-
trolled will and sovereign prerogative. We . . . can not answer to
anyone else in respect of it. We use it when, as, and to the extent
we need it. There can be no limitation upon it except our requirements, our will, and our force of arms. Whatever security we may
need within its purview it must give if we ask it." The League
would transform the Doctrine from a policy into an agreement,
which could not be allowed to happen.[43]

Although Knox's resolution remained popular with most Republicans, it eventually was opposed by several of the undecided
senators, including Norris, and Lodge never pushed it to a vote,

41. Ibid., 1372, 1379.
42. Ibid., 1264 (June 18, 1919), 2997 (July 22, 1919), 3024-25 (July 23, 1919).
43. Ibid., 1216-21 (June 17, 1919).

fearing it would split the party as well as be defeated.[44] Wilson rejected Tumulty's urging to make an open attack on it, as he thought that "one of the objects of Knox and his associates is to stir me up, which they have not yet done."[45] Knox may indeed have hoped the resolution would have that effect, but his reason for introducing it was related more to Root's letter than to anything else. Furthermore, Knox was only reiterating previously expressed ideas. While the President was wise not to let the resolution provoke him into an intemperate outburst, he should have been provoked enough to realize that the resolution's lack of a majority did not indicate any weakening of opposition to the League. If a simple majority could not be mustered to separate the Treaty from the League, it did not follow that a two-thirds majority could be found to support a united Treaty and League.

Most importantly, the failure of the Knox resolution to rally all Republicans brought Elihu Root into the service of the party once again. Meeting together for several hours on June 20, Root, Lodge, Knox, and Brandegee devised a strategy which it was hoped would unite the Republican senators and, Root believed, provide a constructive approach to the League. In a letter to Lodge, made public on June 21, Root stated his support for separation of the League from the Treaty; his major point, however, was the need for a series of Senate reservations to the League. Specifically, he suggested that the Monroe Doctrine should be declared inviolable; that there should be no qualifications on a nation's right to withdraw; and that Article ten should be rejected.[46] In March Root had been willing to accept Article ten on a five-year basis because he thought the United States must assist in restoring peace in Europe and the League needed this article to accomplish its purposes. He had never believed in it, however, as a viable solution to international problems.[47] Now he was, in a sense, coming out in the open, as Brandegee had said he should, and calling for its outright rejection.

44. Knox to Beveridge, June 18, 1919, Knox Papers, Box 7; *New York Tribune*, June 19, 1919.

45. Wilson to Tumulty, June 16, 1919, Wilson Papers, Series 8 A, Box 63.

46. Knox to Beveridge, June 21, 1919, Beveridge Papers, Box 215; *Boston Evening Transcript*, June 23, 1919; Philip Jessup, *Elihu Root* (New York, 1938), 2:401-402; Richard W. Leopold, *Elihu Root and the Conservative Tradition* (Boston, 1954), 138-39. Lodge wrote to Henry White that Root's letter was "more disastrous to the League than any statement that has been made by anyone. It has consolidated feeling in the Senate." Lodge to White, June 23, 1919, Lodge Papers.

47. John Chalmers Vinson, *Referendum for Isolation: Defeat of Article Ten of the League of Nations Covenant* (Athens, Ga., 1961), 69.

Root's new position on Article ten was good news to the irreconcilables, but Borah and Johnson quickly announced that reservations were inadequate and that only amendments would satisfy
them. Knox, however, was reported to believe that Root's reservations would safeguard the United States completely if the other
League signatories were required to accept the Senate's reservations
before ratification of the Treaty of Versailles.[48] None of the irreconcilables was being frank. Borah and Johnson would not accept
the League even with amendments. As Borah remarked on June
30: "I am opposed to any league of nations. With me it is not a
question of amendments of any kind. If my country is to be sold
I am not interested in the details of the bill of sale."[49] Nor would
Knox find Root's reservations satisfactory.

During the next two months there were frequently contradictory
statements by the bitter-enders. An irreconcilable would be quoted
as favoring the League if strong reservations were adopted; soon
thereafter he would declare that reservations were not enough,
that amendments were the minimum price he would accept for an
affirmative vote; soon after that he would demand defeat of the
Treaty no matter what reservations or amendments it included.
For several of those who finally voted as irreconcilables, such
vacillation reflected genuine uncertainty whether they should
accept the Treaty, with the League included, in some modified form
or whether they must reject it unconditionally. With others, such
as Borah, this seeming irresolution was a tactic in the parliamentary
struggle, which now became exceedingly complex.

Following Root's letter, debate about the meaning of "amendment" and "reservation" developed. As usually interpreted, an
amendment constituted a textual change of the Treaty requiring its
resubmission to the other signatories, including Germany; a reservation, on the other hand, placed an interpretation on the subject at
issue and did not textually change the Treaty, consequently avoid-
ing a reopening of the Peace Conference. There was a further distinction between reservations which were incorporated as part of
the actual resolution of approval by the Senate, as were the so-
called Lodge reservations, and reservations, also called interpretations, which were put in a separate resolution, such as Wilson was
willing to accept. The former were generally considered binding
on the signatories, the latter not.[50]

48. *New York Times,* June 24-25, 1919.
49. *Cong. Record,* 66 Cong., 1 sess., 2075 (June 30, 1919).
50. George Henry Haynes, *The Senate of the United States: Its History and
Practice* (New York, 1938), 2:617-18. Jack Kendrick, "The Republican Senate

Although most Republican senators eventually supported one set of reservations, they did so only after much political bargaining. Basically there were three groups among the Republicans: strong reservationists, mild reservationists, and irreconcilables, each with many shadings of opinion; one Republican, Porter McCumber, would accept the Treaty as it stood, but even he preferred mild reservations. In June, 1919, it is impossible to give precise numbers for each group. Nor can it be determined at what exact moment a senator switched from being a strong reservationist to an irreconcilable or from a mild reservationist to a strong reservationist. Fairly close approximations of the size of each group can be arrived at, however, which will show the general nature of the parliamentary divisions and resultant struggle.

Of the three groups, the irreconcilables at this time comprised only a small minority. In June one could cite Borah, Johnson, Sherman, Poindexter, and Brandegee as virtually certain to reject the Treaty, if the League were a part of it, even with the adoption of amendments or reservations. McCormick, Moses, and Fall also may belong with the above. Norris still seemed likely to accept the Treaty, including the League, provided it was qualified by amendments or reservations. The other future Republican bitter-enders probably had not yet decided what to do. Next to the bitter-enders and in the center of the Republican party stood those who became known as strong reservationists. Many in this group were almost if not equally as opposed to the Treaty as the irreconcilables, but for a variety of reasons did not want to go on record as totally opposed; other strong reservationists favored the Treaty but insisted on amendments or, if amendments failed, strong reservations. The strong reservationists numbered about thirty. The mild reservationists, in contrast, very much wanted the League approved but with certain reservations that were fewer in number and more mildly worded than those desired by the strong reservationists. In June there were approximately as many mild reservationists as irreconcilables.

The Democratic senators were also divided though not as badly. About forty approved of the Treaty and opposed any reservations. Only one, Reed, was at this time an unequivocal opponent of the League. Thomas, along with about a half dozen others, supported it with amendments or reservations.

The irreconcilables had failed to separate the League from the rest of the Treaty, and Root's call for reservations made it highly

and the League of Nations, 1918-1921" (Ph.D. diss., University of North Carolina, 1952) 177-80.

improbable either that separation would ever be accomplished or that the Republican party would take an implacable stand against the League. Therefore, while the bitter-enders would neither give up on the idea of separation, nor give up trying to commit the Republican party to their viewpoint, nor give up, especially in the case of Borah and a few others, pushing for a national referendum on the League, it soon became clear that they would have to adopt other methods if they were to have any chance of defeating the Treaty. There were only two possible approaches; each had its drawbacks and in June neither appeared likely to succeed.

The first, and the one the irreconcilables finally followed, was to support the adoption of amendments, or if these were defeated, reservations, in the hope that a large number of Democrats could not accept the Treaty as thus modified. The irreconcilables, after helping put through reservations, would then join the Democrats in voting against the Treaty with those reservations. For this plan to succeed several things were necessary. In the first place a majority—only a simple majority, not two-thirds—had to be secured for the reservations. This meant finding language acceptable to each of the three factions. Not every conceivable reservation would do; reservations useful to the irreconcilables' purpose had to be so worded and in such a form as to make them unacceptable to Wilson and the pro-League Democrats. Otherwise, the Treaty would be overwhelmingly approved. But if the irreconcilables insisted on reservations that were too strong, the mild reservationists would join with the Democrats to vote down all reservations or to vote through mild reservations. If that happened, enough of the strong reservationist Republicans under Lodge might join the Democrats and mild reservationist Republicans to form a two-thirds majority for the Treaty. Again the bitter-enders would lose.

The second possible approach was to join with the Democrats in voting down all amendments and reservations in the hope that enough Republicans would then be persuaded to defeat an unreserved Treaty. Most irreconcilables probably would have preferred to do this, for it was simple and direct: Senators would be forced either to support or reject the League as it was written. This approach, however, also had serious disadvantages. Lodge and the rest of the Republicans, in addition to a handful of Democrats, would be forced to choose between flat rejection and full acceptance. The Massachusetts majority leader had never been willing, in spite of constant pressure by the irreconcilables, to take an out-and-out stand against the League. Rather he was determined to maintain party unity and assume a stance on the League that was not unpopular with the public, provided he did not have to accept the League unqualifiedly. Reservations clearly offered the best chance of achieving these aims. Also, of course, as Lodge tried to convince the bitter-enders, reservations could result in the League's defeat if Wilson was unwilling to compromise and swallow a "Republicanized" League. But if the irreconcilables presented Lodge with an either-or situation, he might not join them in voting against an unreserved League and might instead swing toward the mild reservationists, in which case the Democrats, seeing the irreconcilable strategy, could come to terms with the reservationist Republicans. In fact, when the bitter-enders hinted of joining the Democrats to vote down reservations, Lodge indicated he might align himself with the mild reservationists. The irreconcilables could always counter by threatening to bolt the party in the 1920 election. This threat Lodge could not disregard, but he knew and the bitter-enders knew that their bolting probably would not affect the Senate's action. Furthermore, if the Republicans were to win the 1920 election, notwithstanding an irreconcilable defection, the latter group would find itself cut off from party leadership. In the final analysis, therefore, the bitter-enders rested their hopes on Lodge's ability to steer through strong reservations without alienating the mild reservationists, and on Wilson's willingness to reject the League with strong reservations attached.

The Democratic senators were well aware of these Republican divisions and tried to widen them. Hitchcock, the Democratic minority leader, portrayed Lodge and his followers as devious and dishonest, as men pretending to favor the League but actually maneuvering to defeat it; he then contrasted them with the irreconcilables. The latter were straightforward and honest; they admitted they wanted to defeat it: "at least they are candid, at least they are sincere, at least they are courageous . . . and that leadership of the Senator from Idaho [Borah] is a leadership which can be understood; it is a leadership that can be defended." Hitchcock suggested to Borah that if he wished to belong to a party that would stand squarely and openly against a League, he would have to desert the Republicans. Borah replied that if necessary he would leave his party, even if there were only one other person who shared his view, and he said he knew of one, referring probably to Johnson. "We would have a party of our own." Hitchcock said that he admired "the Senator for his stalwart courage."[51]

But such rhetorical devices were doomed to failure. The irrecon-

51. *Cong. Record*, 66 Cong., 1 sess., 790-91 (June 9, 1919), 1505 (June 21, 1919).

cilables would not be prompted to bolt Lodge's leadership by
Democratic praise for their independence of thought or by shame
for continuing to work with their devious colleagues. If the Democrats wanted to profit from the Republican differences, they would
have to make advances to the mild reservationists, not the irreconcilables. The irreconcilables could only hope they would not
make these efforts in time. For the moment they were encouraged
by the news from Paris. Upon receiving the report of Root's call
for reservations, Wilson quickly answered: "My clear conviction
is that the adoption of the Treaty by the Senate with reservations
would put the United States as clearly out of the concert of nations
as a rejection. We ought either to go in or to stay out."[52] Hitchcock
was soon proclaiming a "no compromise" stand on all reservations.

On June 28, 1919, Germany signed the Treaty. Wilson took the
opportunity that the occasion provided to send a brief message to
the American people in which he declared the Treaty, containing
the League, to be "a great charter for a new order of affairs in the
world," but only if it was "ratified and acted upon in full and
sincere execution of its terms."[53] There was no mention of any
further modification by the Senate. Newspapers polling Republican
senators found them almost unanimous in support of reservations.[54]
Norris, accepting the President's desire for "a new order of affairs,"
could not, however, reconcile these words with the disposition of
Shantung, and said he would insist on reservations.[55] Brandegee,
at odds with the idealism of both Wilson and Norris, vowed never
to "vote for it until hell freezes over." He was "not to be buncoed
by any oleaginous lingo about 'humanity' or 'men everywhere' or
'pooling the naval forces of the world' or . . . somebody's interpretation of the 'cries of the populace' as he motors down the Champs
Elysees." Like the man from Missouri, he had to be shown. And he
had not been shown by the "international bankers" or the "maudlin
sentimentalists" or "the poor deluded clergymen who are always
for virtue in the abstract, but fail to recognize vice in the concrete"
or by "the college professor who mistakes the eructations of an acid
stomach for the birth of a great purpose."[56]

Wilson boarded ship on June 29 to return to the United States
with the completed Treaty. Colonel House spoke to him just before
leaving. "Meet the Senate in a conciliatory spirit," his friend and
adviser pleaded. "House," the President replied, "I have found

52. Wilson to Tumulty, June 23, 1919, Wilson Papers, Series 8 A, Box 65.
53. Baker and Dodd, eds., *War and Peace*, 1:523-24.
54. *New York Times*, June 29, 1919; *New York Tribune*, June 29, 1919.
55. Ibid.
56. *New York Sun*, June 30, 1919.

one can never get anything in this life that is worth while without fighting for it."[57] Four months earlier House had given similar advice when Wilson came back with the League Covenant, and Wilson had responded with his "I have fighting blood in me" speech in Boston. On that trip home the irreconcilables had been happy to trade blows with him, and they felt they had got the better of the exchange. They were more than willing to continue the fight. Indeed, their only hope was that the President would not stop fighting and start negotiating.

After having been away from the United States for seven months and four days, except for his brief visit between February 24 and March 5, the President landed in Hoboken harbor on July 8. Two days later he formally presented the Treaty to the Senate. Instead of explaining and defending certain of the Treaty's more controversial features, he offered to make himself available to the Foreign Relations Committee for whatever information was desired. The burden of his remarks was an elaboration of the wartime ideals which he had enunciated and for which he had fought at Paris. America's isolation, he said, ended with the Spanish-American War, and America could not avoid being a world power. "The only question is whether we can refuse the moral leadership that is offered us, whether we shall accept or reject the confidence of the world." Thus, he continued: "The stage is set, the destiny disclosed. It has come about by no plan of our conceiving, but by the hand of God who led us into this way. We cannot turn back. We can only go forward, with lifted eyes and freshened spirit, to follow the vision. It was of this that we dreamed at our birth. America shall in truth show the way. The light streams upon the path ahead, and nowhere else."[58]

Several bitter-enders made typically caustic comments on the address. "Soothing, mellifluous, and uninformative," said McCormick. "Soap bubbles of oratory and soufflé of phrases," retorted Brandegee. Yet not only the hardened enemies of Wilson found the address wanting. Norris, who was probably the fairest-minded Republican bitter-ender, pronounced it "a fine lot of glittering generalities."[59] On July 15 he attacked the Treaty in the Senate. He still was sympathetic to the idea of a league, but only a league that provided for disarmament, abolished the right of conquest, decreed the end of secret diplomacy, and established a system of

57. House Diary, June 29, 1919, Edward M. House Papers (Yale University Library, New Haven, Conn.).

58. Baker and Dodd, eds., *War and Peace*, 1:537-52.

59. *Chicago Tribune*, July 11, 1919; *Boston Evening Transcript*, July 11, 1919.

international arbitration. Even a perfect league would be corrupted when attached to a treaty containing such indefensible provisions as those giving Shantung to Japan. He would not vote for the Treaty without amendments.[60]

When other Republicans who had been considered friends of the League also spoke critically in the days following his address, the President made conciliatory gestures. Uncommitted senators as well as those supposedly sympathetic to the League were invited to the White House to express their opinions and hear the President's explanations. Norris received an invitation to see the President on July 21. Since his speech on the fifteenth he had received extensive coverage in the press. Wilson and Hitchcock believed that if they could persuade him that the Shantung issue had been decided in the only feasible manner, his and others' opposition to this section would decline. But Norris rejected the invitation, saying that he did not wish to hear any information that would need to be kept confidential and that if the President had anything to say he should transmit it to the Senate in the normal manner.[61]

On the twenty-eighth Wilson met with Charles Thomas, the Colorado bitter-ender. While neither man commented on what was said, Thomas's views apparently "came as a great shock and surprise" to the President.[62] What Thomas told the President may be inferred from his Senate speech on the twenty-ninth. The Colorado senator maintained that his remarks were not to be interpreted as an attack on the Treaty, but only as an examination of the causes of war and peace. Nevertheless, he had few kind remarks for the League, and he criticized many features of the Treaty. His analysis of the effect the Treaty's terms would have on Germany was both eloquent and prescient. It was understandable, he said, that the Allies had imposed a harsh, vindictive settlement. No amount of reparation could compensate for the damages done by Germany. Nevertheless, "the Germans are human beings, possessed of human attributes, influenced by human motives, and inspired by human impulses." They would respect a dictated peace treaty only so long as the Allies had the power and the will to enforce it. When that power disappeared Germany would repudiate the treaty regardless of whether she was a member of the League of Nations. "The aspiration of Germany will be the coming of that hour. She will prepare for it . . . and we may be sure that her preparations will not

60. *Cong. Record*, 66 Cong., 1 sess., 2592-96 (July 15, 1919). Fall, Moses, and La Follette also denounced various parts of the Treaty in July.

61. *New York Tribune*, July 21, 24, 1919.

62. *Washington Post*, July 29, 1919; unpublished Thomas autobiography, Thomas Papers.

be discouraged by a world's assurance that the horizon of the future shall not be overcast by the gathering clouds of war. For it is everlasting truth that no peace of force has ever outlived the force which imposed it." Moreover, Thomas continued, the spirit of nationalism, which had never been stronger, endangered any hopes for a new world order organized around the principle of brotherhood. Nationalism was "a condition not easily controlled. It must expand its energy before it subsides, and will do more to exorcise the spell of internationalism than all the fleets and armies of men." Ironically, he concluded, it was Wilson's promotion of the right of self-determination which had done so much to foster the spirit of nationalism and thereby undermine his larger goal of an international organization.[63]

Thomas still preferred a league confined to the English-speaking nations, a league resting on self-interest and common goals. In that respect his views should not have surprised the President, if the President had been listening. Thomas had advocated such a league for many months, just as Norris had frequently spoken out over the last several years in favor of his quite different conception of an international organization. Both were consistent with their earlier positions.

The final irreconcilable to see the President was Bert Fernald, a senator from Maine, who had said nothing to indicate where he stood. The meeting did not last long. Fernald informed Wilson that he had decided to oppose the League unless reservations were added, and that there were forty-two other senators who would do the same. Wilson said that he had hoped there were at least sixty senators "who took a world view" of the issues confronting mankind. When Fernald replied that at least sixty senators did take this position, but that their world view included in its scope the United States, Wilson terminated the interview.[64]

The President made no headway with Norris, Thomas, and Fernald. But his talks with the mild reservationists greatly worried the bitter-enders. In an attempt to discredit the talks, Borah referred to "secret conferences behind closed doors," while Brandegee invidiously suggested Wilson was engaged in jury tampering.[65] What discouraged the irreconcilables most was Wilson's failure to reject all reservations on their merits; instead he maintained that if the United States formally attached reservations to the Treaty, other

63. *Cong. Record,* 66 Cong., 1 sess., 3316-20 (July 29, 1919).
64. *Washington Post,* July 31, 1919; *Boston Evening Transcript,* July 31, 1919.
65. *New York Tribune,* July 18, 1919; *Cong. Record,* 66 Cong., 1 sess., 3077 (July 24, 1919).

nations would follow suit and negotiations would have to be re-opened.[66] Fortunately for the irreconcilables, this argument did not persuade the mild reservationists to change their minds about the need for reservations which would become part of the official resolution of approval.

The bitter-enders made efforts of their own to prevent the mild reservationists from capitulating. Borah urged his friends around the country to write to those senators who might be susceptible to Wilson's blandishments. Beveridge hurried off letters to several senators. Warning Albert Cummins, for example, that a trap was being set, he explained that the President intended "to find out just how little change in the Covenant enough of our men will stand for to give the Democrats, in conjunction with those of our men who fall for his plan, enough votes to ratify this sell out of the country; then he will make a speech or give out an interview or something like that, stating his 'interpretation' of the Covenant; thereafter, if the Covenant is reported with 'reservations' he will say that such modifications are what he has been for all along—and he will get away with it."[67] Had Wilson performed as Beveridge anticipated, the Treaty would have been approved.

While they were trying to stiffen the mild reservationists, the bitter-enders at the same time attempted to convince the Democrats that compromise talks were useless. In the Senate on July 25 Borah asserted that reservations had no value, would not protect the United States once in the League, were only "to get votes," and should be opposed by the Democrats.[68] This statement aroused the wrath of Lodge as had nothing before. Lodge had made "strong efforts," the *New York Tribune* reported, to pledge Republican senators to vote against the Treaty if reservations failed, but he did not want to be put in that position.[69] To show his indignation he met with seven of the mild reservationists immediately after Borah's speech. These seven had already begun drafting a set of reservations. Lodge was being kept informed of their progress.[70] The majority leader also told Borah that he would not cooperate in delaying the Treaty if any further such references were made about reservations.[71] Lodge could not let the irreconcilables obtain

66. *New York Tribune*, July 18, 1919.

67. Borah to Paul Conwell, July 14, 1919, encouraging Conwell and other Missourians to write to Missouri Republican Selden Spencer, Borah Papers, Box 550; Beveridge to Albert Cummins, August 1, 1919, Beveridge Papers, Box 214.

68. *Cong. Record*, 66 Cong., 1 sess., 3142-43 (July 25, 1919).

69. *New York Tribune*, July 27, 1919.

70. Ibid., August 1, 1919.

71. Gus Karger to William Howard Taft, July 31, 1919, Taft Papers, Box 465.

control, for if they did the party would be branded as totally negative; even more ominous was the possibility of a party split, which would allow the Democrats to win the 1920 election. The irreconcilables, for their part, had to make Wilson think that they exercised a controlling influence if they were to persuade him of the futility of compromise. Lodge's actions did not prevent the bitter-enders from continuing to criticize reservations, but Borah never joined the Democrats in voting down reservations, and probably never had any intention of doing so.

As the skirmishing continued over reservations, the Treaty was being considered in the Foreign Relations Committee. Here the irreconcilables had an excellent opportunity to show Wilson how much influence they wielded. Lodge did much of the delaying, as he read the entire Treaty aloud for two full weeks, even though all the members of the Committee possessed copies.[72] The irreconcilables were responsible for calling many witnesses representing almost every group and nationality that had some complaint against the Treaty, as well as some persons who had firsthand information from the Peace Conference. The testimony, which was taken in open hearings, lasted for six weeks. Since the Treaty was in both English and French, Lodge, the self-styled "scholar in politics," was enabled to demonstrate his linguistic proficiency by comparing supposedly subtle differences in the two texts. Such analysis also consumed more time. The Committee stenographer, unaccustomed to the use of French phrases, was often unable to keep up. Thus, although the published Committee hearings ran to 1,297 pages, "much of the discussions anent the nuances of the French text" were probably never recorded, according to the *Philadelphia Public Ledger's* sardonic reporter, Robert Small.[73]

The bitter-enders were not successful in getting all the witnesses they wanted. They would have liked to have called Colonel House, Tasker Bliss, and Henry White, three of the four members of Wilson's Peace Commission, but a motion to subpoena them was defeated.[74] The fourth member of the Commission, Secretary of State Robert Lansing, did testify, and in a way most damaging to the cause of the Treaty. Upon sharp questioning by the Committee, particularly by Johnson, Lansing said that he believed the Shantung agreement was inconsistent with Wilson's Fourteen Points and that the President had known of the secret treaties between Japan and the Allies before he went to Paris. He also thought that Japan's

72. *New York Tribune*, July 29, 1919. Also see *Literary Digest* 62 (August 23, 1919): 52-55.
73. *Philadelphia Public Ledger*, August 4, 1919.
74. *Proceedings of the Committee on Foreign Relations*, 160-61.

agreement to the Treaty could have been secured without the concessions that were made to her.[75]

The star witness was Wilson himself, who, following Lodge's invitation, suggested that the Committee come to the White House for a luncheon meeting on August 19. Before the questioning began, the President presented a brief interpretation of the League. Article ten, he reiterated, was the key provision, and he thought no doubt should exist as to its meaning. The executive council could only advise on the means by which the article's obligations were to be fulfilled. Of course, he added, the United States did have an obligation " 'to respect and preserve as against external aggression the territorial integrity and existing political independence of all members of the League,' " but this was "a moral, not a legal obligation, and leaves our Congress absolutely free to put its own interpretation upon it in all cases that call for action. It is binding in conscience only, not in law." As for reservations, he would not object to them if they were in a separate statement and not made a part of the actual resolution of ratification.

Much of the Committee's interrogation was devoted to clarifying the distinction between a legal and moral obligation. If there was one central issue in the long debate over the meaning of the League, it was that regarding collective security, especially the nature of the obligation under Article ten. The questions asked of Wilson, like those that had been asked of his Senate supporters, while surely in some cases designed to embarrass and irritate, did reflect legitimate doubts. Moreover, the questions were often penetrating and the senators' comments did expose some of the confusion inherent in the concept of collective security.

Borah began by asking about withdrawal from the League. Wilson replied that the executive council had nothing to say about a nation fulfilling its international obligations, that "the only restraining influence would be the public opinion of the world." McCumber asked why not put in a reservation saying this. Wilson answered: "Only we can interpret a moral obligation. The legal obligation can be enforced by such machinery as there is to enforce it. We are therefore at liberty to interpret the sense in which we undertake a moral obligation."

Knox then spoke: "Suppose that it is perfectly obvious and accepted that there is an external aggression against some power, and suppose it is perfectly obvious and accepted that it can not be repelled except by force of arms, would we be under any legal obligation to participate?" Wilson answered: "No, sir; but we would

75. *New York Tribune*, August 7, 12, 1919.

be under an absolutely compelling moral obligation." Warren Harding, senator from Ohio and Wilson's successor as President, interrupted: "If there is nothing more than a moral obligation on the part of any member of the league, what avail articles 10 and 11?" Wilson voiced surprise that the question should be raised, for, he explained, "a moral obligation is of course superior to a legal obligation, and . . . has a greater binding force. . . . In every moral obligation there is an element of judgment. In a legal obligation there is no element of judgment." When Harding still expressed unbelief, Wilson seemed to become a trifle short with him. You are assuming, he told the senator, that the United States would "not concur in the general moral judgment of the world. In my opinion, she generally will." Had it been known, for example, that war was approaching in 1914, "her moral judgment would have concurred with that of the other Governments of the world." When McCumber asked if the President believed the United States would have gone to war had Germany not committed aggressive acts against American citizens, Wilson replied affirmatively. Brandegee totally disagreed. It was naive, he said, to believe the League would be effective if every member were at liberty to interpret its moral and legal obligations in the way suggested by the President, and particularly so if it were "known in advance that is the construction placed upon Article 10 by those who framed it." Brandegee could not envision how "the terror to wrongdoers by what is hoped to be the united, concerted action of the members of the league" would materialize with every member having the right to interpret its own obligation. To the Connecticut bitter-ender, the League as Wilson defined it was "a rope of sand and not an effective tribunal." The President had already stated his views and had no reply.

The other main points of interest in the meeting concerned Shantung and the secret treaties. Wilson admitted that the Shantung section was a disappointment to him, but he said it was the best possible agreement under the circumstances. Contrary to what Lansing had argued, Wilson maintained that Japan would have been satisfied with nothing less than the concessions she received. Both Borah and Johnson probed into the nature of the secret treaties, and in answer to repeated questions the President denied any knowledge of them prior to his arrival in Paris.[76] This statement was untrue, as the irreconcilables well knew, but they did not contradict the statement. As Borah wrote to Amos Pinchot two days later: "Are we not as a matter of patriotism bound to accept the

76. All the foregoing testimony is in *Senate Documents, No. 10,* 66 Congress, 1 session (Washington, D.C., 1919), 499-549.

President's statements as against either Mr. Balfour or the facts!"[77] Subsequently, La Follette correctly stated in the Senate that the treaties had been published in American newspapers as early as 1917. Wilson, he said, was either woefully ignorant of the facts, and thus incompetent, or he was dishonest in not admitting he knew of the treaties.[78]

Notwithstanding his lapse of memory (or prevarication) about the secret treaties, Wilson maintained his composure well during the grilling. He did not, however, succeed in clarifying the issue of Article ten to the satisfaction of the Republican senators, including McCumber and other mild reservationists.[79] Democrats told reporters they were inspired by the President's performance and had renewed enthusiasm to stand firm against any reservations that were directly incorporated into the Treaty.[80] Paradoxically, this may have been the greatest benefit that the meeting conferred upon the irreconcilables. It certainly failed to produce any new spirit of cordiality between Wilson and the irreconcilables. On the contrary; within a week of the meeting the press announced that Fernald, Gronna, and La Follette would vote no on the Treaty regardless of reservations.[81] The resentment of the two peace progressives had been growing steadily since the first published reports of the Treaty's terms. Neither had yet delivered a major speech on the Treaty, but in the July issue of *La Follette's Magazine* the Wisconsin senator had denounced Wilson in strong language.[82] The President's statements at the White House conference may have angered him sufficiently to come out for total rejection. On August 22 Thomas added his voice to the growing dissent by condemning section thirteen of the Treaty, which established the International Labor Organization. The I.L.O., Thomas contended, would reduce American labor standards to those of European and Asiatic workers.[83] A week later Knox attacked the Treaty as unjustifiably harsh on Germany.[84] Meanwhile, the Foreign Relations Committee had passed an amendment on August 23 that would restore the Shantung province to China.[85]

77. Borah to Amos Pinchot, August 21, 1919, Borah Papers, Box 550.
78. La Follette and La Follette, *La Follette,* 2:978.
79. Le Baron Colt, a mild reservationist from Rhode Island, wrote that after careful study he was convinced Wilson's position on Article ten was "inconsistent and irreconcilable." Colt to Elihu Root, September 2, 1919, Root Papers, Box 231.
80. *New York Tribune,* August 20, 1919.
81. Ibid., August 22, 1919.
82. *La Follette's Magazine* 11 (July 1919): 101-102.
83. *Cong. Record,* 66 Cong., 1 sess., 4152-58 (August 22, 1919).
84. Ibid., 4493-4501 (August 29, 1919).
85. *Proceedings of the Committee on Foreign Relations,* 164.

Wilson, too, reacted negatively to the White House Conference, and the subsequent flurry of criticism convinced him that the only purpose of many senators was to humiliate him by demanding additional changes in the Treaty after he had already labored in Paris to satisfy them. Consequently, he decided to forsake further talks in favor of more action. He would "appeal to Caesar." By going directly to the people—a move he had considered since late March—he would make the senators quail before their masters.[86]

The bitter-enders were not surprised. They had, in fact, anticipated the tour would come sooner, and they had been laying plans to meet the challenge. What did surprise them was an announcement that Wilson intended to speak out against reservations as well as amendments. They had expected him to denounce amendments but then accept reservations as a face-saving compromise. Obviously they were not displeased with his firm stand against all changes in the Treaty. As one had earlier remarked: "I am glad to see the President's spine is stiffening. I hope it becomes rigid. I would much rather break it than bend it."[87]

Thus the stage was set for a clash on the hustings. While the climax was not yet in view, in reality the irreconcilables had victory within their grasp. The bitter-enders could defeat the Treaty if they tempered their desire for an outright vote on the issues and instead followed Lodge's advice to support reservations. If reservations were adopted—and there no longer was much doubt they would be—an impasse was certain to be reached between the two political parties from which only one man, the President, could direct the escape. To do so, he would have to take the irreconcilables' course, that is, accept something less than a clear vote for or against the Treaty. Regrettably, from the point of view of the friends of the Treaty, Woodrow Wilson was being driven into a state of mind that was unconducive to intelligent leadership. The irreconcilables hoped to keep him in that state.

86. Walworth, *Wilson*, 2:354, 359.
87. *Boston Evening Transcript*, August 28, 1919; *New York Tribune*, August 16, 1919.

6 THE TREATY'S FIRST DEFEAT

THE ITINERARY that the President had mapped out for his "swing around the circle" was ambitious, too ambitious for one who was never robust and whose physical vitality had been lowered during the long months in Paris and the constant bickering with his senatorial opponents. Wilson planned to visit twenty-three states, travel some 8,000 miles, deliver about forty speeches, and make the inevitable impromptu remarks from the rear platform of his train, all in less than a month.[1] Even had he been in perfect health, the ordeal would have been exacting. In his present condition, as his doctor warned, the trip might prove fatal.

The tour was also too ambitious in another sense. Wilson's schedule called for him to invade seven states represented by irreconcilables: Missouri, Nebraska, North Dakota, Idaho, Washington, California, and Colorado. If he hoped to persuade Reed, Norris, Gronna, Borah, Poindexter, Johnson, and Thomas to accept the Treaty as it stood or with only mild reservations not a part of the formal resolution of ratification, his hope was illusory. Yet it appears he intended to try to do just that, for there was no need to convert the other senators in several of the irreconcilable states. Perhaps Wilson thought that if he could win rousing receptions in the states of his harshest critics, it would demonstrate to his less militant adversaries how popular the Treaty really was. That these latter senators, however, would be affected by the constituents of the bitter-enders was extremely dubious. On the day Wilson left Washington, Lodge wrote to Root that forty-eight Republicans and three or four, possibly five, Democrats were committed to vote for reservations. Moreover, he said, sentiment was growing for outright rejection.[2]

Given Wilson's attitude toward reservations, it was almost impossible for the tour to succeed. His mind was not closed to any changes in the Treaty; he was willing to accept interpretive reservations. Before leaving Washington on September 3 he typed out four that were acceptable to him—on Article ten, the Monroe Doctrine, withdrawal, and domestic questions. These he gave to Hitchcock, to be used if necessary, but without revealing their source.[3] These reservations, however, were meant only as interpretations, not to be a part of the formal resolution approving the Treaty. As mere interpretations, they were already unacceptable to the mild reservationists.

Most scholars have praised the quality of Wilson's speeches on the tour, especially considering that they were prepared as he traveled and that he was suffering from severe headaches and fatigue. Still, the speeches were not without occasional factual errors and certain indiscretions of language, which the irreconcilables were quick to note. Frequently the President abandoned his usually polished style for the vernacular, as when in Indianapolis he declared that his foes must either "put up or shut up," that is, offer alternatives to the League or stop criticizing. In St. Louis he spoke of the "absolute, contemptible quitters" who had endorsed his ideas during the war but had now turned against him. Such men, he said in Kansas City, deserved to be "gibbeted" by historians. They were like the Bolsheviks: always destructive.[4] A central theme running throughout the speeches was Wilson's insistence that his opponents were betraying him. They had gone into this great enterprise with fervor; now they were backing out of their commitments.

These expressions were ill-chosen. Even more unfortunate were the Chief Executive's lapses when describing the Treaty. When he explained that under Article eleven of the League, the United States could "mind other people's business,"[5] the bitter-enders easily countered by saying that if that was true, other nations surely could reciprocate by interfering in American affairs. In St. Louis the President stated that in secret treaties with Great Britain and France in 1917 Japan had been promised rights in Shantung in return for her entry into the war against Germany.[6] He was incorrect. Japan actually had entered the war in 1914, more than

1. Thomas A. Bailey, *Woodrow Wilson and the Great Betrayal* (New York, 1945), 91-102.
2. Lodge to Root, September 3, 1919, Root Papers, Box 231.
3. Bailey, *Wilson and the Great Betrayal*, 172.
4. Ray Stannard Baker and William E. Dodd, eds., *War and Peace: Presidential Messages, Addresses, and Public Papers, 1917-1924* (New York, 1927), 1:619, 624; 2:9.
5. Ibid., 1:617.
6. Ibid., 1:630.

two years before the secret treaties. Norris noticed the mistake and called attention to it in the Senate.[7] At the same time or shortly thereafter he sent Wilson a telegram pointing out the inaccuracy, which the President privately acknowledged, thanking the senator for correcting him. Norris did not immediately disclose the President's reply, for he hoped Wilson would make a public repudiation of his statement.[8] Instead, Wilson only partly corrected himself in subsequent speeches.[9] When Norris finally made the telegram public, he minced no words in discussing the incident. Wilson, he said, had denounced his critics for misstatements about the Treaty, yet he himself had made a gross error, had privately admitted it, but still had the effrontery to go on repeating it before thousands of uninformed citizens.[10]

The President's misstatements of fact and extreme characterizations of his opponents aroused strong protests, but the irreconcilables were privately quite happy with his general attitude toward reservations. Time after time he told his audiences that the Treaty must be either accepted or rejected. He wanted no halfway proposition whereby the United States attached reservations that would necessitate reopening the peace negotiations. The only popular sentiment for "serious reservations," he stated in Salt Lake City, "proceed[s] from exactly the same sources that the pro-German propaganda proceeded from."[11] He was referring in this instance not to any proposals of the irreconcilables, but to a proposed reservation to Article ten that had been drawn up by several of the mild reservationists and Lodge and submitted to him by an official of the League to Enforce Peace.[12]

Wilson gave his final address of the tour at Pueblo, Colorado, on September 25. Completely exhausted by this time, he reluctantly accepted the orders of his doctor to cancel his remaining speeches, after protesting that his enemies would accuse him "of having cold feet" for not finishing what he had begun.[13] Less than a week after

7. *Cong. Record,* 66 Cong., 1 sess., 4960 (September 6, 1919).

8. *New York Tribune,* September 21, 1919.

9. Baker and Dodd, eds., *War and Peace,* 2:24, 223, 317. Wilson sometimes stated that Japan was promised concessions for her "cooperation" in the war rather than for her "entry" into it, and sometimes he used the two terms in the same sentence. See also Rudolph Forster to Tumulty, September 7, 1919, and Tumulty to Forster, September 9, 1919, Wilson Papers, File 6, Box 318. Tumulty suggested the use of the word "cooperation."

10. *Cong. Record,* 66 Cong., 1 sess., 6811 (October 13, 1919).

11. Baker and Dodd, eds., *War and Peace,* 2:356.

12. Denna Frank Fleming, *The United States and the League of Nations, 1918-1920* (New York, 1932), 353.

13. Cary T. Grayson, *Woodrow Wilson: An Intimate Memoir* (New York, 1960), 97-100. The irreconcilables may have felt that Wilson had quit his

returning to Washington, the President suffered a severe thrombosis which paralyzed the left side of his body. Before the trip he had told friends that he was willing to die making the supreme effort for the Treaty. But death did not come now; instead he would be consigned to "a living martyrdom."[14]

Like the President, the irreconcilables were also making a bid for public opinion. They had been taking the stump frequently throughout the fight, but now they greatly stepped up their efforts. Johnson, Reed, Borah, Poindexter, and McCormick left Washington soon after the President departed, fanning out in all directions though sometimes coming together for mass meetings. Johnson, having won the recognition of his fellow bitter-enders as the most effective orator before large audiences, was given the heaviest speaking burden, a pleasant assignment for one also campaigning for the Presidency.[15] Some Republican conservatives were uneasy about the California progressive's rising star, and Henry Clay Frick and Andrew Mellon apparently balked at allowing their anti-League money to be used to underwrite his tour.[16] Financial backing came from the League to Preserve American Independence, the Friends of Irish Freedom, and various individual donors. The two anti-League organizations also arranged to rent the auditoriums and provide advance publicity, such as running full page newspaper advertisements, putting up billboards, hiring brass bands, and holding patriotic rallies.[17] In St. Louis, for example, Johnson was escorted to his hotel by a truck emblazoned with banners bearing excerpts from Washington's Farewell Address.[18]

The irreconcilables spoke mainly in the Middle and Far West, where senators seemed less certain of their course than did those

---

tour for reasons other than those officially given, but publicly they withheld comment. See E. T. Peterson to Borah, September 26, 1919, and Borah to Peterson, October 2, 1919, Borah Papers, Box 550, for comments on Wilson's tour.

14. Bailey, *Wilson and the Great Betrayal*, 135.

15. *New York Tribune*, August 31, 1919. Johnson's correspondence in September and October, especially that with his friend Charles K. McClatchy, leaves no doubt that his tour against the Treaty was also a major campaign for the Presidential nomination.

16. Archibald John Dodds, "The Public Services of Philander Chase Knox" (Ph.D. diss., University of Pittsburgh, 1950), 474.

17. Lodge to Beveridge, September 9, 22, 1919, Beveridge Papers, Box 216; League for the Preservation of American Independence to Borah, September 6, 1919, Borah Papers, Box 550; Johnson to Raymond Robins, September 9, 1919, and Frank Havenner to Alexander McCabe, September 28, 1919, Johnson Papers; Charles C. Tansill, *America and the Fight for Irish Freedom* (New York, 1957), 332, 335; *Kansas City Star*, September 13, 1919.

18. *St. Louis Globe Democrat*, September 13, 1919; *St. Louis Republic*, September 13, 1919.

in the South and New England. Johnson did most of the "trailing" of the President, timing his visits to follow the President's by four or five days. Often he took the same parade route and spoke from the same platform, and always he tried to turn the President's own words against him. Thus, when Wilson called his opponents "contemptible quitters," Johnson replied that if anyone was a quitter it was the President, who had quit fighting for his Fourteen Points at the Peace Conference. Wilson had told his Sioux Falls, South Dakota, listeners that they must choose "between the League of Nations and Germanism." Johnson answered: "The choice is between the League of Nations and Americanism." To Wilson's claim that he knew nothing of the secret treaties, Johnson did not take issue, but simply said that the President had indicted himself for incompetency and ignorance. When the President pointed out that an amendment on Shantung would not benefit the Chinese, Johnson said: "That may be so, but because you can't prevent a burglary is no reason why you should go into partnership with the burglars."[19] Other irreconcilables found similar openings. Wilson had implied that his critics were pro-German, which led Poindexter to denounce the President as "the greatest pro-German in the country," for having to be forced into the war against Germany and for having tried as late as 1918 to arrange a negotiated peace, thus thwarting the Allies' aims.[20] To Wilson's insistence that the Senate approve the Treaty immediately, Reed retorted: "I never knew a man who wanted to sell a gold brick who didn't want to get rid of it overnight."[21] When they were not replying directly to one of Wilson's statements, the bitter-enders repeated the arguments they had made in the Senate against Article ten, British voting representation, and Shantung.

The receptions accorded the irreconcilables were usually not as enthusiastic as those given Wilson, but few senators can ever out-draw the President. Johnson had capacity crowds in several cities. In Kansas City eighteen thousand were on hand and when he entered the auditorium the ovation lasted for sixteen minutes. In Chicago Borah, Johnson, and McCormick spoke from the same platform to a wildly cheering audience. Eight to ten thousand people had to be turned away for lack of room.[22] Borah drew well

19. *Chicago Tribune,* September 11, 1919; copy of Johnson's Sioux Falls speech in Johnson Papers; *Kansas City Star,* September 14, 1919; *New York Tribune,* September 21, 1919.

20. *Philadelphia Public Ledger,* September 28, 1919.

21. *New York Times,* September 12, 1919.

22. *Kansas City Star,* September 14, 1919; *New York Times,* September 14, 1919; *Chicago Tribune,* September 11, 1919.

in Nebraska and Iowa, as did Johnson on the Pacific Coast.[23] Reed was the only one who had troubles. An Ardmore, Oklahoma, audience threw eggs at him, cut the light wires, and refused to allow him to speak. The Missouri senator made the best of a bad situation. Maintaining his composure, he refrained from denouncing his hecklers, but expressed disappointment that the crowd was denied the right to have its Constitutional guarantees of free speech activated by him; and he commented that if this incident were an example of the way the American people governed themselves, they should meditate seriously before undertaking to govern the world through the League of Nations.[24]

In all, the irreconcilables visited most of the states in which Wilson spoke in addition to several he had avoided, and the total output of their speeches more than doubled the President's. How effective were they? One cannot be certain, but at the very least they helped to prevent Wilson from inspiring any mass uprising in support of the Treaty. The Treaty seemed to lose favor, at least among senators, during September and early October. Several Democrats upon whom the President had counted began to resist his leadership, so that Republicans could say, with only slight exaggeration, "A Democrat a day while the President's away."[25] Wilson was his own worst enemy. By condemning reservations as well as amendments, he further widened the breach between himself and those senators who sincerely wanted the Treaty approved but with changes. The masses of Americans, who first heard Wilson, or read his speeches, and then listened to the irreconcilables, probably concluded that the solution to the conflict lay somewhere between these extreme positions. Lodge and the reservationists probably benefited most from the appeals by Wilson and the irreconcilables, for reservations expressed the middle path toward a solution.

Most of the public's attention in September was riveted on the nationwide tours of Wilson and his foes, but the Senate remained the vital center of activity. There the debate on the Treaty continued. Even the irreconcilables out speaking returned occasionally to Washington to keep abreast of the action and lend assistance to their colleagues, who were managing quite well in their own right.

Sherman, for example, had garnered headlines with a long speech accusing the President and Mrs. Wilson of having accepted gifts

23. Claudius O. Johnson, *Borah of Idaho* (New York, 1936), 240-41; *San Francisco Examiner,* October 2, 1919.
24. *New York Times,* October 2-5, 1919.
25. *New York Tribune,* September 8, 9, 1919.

when in Europe worth half a million dollars; it was later reported that the gifts consisted of a few pieces of old lace and some items of small intrinsic value.[26] Not so farfetched was Sherman's further claim that Wilson planned his "swing around the circle" as the beginning of his campaign for a third-term Presidential nomination. Sherman's statement was ridiculed at the time as preposterous, but subsequent study has shown that Wilson was indeed interested in getting the nomination.[27]

Reed drew even more attention than Sherman when he presented as part of his Senate speech on September 22 a memorandum signed by Wilson, Lloyd George, and Clemenceau, addressed to the Canadian Prime Minister, Robert Borden, in which the three Allied leaders assured Borden that Canada and any other of England's self-governing dominions were eligible to sit in the League's Executive Council.[28] Dated May 9, 1919, the memorandum had been printed in the Montreal papers but had received little coverage in the American press. Its exposure on the Senate floor strengthened the position of those demanding a reservation or amendment to the Treaty that would give the United States voting power equal to that of the British Empire, which conceivably could hold five of the Council's nine seats (four belonged permanently to the United States, France, Italy, and Japan, and the fifth permanent seat was England's, although the Covenant said the British Empire). Reed's speech lasted for more than three and a half hours, but he held the attention of his audience, and when he had finished the applause surpassed that heretofore given to any senator during the fight. Alice Roosevelt Longworth, daughter of the ex-President, led the cheering from the galleries, while on the floor itself, William Kenyon of Iowa, sometimes classed in the press as one of the Republican mild reservationists, showed his appreciation of the speech by pounding on his desk with bound copies of the *Congressional Record*.[29] Reed might experience hostility out in the hinterland, but he was king of the Senate galleries.

La Follette excited no such demonstrations, but both in his Senate speeches and in the pages of his magazine, the Wisconsin bitter-

26. *Cong. Record,* 66 Cong., 1 sess., 5500-5501 (September 16, 1919); Fleming, *The United States and the League of Nations,* 386-87.

27. Wesley M. Bagby, *The Road to Normalcy: The Presidential Campaign and Election of 1920* (Baltimore, Md., 1962), 54-63.

28. *Cong. Record,* 66 Cong., 1 sess., 5710 (September 22, 1919); G. P. Det Glazebrook, *Canada at the Paris Peace Conference* (London, 1942), 66-67.

29. *New York Tribune,* September 23, 1919; *Washington Post,* September 23, 1919; Chandler Anderson Diary, entry of September 22, 1919, Anderson Papers, Box 4; Gus Karger to William Howard Taft, September 23, 1919, Taft Papers, Box 469.

ender attacked the Wilson administration on a wide front during the months of September and October. Unlike most other irreconcilables, La Follette was as much if not more interested in domestic affairs than in the Treaty debate. He freely criticized the President for inaccurate and misleading statements on his speaking tour and for his imperious attitude toward the Senate, but he reserved his sharpest barbs for Wilson's failure to press ahead with progressive legislation at home. Preserving economic and political freedoms, securing the masses from a few greedy corporations, protecting natural resources and civil liberties—all of these, La Follette believed, should transcend the discussion of international affairs. He saw no need for the elaborate peace machinery constructed by the League. Give the people a voice and a vote in deciding on war or peace, abolish conscription, and provide for disarmament, and more would have been done to minimize the possibility of war than any article of the League could do.[30]

Norris, who had once been the President's defender against what he considered the unfair criticisms of other irreconcilables, now made highly intemperate remarks characteristic of Sherman or Poindexter. Wilson, he said, had "spent money like a drunken sailor" as he "cavorted around Europe with representatives of monarchies."[31]

Even Charles Thomas, though he did not abuse the President personally, described the Treaty's deficiencies in an increasingly lurid vocabulary. Replying to a resolution of Colorado's Democratic State Executive Committee asking him to vote for the Treaty as it stood, Thomas called the Treaty harsh and vindictive, "freighted with a ghastly cargo of future wars, only awaiting opportunity for their bloody development."[32] If there was any one part of the Treaty that caused Thomas to be a bitter-ender, it was section thirteen, which created the International Labor Organization. In speech after speech he denounced the I.L.O. as worse than all the other articles of the Treaty combined. His chief objection to it was what he believed to be its establishment of a socialistic supergovernment that would dictate radical labor policies. Only the influence of Samuel Gompers and the A.F. of L., he stated, kept more senators from questioning this section.[33] While several other

30. *La Follette's Magazine* 11 (September 1919): 133-34; (October 1919), 149. *Cong. Record*, 66 Cong., 1 sess., 4756 (September 3, 1919), 8001-10 (November 5, 6, 1919).

31. *New York Tribune*, September 11, 1919.

32. *Cong. Record*, 66 Cong., 1 sess., 5674 (September 22, 1919).

33. Ibid., 5760-61 (September 23, 1919), 6327-30 (October 3, 1919), 6943 (October 15, 1919), 7797-7805 (October 31, 1919).

bitter-enders felt similarly about the dangers of the I.L.O., La Follette, who also wanted section thirteen eliminated from the Treaty, was concerned for precisely the opposite reason: that the organization did not go far enough in erecting safeguards for workers throughout the world.[34] In fact, the I.L.O. was neither so powerful as Thomas feared nor so impotent as La Follette imagined, and the United States finally joined the body in 1934.

An irreconcilable who had not been heard from since the filibuster closing the Sixty-fifth Congress raised his voice again in early October. Joseph France of Maryland, like Thomas, feared that the Treaty augured ill for the future. He believed its harsh terms, especially its assigning to England of mandates amounting to almost a million square miles of formerly German territory, would give the next generation of German leaders an "unparalleled opportunity" to instill "a bitter hatred, the very iron into the souls of her men which makes them fit material to be forged into a mighty weapon" of revenge.[35] As strongly as he felt about the Treaty's injustices, though, France believed it more important to discuss ways to preserve peace, notwithstanding past mistakes. He outlined at this time, and later developed in more detail, a plan for a world federation, universal in membership and subject to popular control. Such a federation would have only advisory powers, but its purposes would be varied and dynamic: to formulate international law; to reduce commercial rivalries; to devise methods for raising the living standards of "backward" countries, specifically by reclaiming waste land, wisely utilizing natural resources, and educating people to assume their rightful place in the world community; to consider the problems of population and attempt to strike a balance between congestion and sparsity; to "localize hostilities between States by cooperative policing of the high seas"; to provide international credits for Germany, Russia, Austria, China, and other countries so that they might purchase needed agricultural materials and resume production.[36]

France was especially interested in seeing the United States adopt a positive policy toward Africa and Russia. It should, at a minimum, assume primary responsibility for administering the formerly German colonies in Africa. "The time may come," he declared, "when the maintenance of an open door in Africa may

34. Belle Case La Follette and Fola La Follette, *Robert M. La Follette* (New York, 1953), 2:976.
35. *Cong. Record*, 66 Cong., 1 sess., 6597-6616 (October 9, 1919).
36. Ibid., 8140 (November 8, 1919), 8633 (November 17, 1919), 2 sess., 3161 (February 20, 1920).

be most important, when our right to make our voice heard in African affairs may result in maintaining the peace of the world, and . . . it would be a grave and perhaps a fatal mistake for us . . . to lose forever our power to exercise that right." Then, in cooperation with Great Britain, Belgium, and other powers with interests in Africa, the United States should create "a permanent, progressive, and upbuilding policy for the development of all of the people and resources" of that continent. It was no less imperative, the Maryland bitter-ender continued, to establish friendly relations with Russia. A first step would be to extend congratulations for her Revolution and to express a desire to assist in establishing institutions of her own choosing. On a more practical level, American troops should immediately be withdrawn from Russia, and negotiations should begin "concerning any explanations or reparations" that might be due to the Allied invasion. In addition, the embargo should be raised on exports, and credits should be made easily available. Only by taking such measures, France concluded, could the foundations be laid for a lasting peace.[37]

In contrast to the relatively liberal and humanitarian outlook of France were the views of Bert Fernald, the onetime factory owner from Maine, who said he approached the Treaty "entirely from a businessman's standpoint." Not surprisingly, he singled out for criticism section thirteen, which he thought contained "infinite dangers to American industry." It was almost certain, he asserted, that the I.L.O. would be dominated by European socialists anxious to destroy free enterprise and undermine the American way of life. The United States must fight any organization that would diminish its nationalism, for in nationalism lay the chief instrument for good in the world. America did not need the League to protect it. It could defeat "all the powers combined of hell and earth" on its own soil, even if its soldiers were inexperienced and drilled with broomsticks. Instead of a bulky document of several hundred pages Fernald would substitute a simple resolution declaring peace between Germany and the United States, and restoring normal relations between the two countries. Such "would be a businessman's proposition. There would be no involved meanings, no complex phrases; the language would be plain and unmistakable."[38]

Asle Gronna, the North Dakota peace progressive, who also spoke at this time, was closer in outlook to France than to Fernald. Although he offered no elaborate alternatives, he did share France's

37. Ibid.
38. Ibid., 7886-90 (November 3, 1919). See also Fernald's article: "Will Nationality Survive?" *The Forum* 60 (October 1919): 459-64.

concern for the weaker and oppressed peoples, who he thought would be denied the opportunity to change their lot under the League. Article ten was designed to maintain the status quo; it was the great powers' instrument to preserve the spoils of war. On the other hand, Gronna did not take serious issue with the Treaty's terms for Germany, and he was far more nationalistic than France.[39]

As individual irreconcilables continued to berate the Treaty, the Foreign Relations Committee finished its hearings. The last witness and one of the more sensational was called on September 12, actually two days after the Committee had reported the Treaty back to the Senate. It was an unexpected session and only six Committee members—all Republicans—were present. The witness was William Bullitt, a twenty-eight-year-old employee of the State Department and a delegate to the Peace Commission who had resigned his position in May, 1919, after becoming disillusioned with the harshness of the Treaty's terms. Reading from notes he had made after confidential conversations with Secretary of State Lansing, Bullitt quoted the Secretary as having called the League "entirely useless." The great powers had "simply gone ahead and arranged the world to suit themselves." England and France had got everything they wanted and the League was powerless to rectify the injustices. Lansing, Bullitt reported, had said that "if the American people could really understand what this treaty means, . . . it would unquestionably be defeated." The Secretary believed that Senator Knox probably would understand it (this brought uproarious laughter from the Committee members who could not contain themselves in anticipation of Wilson's reaction to such testimony), and that Lodge also would grasp its meaning, but that his political biases would render him ineffective. Lodge said he didn't mind and asked Bullitt to go on with his reading. Knox, therefore, said Bullitt, was the man Lansing thought "might instruct America." When laughter again broke out, the witness begged to be excused from further testimony along this line. Brandegee excused him with the comment, "We get the drift."[40] The effect of Bullitt's testimony, as Lodge and Brandegee privately predicted, was to enrage Wilson, destroy Lansing's position, help to bring about his resignation, and further harm the Treaty's chances.[41] George Harvey undoubtedly

39. *Cong. Record,* 66 Cong., 1 sess., 7421-30 (October 24, 1919).

40. *Senate Documents,* No. 10, 66 Cong., 1 sess. (Washington, D.C., 1919), 1276-77.

41. Chandler Anderson Diary, entry of September 21, 1919, Anderson Papers, Box 4.

expressed the irreconcilables' sentiment when he wrote in his weekly magazine that Bullitt was the answer of the Treaty's enemies to Wilson's challenge: "Put up or shut up." Now it was Wilson's turn.[42]

The Committee's report of the Treaty on September 10 was highly critical and loaded with amendments and reservations. The forty-five amendments were largely the work of the irreconcilables. Thirty-six of them had been drafted by Albert Fall, each designed to remove the United States from membership on a committee or commission established by the Treaty to expedite such matters as plebiscites and boundary settlements. Of the other amendments the most important were those dealing with Shantung and the British Empire's six votes.

Amendments had little chance of passing. Most of the mild reservationists, a few strong reservationists, and all but two or three Democrats had announced they would oppose them because their adoption would textually change the Treaty and necessitate reopening the peace negotiations. Notwithstanding their almost certain defeat, Lodge endorsed them. By doing so he partially satisfied the irreconcilables who, except for Thomas, demanded amendments to almost every objectionable feature of the Treaty; and since there was no danger of their passing, the majority leader did not risk losing the support of the mild reservationists. Moreover, once the amendments were defeated, Lodge could offer strong reservations as a compromise between amendments and the mildly worded reservations desired by some eight or ten Republicans.

The more militant and candid irreconcilables left no doubt that they would vote against the final version of the Treaty, even if amendments were adopted. When John Sharp Williams, Democrat from Mississippi, asked Borah if he would vote for amendments and then, assuming the amendments were passed, still vote against the Treaty, Borah said, "The Senator has me right."[43] Sherman frankly discussed his course of action in these words: "I will vote for any pertinent amendment that comes along. I hope every one of them will be adopted. There could not be confusion worse confounded if every amendment offered were voted into the treaty. . . . So vote them in; and then after every one of the amendments is voted into the treaty and the league, I will vote to reject it all."[44] Not all the bitter-enders took this position. Thomas voted against most of the amendments, in part because he thought they were politically in-

42. Bailey, *Wilson and the Great Betrayal*, 126.
43. *Cong. Record*, 66 Cong., 1 sess., 6083 (September 29, 1919).
44. Ibid., 7000 (October 16, 1919).

spired, but also because he saw no need for them. His opposition to the amendments, and subsequently to several of the reservations, stamps him as the least implacable of the bitter-enders. He was, however, unalterably opposed to section thirteen of the Treaty, and when the amendment to eliminate that section went down to defeat, he felt he had no choice but to reject the entire Treaty. Had the amendment passed, it is probable that he would have voted for the Treaty. Norris also might have voted for the Treaty if several amendments had been adopted, particularly the Shantung amendment. Had the Treaty been separated from the League, as the Round Robin signers had urged back in March, it is likely that the Treaty, if amendments or reservations were added, would have won the approval of most bitter-enders, perhaps all but the peace progressives and France. The latter in turn might have accepted the amended or reserved League had it not been tied to the Treaty. More than the League itself, their objection was to the League's being used to enforce the general terms of the Treaty. But all of this is mere speculation. The fact was that however divided the irreconcilables might have been on both general questions of foreign policy and specific features of the Treaty, they all found one or more parts of the Treaty so detestable as to rule out any acceptance of the bad with the good.

One after another the Committee amendments were defeated, usually by margins of twenty or more votes. Senators next introduced amendments of their own, most of them similar to the Committee's. When these, too, went down, the Senate turned to reservations. To the original four proposed by the Committee, covering Article ten, the Monroe Doctrine, withdrawal, and domestic questions—the subjects Elihu Root had mentioned in his June 2 letter to Lodge—the Committee added ten more plus a preamble requiring acceptance of the reservations by three of the four principal Allied Powers. The additional reservations dealt with issues such as the British Empire's six votes, Shantung, the I.L.O., mandates, armaments, and representation on various commissions.

The bitter-enders took little part in the debate over reservations, which they thought would be worthless once the United States joined the League. Other nations would not feel bound by them and even American policymakers would find ways to disregard them. Their only purpose was, in Johnson's words, to "enable those who have been running with the hare and hunting with the hounds . . . to justify themselves to both sides."[45] "A reservation,"

45. Johnson to Beveridge, November 14, 1919, Beveridge Papers, Box 215.

said Reed, "is the last resort of cowardice. It is the hole through which the little soul of a fellow who is not willing to stand up and front the people seeks to escape from responsibility."[46] Lodge was no longer so bothered by such talk. His grip on his party was much surer now than it had been in June and July. The mild reservationists were committed to support the Foreign Relations Committee reservations. Wilson had helped see to that. And the irreconcilables, in spite of their ranting over the ineffectiveness of reservations, which actually helped Lodge with the mild reservationists, had no choice but to support Lodge's policy.

The fourteen reservations were voted through in the first two weeks of November. Informed observers no longer discussed the possibility of unreserved ratification of the Treaty. The Republicans were solidly behind Lodge, and most Democrats were following Hitchcock's leadership. The Democratic minority leader had earlier clarified the position of his party, declaring that the Democrats would vote against the Treaty if the Committee's reservations were adopted.[47] This statement pleased the bitter-enders immensely, but they could not quite believe Hitchcock meant what he said. It was too good to be true. Borah was "hoping and praying" that the Democrats would carry through with their threat, but he had no great hope they would do so.[48]

The Democratic senators engaged in some last-minute maneuvering to split the Republicans. Hitchcock presented the four reservations Wilson had given him before his tour, and added one more of his own, relating to voting rights. They differed little in wording from the Lodge reservations. Each set would have left Article ten, the Monroe Doctrine, domestic questions, and withdrawal as matters for the United States Congress to interpret and act upon. The Wilson–Hitchcock "reservations" were not to be part of the Treaty, and were therefore unacceptable to the Republicans; but even if they had been actual reservations rather than interpretations, the Republicans almost certainly would have rejected them. Events had gone beyond the point of easy compromise. Porter McCumber, the mildest of the mild reservationists, now refused to accept a Democratic-sponsored reservation to Article ten that was identical to one he had earlier submitted.[49] McCumber explained that when he had first proposed his reservation, a chance existed for compromise between the Democrats and mild reser-

46. *Cong. Record,* 66 Cong., 1 sess., 7959 (November 5, 1919).
47. *New York Times,* October 8, 1919.
48. Borah to Alfred J. Dunn, October 9, 1919, Borah Papers, Box 552.
49. *New York Tribune,* November 11, 1919.

vationists. But the Democrats had then rejected all such reservations. To accomplish his purposes, McCumber said, he had been forced to work with the Republican strong reservationists. An agreement had been reached among the Republicans, and while he admitted that the Committee reservations were stronger than he desired, he could not now desert his colleagues. For if these reservations were defeated, more than a third of the Republican senators would vote to reject the Treaty.[50]

Having failed to separate the mild and strong reservationists, the Democrats next attempted to lure the irreconcilables away from the two groups of reservationists. Thomas Walsh, a strong supporter of the League, slyly proposed an amendment to Lodge's reservation to Article ten which would have freed the United States from participating in any proceedings of the League's executive council and have released all other League members from any obligation to the United States under Article ten. This amendment appeared suited to the bitter-enders' tastes. The United States would not dirty its hands with the League's business, and the rest of the world would not be expected to concern itself with purely American affairs. Walsh's amendment caught the bitter-enders, and apparently most Democrats, by surprise. Borah asked the clerk to read the amendment again. Upon a second reading, the Idaho senator praised it and said it should be adopted. Fall, McCormick, and Reed agreed. But when Key Pittman, the Nevada Democrat (who was ignorant of Walsh's purpose), bluntly stated that he would vote for the Walsh amendment, then against the Lodge reservation, Borah became suspicious and then indignant. He again indicated his willingness to support Walsh's amendment, but said he had "no desire to indulge in child's play." When Hitchcock was asked Walsh's purpose, he said he assumed the amendment was intended "to reveal the vice of" Lodge's reservation. Thereupon Fall withdrew his support of the amendment.[51]

As this exchange was taking place, Lodge was conferring with individual irreconcilables, pointing out to them that if the Walsh

50. *Cong. Record,* 66 Cong., 1 sess., 8419-23 (November 13, 1919). This reservation that McCumber had once proposed was resubmitted by Charles Thomas. Thomas probably had no expectation that McCumber or other Republicans would accept it, but Thomas had nothing to lose by offering it. He was going to vote against the Treaty anyway, and since it seemed certain the Treaty would be defeated, he could afford to embarrass the Republicans, whose motives he questioned. Besides, he thought Article ten should be accepted on a five-year trial basis. Since the United States had, through Wilson, helped bring into existence many of the new states of Europe, she must not abandon them until they were on their feet.

51. Ibid., 8213-18 (November 10, 1919).

amendment were adopted, the mild reservationists along with the Democrats would then defeat the Committee reservation. That in turn would force the strong reservationists either to vote against the Treaty or to accept it without any effective reservation to Article ten. Not knowing how Lodge would vote, several more irreconcilables reversed their stand on the amendment. On the following day Lodge hinted to Democratic leaders that if they succeeded in defeating his reservation, he might vote against the Treaty. Democrats were as uncertain as the irreconcilables of what Lodge would do. The Massachusetts majority leader was in the enviable position of being able to threaten both the bitter-enders and the pro-Treaty senators. When the amendment came to a vote it was soundly defeated, with only two Democrats—Walsh and Pittman—and two irreconcilables—La Follette and Norris—supporting it. Walsh's effort had served only to demonstrate Lodge's control and reveal Democratic ineptitude.[52]

Hitchcock tried his own hand at divide-and-conquer tactics, with no more success than Walsh. His ploy was to offer as an amendment to a Lodge reservation the controversial section five of Knox's resolution of June 10. This section would have pledged the United States to consult and cooperate fully with the European powers to devise means for removing any threat to the peace and stability of Europe. Section five had been stricken from the resolution by the Foreign Relations Committee due to the opposition of Borah and Johnson. Knox now said he would oppose the amendment, not because he no longer favored section five but because Hitchcock had lifted it out of context and was only playing politics. The amendment failed, although thirty-four Democrats supported it, including Kenneth McKeller, who had been section five's most severe critic when it was first proposed.[53]

By November 18 the fourteenth and final Committee reservation had been adopted. The President, still bedridden but well enough to see Hitchcock on November 7 and again on the seventeeth, set himself adamantly against the reservations. In a letter to Hitchcock on the eighteenth, which was read to the Democratic party caucus, Wilson stated that the Lodge reservations nullified the Treaty and that the Treaty with the reservations attached should be defeated. That done, he expected the introduction of "a genuine resolution of ratification," that is, either a resolution for the Treaty without any reservations or one with only the interpretative reservations. The ir-

52. *New York Times,* November 12, 1919; *New York Tribune,* November 12, 1919.

53. *Cong. Record,* 66 Cong., 1 sess., 8435-36 (November 13, 1919).

reconcilables, however, were still afraid that at the last minute Wilson would change his mind and advise his party faithful to accept the Treaty. Borah went to Senator Swanson of Virginia, one of the Democratic leaders, and asked him to do all he could to prevent Wilson from capitulating to Lodge.[54]

Preparatory to the final voting on the nineteenth, several irreconcilables made brief speeches. Borah was eloquent in summarizing his opposition: "In opposing the treaty I do nothing more than decline to renounce and tear out of my life the sacred traditions which throughout 50 years have been translated into my whole intellectual and moral being. I will not, I can not give up my belief that America must, not alone for the happiness of her own people, but for the moral guidance and greater contentment of the world, be permitted to live her own life."[55] Brandegee and Sherman relied on sarcasm to make their points. The former told the packed galleries that the League of Nations was "nothing but a mind cure," a "pipe dream" that had momentarily caught the public's fancy. It would never work. Whenever an emergency arose "it will blow up, just like an automobile tire when it is pumped too hard, and those who are riding in the vehicle will have to make other arrangements." Unwilling to ride in that vehicle, Brandegee said he would accept instead, as alternatives to the League, section five of Knox's resolution, the establishment of an international court, and some obligation to protect France against a resurgent Germany.

Sherman used fewer mixed metaphors to convey his sentiments. His address he called "a funeral oration over the defunct remains" of the Treaty without the customary kind words for the departed. Reflecting on the fight, he saw both tragedy and farce. The tragedy was embedded in the Treaty itself, a document that "bristles with the selfish philosophy of Abe Potash, sharpened with the cruel avarice of Shylock, and interwoven with the crude commercialism of David Harum. Under it, we would be done first, without a chance to do anybody or anything in return." The farce came from watching the Treaty's Democratic enthusiasts prepare to vote against it alongside the irreconcilables. It was, Sherman said with great delight, one of the few times he had found himself in agreement with Wilson.[56]

Spokesmen for the other three groups presented their cases. Hitchcock asserted that the reservations had been written by the Treaty's enemies. Frank Kellogg, speaking for the mild reserva-

54. Bailey, *Wilson and the Great Betrayal,* 183.
55. *Cong. Record,* 66 Cong., 1 sess., 8781-84 (November 19, 1919).
56. Ibid., 8774-76, 8769-71 (November 19, 1919).

tionists, angrily denied this was so. The Democrats were the villains, he said, for refusing to compromise with those Republicans who truly wanted the Treaty ratified. Amid these charges and counter-charges the irreconcilables sat contented.

The voting began shortly after 5:30 in the afternoon. The first motion was to accept the Treaty with the reservations. As the clerk called the roll, there were no surprises. Thirty-five Republicans and four Democrats voted in favor of it; the remaining Democrats joined with the irreconcilables to total fifty-five negative votes. Needing a two-thirds vote, the Treaty had not received even a simple majority. Before adjourning, two more votes were taken. One was on the same motion, the Treaty with reservations. The lines again held firm except for two Democratic senators who crossed over to support the Treaty. Certain of his hold, Lodge permitted a third vote to be taken, this time on approving the Treaty without reservations. The irreconcilables now sided with the reservationists to defeat this motion by a 38 to 53 tally.[57] Shortly thereafter, Vice President Marshall rapped his gavel and the first session of the Sixty-sixth Congress was adjourned. What the vast majority of Americans had once believed impossible had happened: the United States had rejected the Treaty of Versailles; it would not be a member of the League of Nations.

It should be noted that the votes of the irreconcilables did not constitute the margin by which the Treaty was defeated. All three resolutions lacked the necessary two-thirds majority by several more than sixteen votes. The Treaty failed because of the deadlock between the Wilsonian Democrats and the Republican reservationists. The former would not accept the reservations and the latter would accept nothing less than the reservations. As long as this deadlock persisted the irreconcilables had nothing to fear. But should the two factions reach a compromise or should one accept the other's position, the irreconcilables would be doomed. Thus it was the bitter-enders who were now interested in preserving the parliamentary status quo, and in the coming months they would do everything possible to prevent its disturbance.

In the meantime they congratulated themselves on their victory. On the night of the Treaty's defeat, a great celebration was held at the home of Alice Roosevelt Longworth.[58] As they exulted in their triumph, it still was difficult for them to realize what had been

57. Ibid., 8786, 8802-8803 (November 19, 1919).
58. Alice Roosevelt Longworth, *Crowded Hours* (New York, 1933), 292. Lodge and several of the strong reservationists were also present, and seemed no less exuberant than the bitter-enders.

accomplished. Indeed, for days afterward they expressed amazement at the way the Treaty had been beaten. "It is the most ridiculous and laughable situation I have ever encountered," Johnson wrote, referring to the unwillingness of the Democrats and the reservationist Republicans to work out a solution. Of course, Johnson added, "I can not laugh publicly, unfortunately, because I don't want to bring these two forces together, and the whole strategy of the situation now is to keep them apart."[59]

59. Johnson to John Francis Neylan, November 24, 1919, Johnson Papers.

7 NO COMPROMISE AND NO TREATY

THE TREATY OF VERSAILLES had been voted down three times, but it was not yet dead. Before the Senate passed final sentence, the Treaty's friends made one last effort—perhaps their first serious one —to bridge their differences. They ultimately failed, but not by much, and not before they had caused the irreconcilables to expend themselves to the utmost.

Pressures for a compromise came from many sources after Congress had adjourned on November 19, 1919. Republican mild reservationists informed Lodge that they could not follow his leadership unless he made some attempt to reach an understanding with the Democratic senators. Elihu Root, angry that the irreconcilables had "used" him by applauding his suggestions for reservations and then voting against the Treaty, advised Lodge to make concessions in order to dispel the impression that the bitter-enders were in control of the Republican party. Lodge himself discovered on a trip to Massachusetts in late November that his constituents favored another attempt to pass the Treaty.[1] Democratic senators were also anxious to try again. Hitchcock, unable to see the President for at least two weeks after the final vote, nevertheless wrote letters to the White House urging further talks with the mild reservationists. Oscar Underwood of Alabama, a Democratic wheelhorse and a claimant for Hitchcock's job as minority leader, wanted to go even further. If an agreement could not be reached on reservations, Underwood thought the Senate should follow Knox's advice, that is, separate the Treaty from the League, pass the former, and continue debate on the latter. Colonel House and Wilson's Cabinet ministers also advised compromise.[2] Public opinion polls of various kinds reflected the same sentiment, while newspapers solemnly editorialized that if the avowed enemies of the Treaty, representing only one-sixth of the Senate's membership, could have their way, something was fundamentally wrong with American democracy. Some writers saw the stalemate over the Treaty as being responsible for the nation's rash of labor strikes, the high cost of living, the alleged spread of Bolshevism, and other afflictions. Not until peace was officially restored by the Treaty's ratification, they maintained, could proper attention be given to domestic problems.[3]

Long before these cries for compromise had reached their peak, the irreconcilables had launched a counteroffensive of their own. Their primary target naturally was Lodge. He had to be persuaded not to retreat one inch from the ground he already held. The bitter-enders did not at first, however, threaten to bolt Lodge's leadership if he yielded; nor did they, as they earlier had, criticize his reservations as ineffective and politically inspired. Rather, they shrewdly appealed to his partisan nature by praising his reservations as "American," and by enumerating the great advantages to be gained for the Republicans if he stood firm. A similar plea was addressed to Will Hays, the party's National Chairman. It was necessary to have Hays proclaim that the Republican party would make the Treaty an issue in the 1920 election, and that it would stand for nothing weaker than the Lodge reservations. In a long letter to Lodge on November 27, Brandegee spelled out these points in detail. "Wilson is in an awful hole and so is his party. Will Hays ought to have sense enough to keep them there." Wilson, Brandegee thought, would accept reservations if they were changed only slightly in wording. The strategy was to squelch any talk of conciliation or compromise by Republicans. "Mushy patriots" such as Root and Taft must be kept out of the Senate struggle. If the Democrats and mild reservationists would not accept Lodge's reservations just as they stood, "let their blood be on their own heads." The Republicans could go to the country in 1920 "with your American reservations and the American Flag as the issue. When

1. Root to Lodge, December 1, 1919, Root Papers, Box 231; Richard W. Leopold, *Elihu Root and the Conservative Tradition* (Boston, 1954), 142.
2. Thomas A. Bailey, *Woodrow Wilson and the Great Betrayal* (New York, 1945), 209; *New York Tribune*, December 17, 1919; Arthur Walworth, *Woodrow Wilson*, 2d ed., rev. (Boston, 1965), 2:387; Josephus Daniels, *The Wilson Era: Years of War and After, 1917-1923* (Chapel Hill, N.C., 1946), 461-62; Kurt Wimer, "Senator Hitchcock and the League of Nations," *Nebraska History* 44 (September 1963): 198, n. 27.
3. See the results of the poll in which forms prepared jointly by Lodge and Hitchcock were sent to over four hundred colleges, *Cong. Record*, 66 Cong., 2 sess., 1695 (January 20, 1920). Further evidence of public sentiment came on January 13 when representatives of organizations comprising twenty million American citizens called on the White House and Senate for compromise, *Philadelphia Public Ledger*, January 14, 1920.

we get done, the Wilson internationalists will be in the position in which the Tories of the Revolution found themselves."[4]

Lodge's initial statements reassured the bitter-enders. Shortly after the Treaty's defeat on November 19, he declared that his reservations would not be changed and that he was willing to take his case to the people in the upcoming election. Ten days later he was quoted as saying that his reservations constituted "the irreducible minimum" and that "immaterial verbal changes [in the reservations] would be foolish and needless."[5] He was equally unbending in private. To Root's letter advising concessions, Lodge replied that it would be "silly" to make verbal changes in the reservations "to save the Democrats' faces. . . . That would weaken our position in regard to the Treaty and also our party position, for we have been forced into an attitude of standing as a party for American reservations." Substantive as opposed to mere verbal changes could not be made even if desirable, he said, since there were many Republicans who would join the irreconcilables if the reservations were diluted to any extent.[6]

Thus, when Congress reassembled on December 1, 1919, the irreconcilables felt reasonably confident about Lodge. They thought he had committed himself too explicitly to allow any reversal. One could not reduce an "irreducible minimum" without betraying his country, as Johnson told a New York audience. Hays, however, refused to do more than praise the Lodge reservations; he would not come out flatly against compromise.[7]

In addition to riding herd on Lodge and Hays, some of the irreconcilables strove to check the compromise sentiment which rested on the assumption that delay in peacemaking caused or aggravated domestic troubles. To meet this charge of delay, Knox once again introduced his resolution providing for separation of the League from the Treaty. In addition, he called for the Senate's "unreserved" approval of the Treaty and for the United States to become a consulting member of the League, "with the probability that as time goes on . . . we would become a full member."[8] This latter proposal went much too far for Borah and Johnson, and there were other bitter-enders who objected to swallowing the

4. Brandegee to Lodge, November 27, 1919, Lodge Papers; Brandegee to Beveridge, November 28, 1919, citing his letter to Hays, n. d., Beveridge Papers, Box 214.

5. *New York Tribune,* November 22, December 1, 1919; *New York Sun,* November 22, 1919.

6. Lodge to Root, December 3, 1919, Root Papers, Box 231.

7. Brandegee to Beveridge, December 9, 1919, Beveridge Papers, Box 214; *New York Evening Post,* January 16, 1920.

8. *Cong. Record,* 66 Cong., 2 sess., 540, 544 (December 13, 1919).

Treaty even if it resulted in the League's defeat.[9] But the resolution in this form did not survive. The Foreign Relations Committee's amendments changed it to a resolution that reserved to the United States all the rights and benefits of the Treaty without any of its obligations. Nothing was said about the League, although the President was instructed to convene an international conference which would both formulate plans for an arbitration tribunal and consider disarmament.[10] Even as amended, the resolution lacked strong support from the irreconcilables, and Lodge did not try to push it to a vote. He was especially sensitive now to the wishes of the mild reservationists, who along with many Democrats, refused to consent to anything until they had tried to work out a solution assuring the Treaty's passage with the League included.[11]

Beyond everything else, Wilson's attitude remained the crucial factor. Perhaps most Democrats hoped he would soften his views after November 19, but his inaccessibility gave them little on which to base their hopes. Some negative evidence of his thinking could be gleaned from his annual message to Congress on December 2, which he did not personally deliver. As if to show his contempt for the Senate's action, Wilson never even referred to the Treaty. The pedestrian style of the message only added to rumors that the President was mentally as well as physically incapacitated. Fall and Moses questioned whether Wilson had written it and implied that Mrs. Wilson and the President's doctors were withholding or distorting information about his condition.[12]

This uncertainty about the President's health prompted Fall and Moses to instigate a probe to determine if Wilson was able to discharge his duties. A resolution was adopted by the Foreign Relations Committee creating a subcommittee to call on the President, ostensibly to obtain his views on Mexican affairs, but actually to pass judgment on his health. Fall and Hitchcock were appointed, the latter to insure a nonpartisan report. On December 5 Mrs. Wilson ushered the so-called Smelling Committee into the President's bedroom in the White House. As she described the rather bizarre scene: "Senator Fall entered the room looking like a regular Uriah Heap [*sic*], 'washing his hands with invisible soap in imperceptible water.' He said to my husband: 'Well, Mr. President, we have all been praying for you.' 'Which way, Senator?' inquired the President, with a chuckle."[13] The interview lasted for forty-five

9. *New York Tribune,* December 15, 16, 1919.
10. *Cong. Record,* 66 Cong., 2 sess., 960-61 (December 20, 1919).
11. *New York Times,* December 19, 27, 1919.
12. Ibid., December 3, 1919.
13. David H. Stratton, "President Wilson's Smelling Committee," *Colorado*

minutes. At its conclusion Fall told reporters he was fully satisfied that Wilson was "in excellent trim" and up to the demands of his office. Before the senators departed, Wilson asked Fall to inform "Dr." Moses that he was well, which news the President thought would reassure the senator though it might also disappoint him.[14] The knowledge that Wilson was vigorous enough to crack jokes would indeed reassure the bitter-enders. As long as he was still intransigent, it was much better for them that he be strong.

Further evidence of Wilson's stubborn mood came on December 14 in a statement released by the White House, which announced that the President had "no compromise or concession of any kind in mind, but intends . . . that the Republican leaders of the Senate shall continue to bear the undivided responsibility for the fate of the Treaty." The irreconcilables were delighted with the statement. "I hope he sticks to it," Borah remarked.[15]

In spite of Wilson's rigidity the movement for a compromise continued. In mid-December a group of Democratic senators suggested the creation of an informal bipartisan committee to discuss the Treaty.[16] Lodge answered that he was "standing pat," but soon thereafter he began to yield, if only slightly.[17] On the twenty-first, six of the mild reservationists met with him and insisted that he confer with the Democratic leaders.[18] The next day Lodge talked to Oscar Underwood, Hitchcock's rival, about several proposed changes in his reservations which the mild reservationists had submitted. Lodge and Underwood may also have discussed the Knox resolution, which Underwood had said he would accept if compromise proved impossible. The mild reservationists were not appeased; Lodge appeared to be trying to split the Democrats by not working with Hitchcock. When Lodge failed to do anything further in the next few days, the mild reservationists issued an ultimatum: either he met with Hitchcock and discuss ways to resolve the deadlock or they would initiate negotiations on their own.[19] The mild reservationists were finally beginning to subject Lodge to the kind of pressure the irreconcilables had subjected him to for months.

Quarterly 1 (Autumn 1956): 164-84; Edith Bolling Wilson, *My Memoir* (Indianapolis, Ind., 1938), 298-99.

14. *New York Times,* December 6, 1919; *New York Tribune,* December 6, 1919.

15. *New York Tribune,* December 15, 1919. Wilson's statement, coming two days after Knox introduced his resolution, was a strong inducement for the bitter-enders not to accept anything less than total defeat of the Treaty.

16. *Philadelphia Public Ledger,* December 16, 1919.

17. *New York Times,* December 19, 1919.

18. Charles McNary to Taft, December 22, 1919, Taft Papers, Box 475.

19. *New York Times,* December 25, 27, 1919.

The irreconcilables reacted immediately. Johnson, who had been in California promoting his Presidential campaign, made plans to return to Washington to help "stiffen Lodge's spine."[20] Other bitter-enders declared they would fight Lodge with every available means if he compromised. They would accuse him of cowardice, treachery, and sacrificing his country's interests. If necessary they might filibuster to prevent the Senate from reconsidering the Treaty.[21] Borah announced that an organization had been formed to make certain the Treaty was an issue in the election. Calling itself the "American Vigilance Committee," it would demand that all candidates take a clear stand on the League and work to get anti-League delegates elected to the national conventions. When asked what would happen if neither party stood firmly against the League, Borah replied: "There is room in America for more than two political parties."[22]

Nevertheless, Lodge could no longer disregard the pro-Treaty forces, and in late December he agreed at least to listen to their proposals. He wrote Beveridge not to be disturbed by his action. "We could not have afforded" to refuse even to consider modifications, Lodge advised. However, he was still "strongly against" mere "changes in phraseology which would not alter the meaning of the reservations." Finally, the Massachusetts majority leader assured Beveridge by saying "the President . . . is really immovable I think."[23]

The irreconcilables were extremely disappointed and angry at Lodge's reversal. Even if he had no intention of allowing changes in his reservations, it was dangerous that he had consented to talk to the Democrats. Talking would surely lead to minor concessions in the wording of certain reservations, they thought. It was not necessary that the changes be substantive, for if the Democrats could claim credit for changing the reservations in any way, they would be able to support them without losing face. And face-saving was of no small concern to most of the senators. Furthermore, if many Democrats went over to the reservationist side, Wilson might decide that it was futile to hold out. Even should he resist the tide, enough Democrats might join the Republicans to pass the Treaty, in which case Wilson surely could not refuse to ratify its approval. Lodge believed Wilson would never capitulate, either to advise compro-

---

20. *New York Sun*, December 27, 1919; *New York Times*, December 28, 1919. Johnson to Borah, December 30, 1919, Borah Papers, Box 199.
21. *New York Times*, December 28, 1919.
22. Ibid., December 27, 1919; *New York Tribune*, December 27, 1919.
23. Lodge to Beveridge, January 3, 1920, quoted in John A. Garraty, *Henry Cabot Lodge: A Biography* (New York, 1953), 384.

mise or to sign a Treaty with reservations, but the bitter-enders could take no such chances.

At this point Wilson once again proved he was the irreconcilables' best friend. At the Democrats' annual Jackson Day dinner on January 8, 1920, a letter from the President was read to the party faithful. In it he repeated that he had no objection to the Senate's attaching interpretations to the Treaty, so long as they would not be a part of the formal ratification. The Treaty with formal reservations, however, must be rejected. "We must take it without changes which alter its meaning, or leave it, and then . . . face the unthinkable task of making another and separate treaty with Germany." He knew the people had always supported his position, and his recent nationwide tour confirmed that belief. If anyone doubted it, Wilson concluded, let the question be decided by the forthcoming election; let 1920 take "the form of a great and solemn referendum" on the Treaty.[24]

The bitter-enders were at first jubilant over the President's latest action. At the very moment when the compromise movement seemed to be catching fire, he had dashed cold water on it. Moreover, by proposing to make the Treaty an issue in 1920 he was doing exactly what they had urged for months. Once more the two sides found themselves together. The irreconcilables had many kind words for the President. He was "candid and consistent," a man of principle; and they hoped his health would permit him to be the Democratic standard bearer.[25]

The Treaty's friends divided over the message. Mild reservationists said it was incredibly foolish to think the election could settle anything. Even if the Democrats miraculously won every Senate seat that was being contested, they still would lack a two-thirds majority. Many Democrats, including Hitchcock and Underwood, supported the referendum proposal, but three-time Presidential candidate William Jennings Bryan outspokenly opposed it, and other Democrats who preferred not to be named also felt it was a mistake.[26]

Wilson's letter did not have the effect the irreconcilables at first hoped for. Instead of discouraging further talks between the Democrats and Republican reservationists, it seemed to promote them. Even Democrats who praised the letter must have understood the

24. Ray Stannard Baker and William E. Dodd, eds., *War and Peace: Presidential Messages, Addresses, and Public Papers, 1917-1924* (New York, 1927), 2:453-56.
25. *New York Times,* January 9, 10, 1920.
26. Ibid. See the *Christian Science Monitor,* January 17, 1920, for the best analysis of why the "solemn referendum" proposal was doomed to fail.

impossibility of any true referendum on the Treaty. On January 15 the senators wanting a compromise began to hold regular meetings. Lodge reluctantly agreed to participate and named Harry New, a strong reservationist, along with Irvine Lenroot and Frank Kellogg, both mild reservationists, to assist him. The Democrats selected five men: Hitchcock, Robert Owen, Thomas Walsh, Kenneth McKellar, and Furnifold Simmons. The irreconcilables were not only shut out of the negotiations; they also must have observed that Lodge had not chosen a fifth man who, on the basis of the Republican division, should have been a strong reservationist if not an irreconcilable. Thus, it appeared that he had made one more concession. The bitter-enders were further irritated when the conferees decided to keep their discussions confidential. Although the press would manage to secure much general information about what went on, Borah still complained of "secret diplomacy."[27]

On the eve of the bipartisan conferences as they were called, spirits ran high among the Treaty's friends. Newspapers on January 14 carried the story that representatives of organizations numbering twenty million Americans had called on the White House and the Senate for compromise. At the same time the results of a poll conducted in over four hundred colleges showed an unmistakable preference for the Treaty's passage.[28] One mild reservationist remarked: "It is just as sure as anything in the world that we are going to get together." Lodge had already consented, under pressure from the mild reservationists, to modifications in a few of the most controversial reservations, which the Democrats were reportedly prepared to accept in their new form. But when asked to verify this report, an experienced and sagacious Democratic senator replied: "Oh yes, there is plenty of talk of revolt against the President. There are many threats to accept the Lodge resolution [*sic*] and shift the burden of the treaty from the back of the Senate to the shoulders of the President. The difficulty is that all of it is cloakroom courage."[29]

The first meeting of the group on January 15 lasted for two hours. Lodge pronounced the results "encouraging." A short meeting on the sixteenth was followed by a five-hour session on the seventeenth.

27. Lodge curiously misstates the facts in his book *The Senate and the League of Nations* (New York, 1925), 193, saying that there were five Republicans and four Democrats, although he correctly lists by name the four Republicans and five Democrats.

28. *Philadelphia Public Ledger*, January 14, 1920; *Cong. Record*, 66 Cong., 2 sess., 1695 (January 20, 1920). The *Public Ledger* on January 14 and 15 published figures on the collegiate poll.

29. *Philadelphia Public Ledger*, January 11, 1920.

Agreement was reached on several minor points, but nothing was settled on the reservations to Article ten and the Monroe Doctrine. On the nineteenth the senators talked for several hours, trying without success to reconcile their differences over the reservation concerning the British Empire's six votes. January 21 was another unproductive day. Discussion of the Article ten reservation had caused tempers to flare on both sides, and only the tactful efforts of Simmons prevented the meeting from breaking up in acrimony.[30]

Although no significant progress had yet been made, the bitter-enders were worried. Their periodic meetings with Lodge following his afternoon talks with the Democratic senators did nothing to ease their concern. They frequently issued public statements calculated to strengthen him. In New York City on the nineteenth, Reed and Johnson spoke from the same platform, Johnson insisting that Lodge could not compromise after having previously announced that his reservations were the "irreducible minimum." In private the irreconcilables were conferring among themselves and preparing "to loose their heavy artillery" whenever compromise appeared imminent.[31]

On January 22 came the first signs that the conferees had overcome some of their differences. The Democrats drafted three different reservations to Article ten and the Republicans also made some changes in the Lodge reservation to this crucial article. After the meeting Lodge was quoted as saying: "the thing is going to work itself out." New, who was probably more opposed to the Treaty than Lodge, remarked: "at no time in the discussions has the possibility of agreement appeared so bright." The Democrats were equally confident, and Simmons was being praised as "a born compromiser." The New York Times expected that "tomorrow would probably bring an agreement on Article Ten." In response to the good news the price of cotton jumped several points on the New Orleans exchange.[32]

While the conference was still in session on January 22, reports of what was happening reached the Senate floor. Almost immediately a statement was dictated to the press by Joseph Frelinghuysen, the New Jersey strong reservationist who had been the object of such intensive pressure by the Friends of Irish Freedom. If any substantial changes were made in the reservations, Frelinghuy-

30. New York Times, January 16-22, 1920.
31. Ibid.; New York Evening Post, January 16, 1920.
32. Chicago Tribune, January 21-24, 1920; New York Times, January 21-24, 1920.

sen announced, he would join the irreconcilables forthwith, and other Republicans would follow him.[33]

Whether the conferees were actually as close to an understanding as the press indicted is highly doubtful.[34] Moreover, the actions of the bipartisan conference were only tentative and not binding on other senators. Nevertheless, some progress had been made and the prospects seemed good that it would continue. If only a reservation to Article ten could be devised that would satisfy Hitchcock as well as Lodge, agreement would probably follow on the other issues.

The irreconcilables, undoubtedly strengthened by Frelinghuysen's statement, decided that the time had come for action. On the morning of January 23, prior to the afternoon meeting of the bipartisan conference, Borah and Johnson began circulating among senators. In discussing Lodge's behavior, the word "betrayal" was frequently used. If he yielded further, they told their colleagues, they would carry their fight against him into the Republican national convention.[35]

That afternoon the bipartisan conference met as scheduled in Simmons's office. Not far away eight irreconcilables—Borah, Johnson, Knox, Sherman, McCormick, Poindexter, Brandegee, and Moses —assembled in Johnson's office. After allowing the bipartisan conference to get underway, the irreconcilables delegated Moses, who was probably Lodge's closest friend among the battalion of death, to go to Simmons's office and summon Lodge to meet with them. Lodge, after hesitating a bit, agreed to return with Moses, asking the other conferees to take a ten-minute recess. Upon entering Johnson's office and observing the situation, Lodge sent word to New that the bipartisan conference should be canceled for that day. Shortly thereafter New joined Lodge and the bitter-enders.[36]

33. *New York Times,* January 23, 1920.
34. In 1937 Oregon Senator Charles McNary, a Republican mild reservationist, told historian Thomas Bailey that he possessed a copy of a compromise reservation on Article ten to which Furnifold Simmons presumably had agreed and with changes which Lodge had inserted in writing as acceptable to him. The McNary Papers, since opened to scholars, do contain several copies of committee prints of the Lodge reservations, and one of the copies has several interlinear comments in Lodge's handwriting, including changes to the Article ten reservation. The changes were minor and did not weaken the substance of the reservation. Whether the Democrats would have accepted the Article ten reservation in this form cannot, of course, be determined. It is also impossible to say that Lodge would not have agreed to further modifications had not the irreconcilables acted when they did. See Bailey, *Wilson and the Great Betrayal,* 231; and Charles McNary Papers (Library of Congress).
35. *New York Times,* January 24, 1920.
36. Ibid.; *New York Sun,* January 24, 1920. The press reported that the

By all accounts the meeting between Lodge and the irreconcilables was one of the stormiest of the Treaty fight. The irreconcilables minced no words in voicing their displeasure. Lodge, looking pale and nervous, assured them that nothing final had been done and that he fully intended to present for their inspection any changes that were agreed to. That was not enough, they rejoined; he should have consulted them in advance. Were they not more important than the international bankers whose propaganda in behalf of compromise flooded their offices? Was he a coward who lacked the courage to stand up for his own reservations, which were the least he had said would protect the United States? Lodge, badly shaken, said he supposed he would have to submit his resignation as majority leader. " 'No, by God! ' " Borah exclaimed. " 'You won't have a chance to resign! On Monday I'll move for the election of a new majority leader and give the reasons for my action! ' " There were thirty-eight senators, Borah told him, who would reject the Treaty if the reservations were substantially weakened.[37]

When the meeting disbanded reporters rushed up to ask questions. "Are you as hopeful of compromise as you were last night?" Lodge was asked. "We shall see," was his reply. "Did you have a pleasant time?" "Oh, perfectly," he answered, and added that the bipartisan conference would meet promptly the next day. The bitter-enders' comments told a different story. According to one irreconcilable, the group of eight had almost reached a "parting of the ways" with Lodge. Sherman was the angriest and most outspoken. "If the Republican party wants to stand on the Lodge reservations I would accept its decision and support the platform," he stated. "But if there is the slightest yielding I am through with the party. . . . In plain language, I'll bolt."[38] Borah communicated these same sentiments in a letter to Lodge on the twenty-fourth. "You are either changing these reservations or you are not," Borah wrote. If, in fact, no changes were intended, Lodge was "trifling

meeting was held in Johnson's office. Knox and Borah later said it took place in Knox's office. Borah to Pittman Potter, July 19, 1929, Borah Papers, Box 301; and Knox's comments to Chandler Anderson, in Anderson's Diary, entry of December 16, 1920, Anderson Papers.

37. *New York Times*, January 24, 1920. The exchange between Borah and Lodge is taken from Bailey, *Wilson and the Great Betrayal*, 231. Borah's account of the incident, which he related to Bailey in 1937, undoubtedly conveys the tone of the meeting, but it does not ring true in detail. It seems unlikely, for example, that Lodge seriously offered to resign. His subsequent actions suggest instead that he was confident that the bitter-enders would not abandon his leadership even if he defied them.

38. *New York Times*, January 24, 1920; *Chicago Tribune*, January 24, 1920.

with a great and grave subject and doing a foolish and useless thing for insincere purpose." However, if changes were intended, Lodge was "proposing to surrender vital interests of the American people," since he had declared his reservations to be the minimum that would protect those same interests. "I must refuse even by implication to seem to go along with an organization which according to its own annuoncement is now engaged in compromising American honor and security. I propose to appeal from the organization to the voters."[39]

There was no meeting of the bipartisan conference on the twenty-fourth. Lodge told reporters that he had to consult with the irreconcilables, which he did for the next two days. Apparently he tried to persuade them that if they would support the Treaty with his reservations as modified by the suggestions of mild reservationists and Democrats, the Treaty would be approved by the Senate, but not ratified because Wilson would refuse to sign it. Since he had no intention of changing the substance of his reservations and would not allow the reservations to be detached from the formal resolution of ratification, both of which Wilson insisted must be done, the Treaty would never be signed. In that case, Lodge explained, the entire burden of defeat would fall on the President, his refusal to accept the Treaty would split the Democratic party, the Republicans would remain united, and they would have an unbeatable issue for the election.[40]

But the irreconcilables rejected Lodge's argument. It was too risky to depend on the President, especially considering the pressures that would be brought to bear upon him if the Democratic senators assisted in passing the Treaty. Wilson and the Democrats had already had their chance to accept reservations. Why give them a second chance? Furthermore, the Republicans would injure their position for 1920 by agreeing to reservations weaker than those already judged minimal for American security. The public would see through such hypocrisy.

When the bipartisan conference next met on January 26, Lodge informed the group that there was "a very strong feeling among many Senators" against changing his reservations either "in words or in substance," and that any modification of the reservations to Article ten and the Monroe Doctrine would insure the Treaty's defeat. This statement, he asserted, had not been dictated by the irreconcilables; "he had intended at the proper time to make such

---

39. Borah to Lodge, January 24, 1920, Borah Papers, Box 552.
40. Denna Frank Fleming, *The United States and the League of Nations, 1918-1920* (New York, 1932), 409.

a statement of his position; but that in view of the pressure for ratification, and of his own desire for ratification, he could not decline to enter into a conference with men of the opposite party."[41] When "the proper time" would have come Lodge did not specify. Privately he admitted that he was planning to end negotiations whenever the Democrats rejected a reservation to Article ten which denied the obligation of that article. "We [the Republican conferees] were determined that there should be no obligation of any sort left under Article Ten. They went pretty far in offering exceptions to the obligation but they kept the obligation alive. On that we broke off."[42]

Negotiations did not end immediately, but the hopeful spirit in which they began had disappeared. On January 30 Hitchcock, unable to get Lodge's agreement to a reservation to Article ten that William Howard Taft had drafted, said there was no use in prolonging the stalemate. Lodge, he charged, was still in the grip of the irreconcilables.[43]

Pro-Treaty newspapers heaped execrations on the bitter-enders for the next several days. The *New York Evening Post* characterized the group as the "Legionaries of Death," the "Soviet of Eight," and the "Republican Communists." Borah was described as the "Proletarian Commissary," and Johnson was called "Spartacide." The *Post's* Washington correspondent thought the irreconcilables' threat to bolt had been decisive in preventing a compromise. "Hiram Johnson in retrospect," he wrote, "is the man who by his coolness to Hughes elected Woodrow Wilson in 1916; in prospect he is a candidate for the Presidency in 1920. . . . Senator Lodge and his friends hear the bones of that 1916 skeleton rattling in the closet, and are afraid."[44]

The bitter-enders gladly took the credit. Believing now that the

41. *New York Times*, January 27, 1920. Lodge made the same point repeatedly in his private correspondence. See, for example, his letter to F. H. Gillett, July 26, 1920, in which he says that Article ten "brought the break and I meant the break to come on that Article if we had to break." Lodge Papers.

42. Lodge to F. H. Gillett, July 26, 1920, Lodge Papers.

43. *New York Times*, January 28-31, 1920. On January 26 Wilson wrote to Hitchcock rejecting a reservation to Article ten which Senator Simmons had approved. Wilson did not quarrel with its substance but he still insisted that reservations be separated from the treaty in the form of interpretations. This letter undoubtedly dismayed Democratic senators who sought a compromise, though they continued to meet with Lodge until January 30. See James E. Hewes, Jr., "Henry Cabot Lodge and the League of Nations," to be published in the *Proceedings* of the American Philosophical Society.

44. *New York Evening Post*, January 26, 28, 1920. The *Chicago Post*, February 7, 1920, dubbed them "the eight dictators."

crisis had passed,[45] they became more confident. Their public remarks about Lodge were almost condescending. He "was more to be pitied than scorned." Under pressure from Hays and sinister interests, he had succumbed to wills stronger than his own. At the same time, however, they said they would attack him openly again if he weakened. Lodge in turn was resentful at the way he had been treated. The irreconcilables, he as much as admitted, had forced his hand in breaking off compromise negotiations, making it appear that he was under their domination. Not only was it humiliating to him personally, but it was also detrimental to the party's image. In the coming weeks he reasserted his independence. Although there were no further meetings of the bipartisan conference, he continued to talk with the mild reservationists and Democrats, and his reservations subsequently would be modified, the irreconcilables notwithstanding.

One reason the compromise movement did not die following the irreconcilables' threats against Lodge was the disclosure of the attitude of the English government toward the American struggle over the Treaty. What did most to revive the flagging hopes for compromise was the publication of a letter in the *Times* of London on January 31 by Sir Edward Grey, the former British Foreign Secretary. Grey had been sent to the United States in late September, 1919, as a special ambassador for the purpose of bringing Wilson and the Senate into some agreement on the Treaty. His mission was especially delicate because what he had to tell the President directly challenged an argument Wilson had long used against the Lodge reservations: that they would be unacceptable to the other Treaty signatories. Grey waited patiently for three months until Wilson had recovered his health sufficiently to receive visitors. But the invitation never came. Grey then became discouraged and decided to return to England.[46] Before leaving, however, he talked to several senators, including Hitchcock, Lodge, Borah, and Brandegee, and also to George Harvey, the anti-League publisher, who urged him to issue a public statement upon his re-

45. Poindexter to Salmon Levinson, January 26, 1920, Levinson Papers, Box 69; Moses to Beveridge, January 27, 1920, Moses Papers; Borah to James Babb, January 31, 1920, Borah Papers, Box 552.

46. Why Wilson refused to see Grey is not altogether clear. It may have been that he had knowledge of Grey's purpose and simply did not want to talk about any compromise. Or Mrs. Wilson may have been the one who vetoed the meeting, perhaps because she thought her husband was not well enough. Bailey, *Wilson and the Great Betrayal*, 235-46; cf. Walworth, *Wilson*, 2:381, who says that the invitation was not extended because Grey would not dismiss one of his staff officers who had criticized the President.

turn making clear that England would accept the Lodge reservations.[47]

There was much in Grey's letter that indirectly strengthened the irreconcilables' hand. For example, he stated that opposition to the Treaty did not stem primarily from political motives. Many senators had a sincere faith in America's traditional isolationist policy which they feared the Treaty would destroy. Furthermore, Grey conceded, their fears were not unreasonable, for entry into the League would "not merely be a plunge into the unknown, but a plunge into something which the historical advice and traditions of the United States have hitherto positively disapproved." On balance, however, he believed most Americans favored the Treaty and did not want to shirk their obligations; they wanted only to define them more carefully. Grey thought the reservations were unnecessary and that some of them materially altered the Treaty, but they "would not be felt in practice." Even the reservation concerning the British Empire's six votes could be amicably negotiated. The most important consideration was that the United States join the League; without its presence the League would be ineffective.[48]

While badly undermining the Wilsonian Democrats, Grey's letter reinforced the Republican reservationists, although it was obvious that Grey hoped for a compromise between the two groups. To the extent that it caused Democrats to move toward reservations, the letter was a blow to the irreconcilables. On the other hand, Grey testified to the integrity of their motives, or at least to the motives of those he saw as sincere isolationists. He also supported what they had often said about the League being a "plunge into the unknown," and most notably, he confirmed their opinion that, once in the League, the United States would be little protected by the Lodge reservations. The letter provided the bitter-enders an excellent platform from which to attack the President. They now accused him of having surrendered rights and privileges which the British were voluntarily conceding. As Poindexter said, Great Britain was instructing the United States where its self-interests lay, as she might instruct one of her dominions. Knox, whose previous experience as Secretary of State made him appreciate the diplomatic insult that Grey's letter might constitute to Wilson, was glad to see that the British statesman "recognized the existence of an American

47. Garraty, *Lodge*, 387, n. 1; *The Autobiography of John Hays Hammond* (New York, 1935), 2:649; *New York Sun*, February 3, 1920; *New York Times*, February 2, 1920.
48. *New York Times*, February 1, 1920, has the text of the letter.

public opinion independent of the White House." Reed expressed his assent to Grey's statement that the League would be a "plunge into the unknown," but the Missouri bitter-ender argued that a nation must never plunge into the dark unless its very survival was at stake, which was not then the case. Reed also thought the letter honest in admitting that the League would fail without American participation; what Grey meant, according to Reed, was that "conditions being very rotten in Europe," the United States was invited by the Old World nations to enter "this broth of perdition for their benefit to guarantee them in the enormous gains . . . they have recently taken."[49] Thus, as usual, the irreconcilables turned to their advantage as best they could a potentially damaging incident.

Another and even better opportunity for flailing the President came in early February upon the dismissal of Secretary of State Lansing. During Wilson's period of incapacitation, Lansing had called the Cabinet together several times to discuss what he considered important matters. When this news reached the White House, Wilson, already sorely displeased with the Secretary, became incensed and peremptorily asked for his resignation, charging him with insubordination.

The reaction to the firing was almost wholly critical of the President. Newspapers that had backed Wilson throughout the fight now refused to go along with him, and Democratic senators who favored the Treaty preferred either to keep silent or to express disagreement.[50] The irreconcilables had a field day. Norris ventured to suggest that "the mental expert who has been employed at the White House has been discharged too soon." While nobody else said it quite so bluntly, Norris was not alone in this sentiment. Sherman, who had drafted a bill to establish procedures for investing the Vice President with executive authority in the event of Presidential disability, announced he would seek early consideration of his measure.[51] Ironically, however, Wilson's highly unpopular

49. Ibid., February 2-5, 1920; *Philadelphia Public Ledger,* February 2, 3, 1920. Reed believed the letter was a definite help to the bitter-enders, Reed to Salmon Levinson, February 6, 1920, Levinson Papers, Box 74. For Reed's remarks in the Senate, see *Cong. Record,* 66 Cong., 2 sess., 2352-60 (February 2, 1920).

50. Bailey, *Wilson and the Great Betrayal,* 247.

51. *New York Times,* February 15, 1920; *Chicago Tribune,* February 15, 1920. Raymond Clapper, a United Press correspondent, wrote in his diary that Washington was "astounded at President's action. . . . Many believe he is on verge of insanity. No one can understand it. Sympathy entirely with Lansing." Diary entry of February 14, 1920, Raymond Clapper Papers (Manuscript Division, Library of Congress), Box 194.

action seemed destined to harm the bitter-enders, for by weakening the faith of many Democratic senators in the President's judgment, it probably caused them to move closer to accepting the Lodge reservations.

In the midst of these events the Senate on February 9 voted to suspend one of its rules so that the Treaty, technically dead following the November 19, 1919, vote, could again be taken up for action. The irreconcilables had had no expectation of preventing the Treaty's reconsideration, but they were probably surprised that not one strong reservationist joined them in opposition. It seemed to them that Lodge was even more fearful of the pro-Treaty sentiment than they had earlier suspected, for notwithstanding Lord Grey's letter accepting his reservations, he was averse to allowing the Treaty to remain in limbo and have it carried into the election. Lodge, in fact, would have preferred to do what the irreconcilables wished, but he knew the mild reservationists would never permit it. If he wanted to keep the latter group in line and also prove his reasonableness to the general public, he would have to make concessions.[52] As debate on the Treaty resumed it was obvious that Lodge was not merely going through the motions. Not only was he willing to make verbal changes in his reservations, but he also would consent to certain substantive changes.

Directly challenged by Lodge's actions in the face of their earlier threats to bolt his leadership if he compromised any further, the irreconcilables responded by doing nothing different than before. They simply could not risk breaking away if they were to retain any influence over him and have any say in the party's future in 1920. They did, however, criticize him much more frequently and openly. They particularly liked to contrast his political expediency with what they held up to be the great statesmanship of Wilson in remaining steadfast, much as the Democrats had disparaged Lodge in contrast to the irreconcilables' principled opposition. Borah, for example, pictured Wilson as a man who had deep convictions, perseverance, "the invincible faith of Peter the Hermit." However, Borah went on, if the President were to compromise with his foes, "his place in history will descend to that of sheer expediency instead of statecraft." Brandegee took a similar tack. Implying that Lodge had broken faith with the irreconcilables by supporting the motion to reconsider the Treaty, Brandegee said that such irresolution, if not unscrupulousness, must be expected from a man who

52. See Lodge to Louis Coolidge, February 11, 1920, for an explanation of his reasons, Lodge Papers.

was weak and without principles. Wilson "at least knows his mind" and "has some conviction about it."[53]

Such language compelled Lodge to reply. It was not true, he said, that he had wavered from his original purpose. Having always wanted "to ratify the treaty with reservations that . . . would protect the United States," he had never closed his mind to changes in his reservations. While he did not believe that any more changes were necessary, he would nevertheless cooperate in securing them if they would assure the Senate's approval of the Treaty "and put the responsibility for further action . . . where it belongs." Then, addressing the irreconcilables, Lodge remarked that the reservations seemed to have "acquired a sanctity with some of my friends which they did not have . . . until the 19th of November."[54]

Failing to dissuade Lodge from accepting changes in his reservations, all that the bitter-enders could do was to continue their assaults on the Treaty itself. Much of the fire, however, had gone out of their speeches, perhaps because they were physically spent from eighteen months of constant warfare. Also dispiriting was the knowledge that their control over the parliamentary situation was diminishing just as the fight was nearing its close. In addition, the 1920 election demanded the attention of those who were up for reelection or seeking the Presidential nomination.

Some new ammunition came their way in the form of two books published at about this time: John Maynard Keynes's *The Economic Consequences of the Peace,* and E. J. Dillon's *The Inside Story of the Peace Conference.* Keynes was a young economist who had served as a member of the British delegation at the Peace Conference. Disillusioned with the Treaty's terms, he had resigned and written his account of the proceedings. Dillon was a philologist, author of several books in the field of foreign affairs, and veteran correspondent of the *London Daily Telegraph.* Keynes's book made the bestseller lists in the United States and was given greater publicity, but the irreconcilables quoted Dillon almost as frequently and Borah thought his book to be as good as or better than Keynes's.[55] Both books preached a similar message: the peacemakers had betrayed Wilson's Fourteen Points, the commercial and reparations provisions imposed on Germany were excessive, and no foundation had been laid for a lasting peace. What made the sharp-

---

53. *Cong. Record,* 66 Cong., 2 sess., 3182 (February 20, 1920), 3237-38 (February 2, 1920).
54. Ibid., 3238-39 (February 21, 1920).
55. *Philadelphia Public Ledger,* February 14, 1920; *Cong. Record,* 66 Cong., 2 sess., 3004-10 (February 17, 1920).

est impression on the public mind was Keynes's portrait of Wilson as the naive schoolmaster outmaneuvered and bamboozled by Clemenceau and Lloyd George. After reading Keynes, Borah posed a commonly asked leading question: if the great Mr. Wilson had been deceived and taken advantage of, what would be the fate of America's ordinary diplomats at the League of Nations?[56] Though neither of these books contained much that the irreconcilables had not already suggested at one time or another—Moses, for example, as early as July, 1919, had made a detailed examination of the Treaty's terms apart from the League—the books did furnish additional details, and some bitter-enders were prompted to renew their criticisms of the Treaty. Thus, Knox argued that Europe's entire economy was pyramided upon Germany, and that European solvency "either depends upon Germany being able to pay a fair indemnity, or it depends upon the United States advancing more money to keep Europe going; . . . if one or the other of those two things is not accomplished, and speedily accomplished, we have nothing but a prospect of Bolshevism and anarchy throughout the entire continent of Europe."[57] McCormick analyzed the Treaty's economic provisions and concluded that a depression in the United States ultimately would result from Germany's having to pay indemnities, which would render her unable to purchase American agricultural products.[58]

On February 21 voting began on the Lodge reservations, now somewhat revised from the original set that had been adopted the previous November. The principal change came in the preamble or resolving clause, which was modified, over the bitter-enders' protests, to allow the other Treaty signatories to accept the reservations by acquiescence instead of by a formal exchange of notes. Several reservations were reworded without substantially altering their original meaning, and in some cases the new language was even more specific than the old in freeing the United States from obligations under the Treaty. The Article ten reservation, for instance, which provoked the longest and most heated debate, with Borah again threatening to bolt the party if the reservation were changed one iota, was eventually adopted in a revised and strengthened form. When it became apparent that a majority of Democrats and Republicans would force a change in the reservation, Borah reversed his tactics and demanded a hand in its revision.

56. Ibid., 2699 (February 10, 1920).
57. Ibid., 2696 (February 10, 1920).
58. *New York Times*, February 25, 1920.

Lodge, happy to have the Idaho irreconcilable in harness, managed to persuade the mild reservationists to accept his suggestions.[59] Seven of the original fourteen reservations, including that exempting the Monroe Doctrine from League jurisdiction, were left intact. Anxious to placate the mild reservationists, Lodge tried to effect a substantive change in the reservation concerning withdrawal from the League, but the Democrats wanted the reservation modified even further and they joined the bitter-enders, who opposed any change, to thwart Lodge's efforts.[60] A fifteenth reservation, expressing the Senate's adherence to the principle of self-determination and in particular its sympathy for Irish independence, was introduced by a Democrat and passed with the aid of the irreconcilables, against Lodge's wishes. The reservation was irrelevant and also insulting to England, but the Democrats hoped that the Republican reservationists would be unable to vote for the Treaty with this reservation added to the other fourteen. The irreconcilables, Thomas excepted, were glad to cooperate with their enemies and also please their Irish constituents, knowing full well that the Democrats' strategy would prove futile.[61]

As the voting on reservations proceeded, the irreconcilables became more optimistic about the outcome. Although many northern and western Democrats indicated they would accept the Treaty with reservations, most southern Democrats remained loyal to Wilson, and there seemed to be enough of the latter group, combined with the bitter-enders, to defeat it. If, for some reason, the southerners swung over, there was always Wilson as the last and perhaps the best hope. "We have two points, therefore, upon which to hang our prayers," wrote Borah.[62] As if in answer to their prayers, Wilson in early March spoke out strongly against any weakening by the Democrats. "I hear of reservationists and mild reservationists," he declared, "but I cannot understand the difference between a nullifier and a mild nullifier." For this ringing statement the bitter-enders extended the President their customary encomiums. At the same time Wilson let it be known that if the Treaty were approved with the Lodge reservations, he would refuse to sign it.[63]

59. Ibid., March 13, 14, 1920. Lodge to Louis Coolidge, March 13, 1920, Lodge Papers.

60. Garraty, *Lodge,* 388. *New York Times,* February 22, 1920.

61. *Cong. Record,* 66 Cong., 2 sess., 4522 (March 18, 1920). Lodge objected to the self-determination clause of the reservation, not to the favoring of Ireland's independence. *New York Times,* March 19, 1920.

62. Borah to A. L. Dunn, February 24, 1920, Borah Papers, Box 552.

63. *New York Times,* March 9, 1920; *New York Tribune,* March 1, 1920.

Following this latest demonstration of Presidential firmness, the Republican reservationists implored the irreconcilables to vote for the Treaty with the reservations. The irreconcilables' votes, added to those of the many Democrats who appeared ready to accept the Treaty with reservations, would provide the necessary two-thirds majority. The Treaty could then be sent to the President. Since he was certain to veto it, the full responsibility for the Treaty's defeat would be his, the reservationists argued; ipso facto, all thoughts in the minds of the people that the Republican party was irresponsible and negative would be removed.[64] These entreaties received no serious consideration from the battalion of death. They had not come this far to hazard everything on one man, even though that man had never failed them yet. Moreover, they, like Wilson, had principles to uphold. To vote for the Treaty even if it was certain to be rejected by the President would be a gross betrayal of their convictions. Not that they were above political considerations. Indeed, they surely realized that to switch their votes at the last minute, after having repeatedly denounced the Treaty, might be politically harmful to them, however much it improved the party's image. Furthermore, there were some among them who counted the Treaty's defeat and their conspicuous part in that defeat as major assets in their bid for the Presidential nomination. Were the Treaty to be adopted or even were they to vote for it, they would lose key issues that distinguished them from other potential candidates. To be sure, these irreconcilables had taken their unpopular stand originally when to do so appeared politically suicidal for anyone with Presidential ambitions; and the irreconcilable position was still not favored by most Americans. But it seemed less unpopular than it had been,[65] and those bitter-enders who had remained steadfast from the beginning did not intend to change their course at this time when there was a chance of riding the wave of the future.

64. *New York Tribune*, March 1, 1920.
65. Whether the irreconcilable position had become less unpopular is questionable. The two most thorough samplings of public opinion, the first published in the spring of 1919, the second in January, 1920, do not show any significant change in the percentage of people favoring outright rejection. The earlier poll was strictly on the League, the later one on the Treaty as a whole. In both polls, the irreconcilable position received about 12 percent of the total. See *The Literary Digest* 61 (April 5, 1919): 13-16, 120-28; and *Cong. Record*, 66 Cong., 2 sess., 1695 (January 20, 1920). In the collegiate poll, published in the *Record*, I have counted as irreconcilables those favoring the Knox plan for separation as well as those supporting outright rejection. If one eliminates the votes of the former the irreconcilable support actually declined to less than 10 percent.

The Democrats also appealed to the irreconcilables in much the same way as they had the previous November. Thomas Walsh tried to get Borah to state that the issue of the League should be made clear-cut in the forthcoming election, even if it required forming a third party. Borah at first agreed that "that might happen," but then he remarked that public opinion exerted a great force on Presidential candidates and he was "perfectly willing" to take his "chances in the next campaign regardless of what may be said at these conventions." Later, Walsh attempted to split the Republicans by presenting Knox's "New American Doctrine" as an amendment to Lodge's Article ten reservation. Knox had first proposed his "doctrine" in December, 1918, and later incorporated it as the controversial section five of his resolution of June, 1919, calling for separation of the League from the rest of the Treaty. This "doctrine" would have pledged the United States to regard a threat to the European status quo as a potential threat to its own security and to consult with the European powers for the purpose of removing such a threat. The Pennsylvanian objected to Walsh's amendment. When he had first made his proposal in December, 1918, Knox explained, he had offered it as an alternative to the League in conjunction with an immediate declaration of peace. It was not intended to be a part of the League but to stand on its own merits. Other irreconcilables who had once supported Knox's proposal took their cue from the Pennsylvania bitter-ender, while Borah and Johnson along with the peace progressives—who had never liked the "doctrine"—joined their comrades to defeat the amendment.[66]

As the time approached for the final vote, tempers grew short on all sides. Senator Simmons bitterly charged Lodge with having killed any chance for compromise by his repeated submission to the irreconcilables. Lodge's followers and the battalion of death, Simmons complained, had made "an ironbound agreement of some sort, which they solemnly entered into at the very inception of this controversy," and this pact prevented either group from voting "their own convictions unless they got the consent of Senators who disagreed with them."

Lodge heatedly denied the charge. "There has been no conspiracy," he replied. "If there had been, it would have saved one member on this side a great deal of trouble. We have been

66. *Cong. Record,* 66 Cong., 2 sess., 3234 (February 21, 1920), 4330-31 (March 15, 1920).

endeavoring to act together. The Senators who are 'irreconcilables,' numbering 15 or 16, are among the ablest Senators of this body, men of deep convictions on this subject, and they have exercised the influence which their numbers, their ability, and their character entitled them to wield in our councils—that and no more."[67] Let the Democrats examine their own behavior, Lodge countered. "We cannot conduct matters on this side of the aisle as they are conducted on that side. We have no one to write us letters."

Simmons retorted that no letter writing was necessary on the Republican side: "the Senator from Idaho has only to tell you what to do."

Borah then got into the fray. There was no reason for Simmons to attack the irreconcilables, Borah said, since they were "standing shoulder to shoulder with the President to assist him in every way [we] can to defeat the Treaty." "There is just as much of an understanding between the President of the United States and myself as there is between the Senator from Massachusetts and myself."[68]

In this exchange was summarized much of the fight: the Democrats charging partisan conspiracy by the Republicans; the rebuttal by Lodge, denying any "iron-bound agreement" with the irreconcilables, but admitting his efforts to get Republicans united and adding a countercharge against Democratic subserviency to Wilson; finally, the battalion of death savoring the irony of its alliance with Wilson, each committed to principles, each less concerned with politics than ideology, but with only the irreconcilables able to realize their goal.

The final vote came on March 19, 1920, three months to the day after the Treaty's first defeat. Although no one held much hope for its passage, a rumor swept the floor that only four more votes were needed.[69] Democratic Senators Thomas Walsh and Joseph Ransdell delivered impassioned speeches urging their fellow Democrats to accept the Treaty with the Lodge reservations rather than have no Treaty at all. Once the United States was in the League, they contended, reminding their colleagues of Lord Grey's letter, the reservations would be of little practical significance. Another effort was made by the Republicans to persuade the irreconcilables to line up with them instead of with the Wilsonians. It was all to no avail. Of the eighty-four senators present and voting, forty-nine registered yea votes, including twenty-one Democrats who deserted

67. Ibid., 4634-35 (March 18, 1920).
68. Ibid.
69. *Chicago Tribune*, March 20, 1920.

the President. That left thirty-five nay votes cast by the loyal Democrats and the battalion of death. The Treaty had received a majority of fourteen votes, but fell seven short of the necessary two-thirds.

Some frantic parliamentary maneuvering followed as the Treaty's friends tried to pass a motion to reconsider the vote. Lodge stated that he would not block another vote, but the irreconcilables vehemently objected; and when the president of the Senate pro tempore declared the motion to reconsider out of order, no one appealed his ruling. All that got through was a resolution instructing the Secretary of the Senate to return the official copy of the Treaty to the President. It was duly delivered on the morning of the twentieth, Joseph Tumulty giving the Secretary a receipt for the copy. As the Secretary was returning to the Senate, one of the first persons he met was Borah. When shown the receipt, the senator's face beamed.[70] And well it might, for never again would the Treaty of Versailles be formally considered by the United States Senate.

The bitter-enders tried on the night of the nineteenth to repeat their victory party of the previous November. It should have been an even more joyous celebration than the first, since on this latter occasion the irreconcilables' votes provided the margin of the Treaty's defeat. But the party lacked spontaneity and enthusiasm;[71] the fight had left them exhausted, and their immediate thoughts were on the approaching election. Some of the senators had already left the capitol to begin their political campaigns. Borah, who would not stand reelection until 1924, decided to remain in Washington "until convinced that the Treaty was so dead that rigor mortis was apparent."[72] His concern was groundless. The real battle had been won. What followed was decidedly an anticlimax.

The press had often speculated and Republican leaders had feared that the election of 1920 would cause calamitous divisions over the Treaty. Certain bitter-enders, most notably Borah, had stated frequently that if their party did not go on record unequivocally against the Treaty in 1920 they would refuse to support it and might even form a third party. Nothing of the sort happened. Instead of widening, the split within the party narrowed. There were several reasons for this.

In the first place, the Republican irreconcilables—whose objections to the Treaty were often diametrically divergent, though

70. *Ibid.*, March 21, 1920.
71. Alice Roosevelt Longworth, *Crowded Hours* (New York, 1933), 303.
72. *Philadelphia Public Ledger*, March 21, 1920.

blurred by their tactical cooperation—now had to take a positive stance. They could no longer respond merely to Wilson's proposals. Rather, they had to help choose a Presidential candidate and write a platform that would enunciate a program the country could follow in domestic as well as foreign affairs. In this new situation, the group, always a coalition, could not remain united. They were further divided by a rivalry among themselves for the Presidential nomination. No fewer than six of them—Johnson, Poindexter, France, La Follette, Knox, and Borah—received consideration for the nomination.[73] In addition, some irreconcilables supported nonirreconcilable candidates for the nomination, while nonirreconcilable politicians supported bitter-enders. For example, two mild reservationist senators—Charles McNary and William Kenyon—favored Hiram Johnson.[74] When the convention opened, therefore, the irreconcilables were more concerned with their own candidacies or those of their favorites than with organizing any rebellion if things did not develop to suit them.

The second reason for Republican harmony was the nomination of Warren G. Harding, a conservative senator from Ohio whose position on the Treaty had been that of a strong reservationist but who might have been an irreconcilable had he not feared the political consequences.[75] Harding's nomination came after the leading candidates canceled each other out. Never one of the front runners for the nomination, Harding was still not quite the dark horse as he is sometimes pictured. As early as December, 1919, his Republican colleagues in Congress judged him as "a man who would appoint a strong Cabinet, take the advice of the leaders in the House and Senate and make an altogether satisfactory—from the political standpoint at least—President."[76] It was this belief in Harding's tractability which in part accounted for his nomination

---

73. Poindexter, who entered several primaries, was the most active of the irreconcilables except for Johnson. France announced his candidacy in May, but did almost no campaigning. La Follette was in the hospital when the Wisconsin delegation put his name in nomination. Knox might have been a strong contender but for his age and his disinclination to run. Borah was the choice of a few delegates who could not support Johnson for personal reasons. See *Baltimore American*, May 13, 1920; *New York Times*, May 19, 1920; and La Follette and La Follette, *La Follette*, 2:996.

74. *New York Times*, April 21, 1920.

75. See Harding to Cornelius Cole, August 12, 1919, in which he admitted he opposed the Treaty as strongly as did the irreconcilables; cf. Harding to Frederick Gillett, August 4, 1920, Harding Papers, Boxes 758, 543.

76. *New York Tribune*, December 11, 1919. Surely the most prophetic comment on the election was that by C. H. Parker of Columbus, Ohio, who on December 1, 1918, predicted Harding would be the Republican candidate and James Cox the Democratic. *Washington Post*, December 1, 1918.

and which also helps explain why the irreconcilables did not bolt. Harding's previous stand on the Treaty—at least in public—was not what they would have ordered, but, given time and assisted by friendly advice, or if need be by criticism, he could be won over, they felt, to their way of thinking.

The platform was a third cause of Republican unity in 1920. The irreconcilables were determined to prevent the adoption of a plank which endorsed the League in any form. When it appeared that the pro-League delegates would succeed in inserting a statement favoring the League with the Lodge reservations, several bitter-enders threatened to take their fight from the confines of the resolutions committee to the open floor.[77] Their threat undoubtedly had some influence in blocking such a statement, but more effective were the actions of Lodge. In his keynote address to the convention, Lodge stressed the contribution of all Republican senators in opposing the League. No one faction was singled out for praise at the expense of another. Lodge also had a large say in the writing of the platform. The plank finally adopted closely followed a draft that Elihu Root had written some time before, possibly at Lodge's urging.[78] It did not support any one viewpoint. Every Republican senator, it read, had performed his "duty faithfully." The irreconcilables claimed, however, and rightly so, that the plank was more in line with their expressed position than with that of the other groups. There was no endorsement of the League and no indication that the Republicans would, if victorious, move to resurrect the Treaty. There was only criticism that the Covenant would produce "injustice, hostility and controversy among nations," that it compromised American sovereignty, and that it "repudiated, to a degree wholly unnecessary and unjustifiable, the time-honored policies in favor of peace declared by Washington, Jefferson, and Monroe." In place of the League the Republican party stood for the development of arbitration and international law. It favored "an international association . . . based upon international justice . . . which shall maintain the rule of public right by the development of law and which shall secure instant and general international conference whenever peace shall be threatened by political action, so that the nations pledged to do and insist upon what is just and fair may exercise their influence and power for the prevention of

77. *New York Times*, June 10, 1920.
78. Ibid., June 10-12, 1920; Garraty, *Lodge*, 392-93; Jessup, *Root*, 2:410. McCormick believed that Lodge had been primarily responsible for getting the anti-League plank adopted. McCormick to Arthur W. Page, August 12, 1921, McCormick Papers.

war."[79] Borah believed that the plank, when carefully analyzed, condemned "any political league," and was broad enough to allow him to construe it as in accordance with his beliefs.[80]

The Democratic convention, which began in late June, paralleled the Republican convention in some ways. A similar contest was waged over the platform. Wilson's followers advocated "the immediate ratification of the treaty without reservations which would impair its essential integrity," whereas those who disliked the President's inflexibility would "not oppose the acceptance of any reservations making clearer or more specific the obligations of the United States to the League associates."[81] A compromise was effected which included both statements.

No strong candidate for the nomination had emerged in the preconvention skirmishing. Wilson, who harbored visions of a third term, was finally persuaded by his doctor and friends to withdraw himself from all consideration.[82] Since he had not indicated whom he preferred to succeed him, the nomination provoked a long struggle. After forty-four ballots the convention selected James Cox, Ohio's competent but colorless Governor. Cox did not share Wilson's enthusiasm for the League nor did he wish to make it the major issue, but after visiting the White House on July 18 he came away talking much like the President.[83] During the campaign Cox maintained that the issue for the voters to decide was whether they wished to go into the League under the Democrats or stay out under the Republicans. The bitter-enders agreed that that was the issue and, characteristically, they praised Cox for stating it so cogently. The Democratic candidate, in turn, commended the battalion of death for their candor in asserting that if Harding were elected he would dump the League.

Neither of the two Democratic irreconcilables played a part in the convention. Thomas was up for reelection but had announced earlier that he would retire rather than run on a platform that promised to be contradictory to his stand on the Treaty. In October he changed his mind and came out on an independent ticket, only to be badly defeated. Reed, on the other hand, not up for reelection, went to San Francisco intending to make his voice heard, but the convention refused to seat him as a delegate even

79. Kirk H. Porter and Donald Bruce Johnson, *National Party Platforms, 1840-1956* (Urbana, Ill., 1956), 231.
80. Borah to Johnson, June 24, 1920, Borah Papers, Box 199.
81. Porter and Johnson, *National Party Platforms*, 214.
82. Wesley M. Bagby, *The Road to Normalcy: The Presidential Campaign and Election of 1920* (Baltimore, Md., 1962), 117-20.
83. Bailey, *Wilson and the Great Betrayal*, 321.

though his district in Missouri had elected him and, by custom, a senator was entitled to one of the party's at-large delegateships.[84] If he had wanted an occasion for bolting, this was surely it. He did not bolt. He denounced the plank on the League as a "surrender of the control of the American Government," and a "treacherous and treasonable undertaking."[85] During the campaign he freely attacked the Treaty and the League. He even went into Wisconsin to assist a La Follette-backed candidate for the Senate who was running as an independent on an anti-League platform.[86] But on election day Reed voted a straight party ticket.[87]

For the Republican bitter-enders the campaign presented more of a tactical challenge. Thomas and Reed had no hope of influencing Cox, but Borah, Johnson, and company not unreasonably expected, given the Republican platform, to pull Harding into their orbit. Actually, he was already there, as far as most irreconcilables were concerned. Like Lodge, he had shifted his ground from the Senate debates. He was no longer talking about ratification of the Treaty with reservations or amendments, only about an "association of nations," the details of which were never revealed. Such talk worried few of the bitter-enders, since most of them had themselves proposed some kind of agreement among nations that committed the United States as much if not more than the platform or Harding's plan.

The only Republican irreconcilables who expressed much dissatisfaction with Harding's stand on the League were Borah and Johnson.[88] This was hardly surprising, for these two had always been reluctant to suggest alternatives and had rejected many of the proposals of their fellow bitter-enders. Johnson was troubled by the fact that, when he told audiences that the platform and Harding's interpretation of it conformed to his views and thus justified his opposition to the Treaty in the Senate, he was obliged, under the pressure of questions, to try to reconcile his statement with those made by Taft, Hoover, and the mild reservationist senators, which also praised the platform and Harding's speeches. Johnson answered

84. Franklin Dean Mitchell, "Embattled Democracy: Missouri Democratic Politics, 1918-1932" (Ph.D. diss., University of Missouri, 1964), 33.

85. *New York Times,* July 2, 1920.

86. La Follette and La Follette, *La Follette,* 2:1016.

87. *New York Times,* November 3, 1920.

88. La Follette was disgusted both with Harding's nomination and the Republican platform, and said so, but he was repelled more by the party's domestic conservatism than by its stand on the League. He considered running for President on a Farmer-Labor ticket. See La Follette and La Follette, *La Follette,* 2:996-1019; *La Follette's Magazine* 12 (July 1920): 98.

by saying he had no objection to Taft and the others trying to save face, but as he complained to Borah, he was "answered in like fashion."[89]

Many Republican friends of the League were also displeased. Having failed to get a plank endorsing the League, they hoped that Harding would at least side with them rather than with the irreconcilables. It appeared in the early weeks of the campaign that he was leaning toward the League's foes. The mild reservationists' demands that he be more affirmative were somewhat met in late August when he spoke earnestly of his "association of nations," suggesting that it might combine the best features of the League and the Hague Tribunal. Even the Democratic *New York Times* took heart, and Taft, receiving private assurances from Harding, entered the campaign.[90] Johnson also liked the speech, feeling that Harding had "scrapped" the League, but Johnson, too, was responding partly on the basis of information supplied him by private sources close to Harding who said that Harding's purposes corresponded to his own.[91] Borah began to have doubts. An association of nations, he said, or a combination, a coalition, or an alliance, was as repugnant to him as the League. In any such organization the United States would lose its "independent action and have to abide by the rules of the game." Asked why, if he felt this way, he continued to support Harding, Borah said there was no choice. But in September the Idaho irreconcilable withdrew much of his support. Asking the National Committee to cancel his scheduled speaking appearances, he explained that he wanted to spend the rest of his time campaigning for the reelection of Brandegee and Moses.[92] If Harding planned to implement his ideas, Borah thought it was essential that these two bitter-enders be back in the Senate.

Harding, apparently concerned by Borah's action and anxious to have Johnson, by far the most popular Republican speaker, take a more active role in the campaign, moved to placate them.[93] On October 7 in what was his strongest denunciation yet of the League, he said that he did not seek clarification of the obligations of the Covenant but outright rejection. The issue between Cox and himself was clear: "he favors going into the Paris League and I favor

89. Johnson to Borah, August 26, 1920, Borah Papers, Box 199.
90. Bagby, *The Road to Normalcy*, 136-37.
91. A. D. Lasker to Johnson, August 20, 1920; Johnson to Lasker, August 31, 1920, Johnson Papers.
92. *New York Times*, October 2, 5, 1920.
93. Harding to Johnson, August 16, 1920, Harding Papers.

staying out." At the same time, Harding renewed his pledge to work for an association of nations. On the following day he praised the Democratic irreconcilable Reed as a man whom the country owed a debt it could never measure.[94]

Thus, as the campaign drew to a close the irreconcilables could not be certain of Harding's long-range commitment, but they were confident that, if elected, he would not ask the Senate to approve the Treaty of Versailles and bring the United States into the League. However much Harding beclouded the nature of America's future policy, the bitter-enders thought that the immediate choice offered to the voters had been defined: it was not a question of *a* league but of *the* League. Wilson had said that that was the issue, Cox had repeated it, Harding had finally spelled it out, the two platforms had confirmed it, and the bitter-enders had made the point again and again.

The returns in November, 1920, gave Harding one of the most overwhelming victories in the nation's history. He won 61 percent of the vote to only 34.6 percent for Cox. (Brandegee and Moses, though trailing Harding, easily won reelection.[95]) The battalion of death quite naturally brushed aside the many other factors that contributed to the result and described the election as the "great and solemn referendum" Wilson had wanted. The verdict, said Borah, signified "an absolute rejection of all political alliances or leagues with foreign powers" and "the re-dedication of this nation to the foreign policy of George Washington and James Monroe, undiluted and unemasculated."[96]

Borah's interpretation was extreme. The people had not registered such a clear-cut mandate. Borah did not speak for Harding nor even for the other irreconcilables, who had never shared his rigid devotion to the doctrines of the Founding Fathers. But the Lion of Idaho was at one with his fellow bitter-enders, Reed and Thomas included, in their feelings of vindication.

The election was to have more significance for the course of American foreign policy in the 1920s and 1930s than for the result of the League fight. The popular interpretation that came to be placed on the massive Republican sweep was that the people had decisively repudiated the League of Nations.[97] Responsibility for

94. *New York Times,* October 8, 9, 1920.
95. Gronna was defeated in the Republican primary, but the League was not the main issue. See Paul Willard Morrison, "The Position of the Senators from North Dakota on Isolation, 1889-1920" (Ph.D. diss., University of Colorado, 1954), 349.
96. *New York Times,* November 4, 1920.
97. Selig Adler, *The Isolationist Impulse* (New York, 1957), 110.

this misreading of history cannot be placed on any one individual or group, but Wilson and the irreconcilables, working in tandem as they had through much of the fight, had as much to do with it as anyone.

Harding did not disappoint the bitter-enders. Two days after the election he stated with considerable firmness that the League was "now deceased." On July 2, 1921, Congress passed a joint resolution declaring the war officially closed, reserving to the United States all of the rights to which it would have been entitled under the Treaty of Versailles but with none of its obligations. The new President happily signed the resolution. The triumph of the irreconcilables had been sealed.

CONCLUSION

SHORTLY AFTER the Senate had voted down the Treaty for the final time in March, 1920, the journalist William Hard wrote in the *New Republic*: "O historian, you will know their names. In whatever age you may live there will be somewhere in your books a little list, and you will ponder every name in it and will wonder what sort of man was behind the name, and I shall silently smile at the joke of the assemblage of those names by fate in any one list for any one vote on any one conviction, but you will sweatingly spade your way through the Congressional Record and will find a band of brothers in glory and will say: 'These were the Irreconcilables.'" Hard went on to make some questionable judgments about the group, but he had properly emphasized its essential diversity. Geographically, the irreconcilables were dispersed: five from the East, five from the West, and six from the Middle West. Politically, it is true, fourteen of the sixteen were Republicans, but one could not have selected fourteen Republicans who differed so widely on both domestic and foreign policy. Conservatives and liberals, pacifists and militarists, imperialists and anti-imperialists, isolationists and internationalists, the battalion of death was more a cross section of the nation than an ideologically homogeneous minority. Objecting to the Treaty for many and often conflicting reasons, offering divergent alternatives, using a variety of means to accomplish their purposes, the bitter-enders revealed themselves as not simply a united little band of naysayers whose horizons were enclosed by the doctrines espoused by the Founding Fathers.

The irreconcilables were united, but only in their conviction that the Treaty must be defeated, not in the nature of their conviction nor in the degree to which they opposed it. A few might even have accepted it had strong amendments rather than reservations been adopted. There were patterns, to be sure, in their opposition. The peace progressives—La Follette, Norris, and Gronna—joined by France, protested most loudly against the Treaty's violations of the Fourteen Points. They saw little or no chance for the Treaty's severe terms to be modified. The League, they thought, would be controlled by the great powers who wanted to freeze the status quo to preserve the spoils of war. This viewpoint was shared to some extent by Borah, Johnson, and Reed, particularly by Johnson, but these three devoted more attention to the League *per se* than to the other parts of the Treaty. The remaining bitter-enders voiced even fewer criticisms of the Treaty's non-League provisions, but they constantly attacked the League. While their criticisms were many, they usually focused upon the League's allegedly utopian character. They were more concerned about the small countries exercising disproportionate power within the League than about great power hegemony.

The bitter-enders were also naysayers, some from long habit and on almost every issue. But on this occasion the parliamentary situation encouraged negativism. The irreconcilables' immediate and strategically necessary task, as they saw it, was to assume the initiative and attack. To suggest substitutes prematurely might be interpreted, as it sometimes was, as a weakening of their resistance. That in turn could affect the actions of Lodge, who saw his role, or one part of it, as that of an honest broker between the irreconcilables and the mild reservationists. If the irreconcilables seemed to be wavering, he might be forced closer to the mild reservationists in order to maintain his position in the center. If that should lead to an overall weakening of the reservations, enough Democrats might be willing to support the Treaty with reservations despite President Wilson's advice to the contrary. The President himself might even agree to accept reservations in this form. Additionally, there was the possibility that alternatives by the irreconcilables would split the group even further and thereby lessen their cooperation on tactical moves.

Nevertheless, the irreconcilables did offer alternatives. Consistency and well-worked-out details were often lacking, partly because of the parliamentary situation but also because of their own intellectual limitations and confusion. The divisions which distinguished their objections to the Treaty were also apparent in their alternatives.

La Follette, Norris, Gronna, and France were philosophical optimists who believed strongly in the effectiveness of nonmilitary force as a means to almost unlimited ends. They were sympathetic

to a league of all nations that was committed to the speedy reduction of armaments, to the abolition of the right of conquest, to
the end of secret diplomacy, and to the creation of an international
court of arbitration. France in particular wanted a league that
would address itself to the problems posed by the population ex-
plosion and attempt to raise the living standards of less developed
countries by economic and technical assistance. These four irreconcilables were less fearful than their colleagues about the threat
such a league would pose to American sovereignty. Self-determination, disarmament, and progressive change were the important
objectives, and a truly democratic and universal league dedicated
to those objectives could perform a noble service in the cause of
peace.

In contrast to this outlook were those irreconcilables who, following Knox's lead, rejected as naively idealistic any association of
heterogeneous nations that placed much reliance on moral force.
These irreconcilables, who tended to be conservative, nationalistic,
and imperialistic, regarded themselves as hard-bitten realists. They
believed that the only solution to evil in the world, and a limited
solution at best, was military power and friendly ties with nations
whose good will counted for something. Many of them, for example,
favored the Treaty of Guarantee which pledged the United States
and England to come to France's aid if she was again attacked by
Germany.

In another category stood Borah, Johnson, and Reed. Like the
realists, they were intensely nationalistic. They did not, however,
accept the argument for an entente or coalition with America's recent Allies. Instead they adhered to a simple creed: America must
be the sole commander of its destiny, proud of its institutions, free
to act as it chose, uncommitted and unentangled, in a world that
respected little else than naked power. More than any of the other
bitter-enders, Borah, Johnson, and Reed invoked not only the
spirit but the literal and permanent worth of the advice given
by the Founding Fathers. Because of their frequent and sensational
Senate speeches against the Treaty, their many stumping tours
around the country, their considerable ability to obstruct or de-
molish what they opposed, their colorful personalities, and their
long careers, Borah, Johnson, and Reed are the best known irreconcilables. But they were not, contrary to the generally accepted view, representative of the group.

What can be said about the strategy and tactics of the bitter-
enders? Clearly they demonstrated a keen understanding of the
possibilities of minority rule. They dominated the debates in the

early stages of the fight and never stopped carrying the attack to the Treaty's defenders. Measured by the number of their speeches both in the Senate and out in the country, the irreconcilables actually worked harder in proportion to the size of their group than any of the other groups. Moreover, their significant part in devising the Round Robin, which helped force Wilson to make changes in the original Covenant, their filibuster, which made certain the calling of a special session thus insuring them an available forum to gain publicity, their formation of an anti-League propaganda organization, and their delaying tactics all contributed to the Treaty's defeat. Above all, they grasped the nature of the parliamentary struggle that confronted them. Finding it impossible to obtain a Senate majority for outright rejection of the Treaty, they worked with Lodge to adopt reservations which the President found unacceptable. Distasteful as it was to some irreconcilables, this indirect method was the only way to defeat the Treaty. In the last analysis the irreconcilables were less rigid than Wilson in the face of political reality. Their success depended, of course, on Lodge's ability to hold his party together. But their own ability to exploit Lodge's obsessive concern for party unity by threats to bolt either the party or his leadership gave them more power than they otherwise would have wielded.

One must detest their often irrelevant, irrational, and demagogic speeches. While every irreconcilable at one time or another appealed to the prejudices and emotions of the people, certain bitter-enders such as Reed and Sherman stood out. However, it is questionable if the irreconcilables were more culpable than those senators who argued that the League should be supported because Jesus Christ had dreamed of it or because George Washington, if alive, would summon a stenographer and dictate an urgent recommendation for its approval. Wilson himself demagogically described his opponents as blind and contemptible men who gave aid and comfort to the Bolsheviks and the Germans. But if the language on all sides was extreme, it was understandable considering the atmosphere in which it was used. Personal animosity and partisan politics, though intense, only partly explain the bitterness of the debates. Too often ignored is the fact that virtually everyone believed the issues in dispute were the most momentous in the nation's history, indeed the history of mankind. There is no reason to question the bitter-enders' motives. They opposed the Treaty because they thought it would do more harm than good, both in maintaining American security and in promoting world peace.

Today the irreconcilables' objections to the Treaty may seem shortsighted, petty, or absurd. Certain of their criticisms, however, particularly those which condemned the harsh treatment of Germany, were, tragically, only too accurate. Moreover, the questions they raised about collective security were fundamental: What was the distinction between a legal and a moral obligation? How could the League promote change and still maintain order? Would the League have compelling power, and if so what became of a nation's sovereignty? If the League lacked such power what was it worth? They did not provide clear answers to these questions, but neither did Wilson or his followers. Those irreconcilables who feared that the League would become a dictatorial superstate were, as events showed, badly mistaken. But as events also showed, their doubts about the League's effectiveness were unfortunately not so mistaken. That the League would have been much more effective if the United States had joined it is possible though not probable. Many of the ambiguities, inconsistencies, and structural weaknesses that the irreconcilables foresaw would plague the League have persisted in the United Nations. That is not to say the irreconcilables were wise in rejecting the League, but they were right to question it as the panacea claimed by so many of its defenders. The questions concerning collective security as well as other methods of promoting a just peace remain unanswered. The irreconcilables' answers, posed in the form of alternatives to the League, ranged from hopelessly traditional to prophetically radical.

Finally, it is not helpful to blanket the irreconcilables as a group with the label of isolationists, as has often been done, even conceding that isolationism was a broad tradition encompassing a variety of emotional and intellectual commitments. Such labels have often substituted for analysis, and in the case of the irreconcilables the label has tended both to obscure their very real differences and to magnify the role of a few at the expense of the many. The bitter-enders were certainly more divided among themselves than they were separated from many of their fellow senators, including Republicans who voted for the Treaty with reservations and Democrats who followed Wilson's advice and rejected the Treaty with reservations. The important thing is their ideas, and, as has long been recognized in the case of the Lodge Republicans and Wilsonian Democrats, votes did not fully reflect ideas. The same was true of the battalion of death.

APPENDIX

William E. Borah of Idaho

Borah has come to be viewed as the most important irreconcilable, and in many ways he was. His own fellow irreconcilables recognized him as something of the spiritual leader of the group. Not only did he take the initiative in opposing Wilson's idea of a league, but until the very end his determination remained steadfast. His strengths were many. He was progressive enough to enjoy the respect of those on the left of his party, yet regular enough, not having bolted to the Bull Moosers in 1912, to satisfy many moderates and conservatives. Almost nobody questioned his sincerity or the depth of his convictions. Despite his loyalty to the party in 1912, he had a reputation as an inveterate objector, an obstructionist who might break the party bonds at any moment. A stock joke in Washington was to express amazement that when Borah took his daily horseback ride in Rock Creek Park, he consented to face in the same direction as the horse. This reputation, not altogether undeserved, was one of his assets during the League fight, since the threat of a bolt was a potent weapon to be used against party-minded senators like Lodge. Still another source of strength was his connection with hyphenate groups, notably the Irish and Germans. Yet his patriotism was unquestioned, for he had voted for war. Finally, there was his oratory. Befitting one who was seen as an inspirational leader and who probably so viewed himself, Borah took enormous and justifiable pride in his speaking ability. The galleries were usually overflowing when he spoke, and the Lion of Idaho, as the press called him, seldom disappointed his onlookers. Tall, powerfully built, with an oversized head topped by a shock of black hair, Borah appeared as a proud but somewhat lonely moral sentinel, a role he preferred the United States to play in the world community.

Frank B. Brandegee of Connecticut

Brandegee was an acid-tongued tory who had condemned Wilson's New Freedom at every opportunity. He was hardly less abusive toward progressives in the Republican party. For those who espoused both progressivism and pacifism, he reserved his most sulphurous phrases. Brandegee was cynical and morose (he committed suicide in 1924), inclined to be lazy, but occasionally brilliant in cross-examination. As a parliamentarian he had few equals, and he was responsible for planning many of the bitter-enders' strategic moves.

Albert B. Fall of New Mexico
Fall was a minor figure among the irreconcilables. Indeed he seemed less interested in the League than in Wilson's Mexican policy which he thought was too weak and conciliatory. His one moment of publicity came when he called upon the President after his stroke to determine his physical and mental fitness to carry on the burdens of office. This, the so-called smelling committee incident, did nothing to enhance Fall's reputation, which would be further reduced in the Teapot Dome scandals. With long black hair, a spider-leg moustache, a broad-brimmed stetson hat, and a combative and reckless nature, he epitomized in both looks and action the hard-driving individualism of the frontier.

Bert M. Fernald of Maine
Easily the least significant of the irreconcilables, Fernald gave only a few pedestrian speeches and claimed no special parliamentary skills. His background was business: business college in Boston, owner of several canning factories in Maine, President of the National Packers' Association, and director of the Fidelity Trust Company. Reflecting this background, his chief objection to the Treaty was its creation of the International Labor Organization, which he thought would destroy free enterprise in the United States.

Joseph I. France of Maryland
France never received the publicity that came to some of the less able but more flamboyant irreconcilables. Yet he presented perhaps the most challenging alternatives to the League of any bitter-ender. His background was uncommon for a senator. A brilliant medical student at the University of Leipzig and Clark University, he went on to become an outstanding physician in Baltimore, after having taught science for a few years at the Jacob Tome Institute. Drawn into politics through his moral indignation over corruption in the state government, he was elected to the Maryland Senate in 1906 and to the United States Senate in 1916. France was a Jeffersonian liberal: chary of federal control over the economy, but a fervent defender of minority rights and civil liberties. He was the strongest advocate in the Senate of recognition of Russia. In 1921 he traveled to Moscow where he interviewed Lenin, whom he admired, talked to Trotsky, made the acquaintance of a widow of a prominent Czarist official, later married her daughter, and returned to Maryland only to find that the voters rejected him for reelection as a radical Bolshevik sympathizer. Although he voted for United States entry

into war, his personal and intellectual ties thereafter were with the peace progressives.

Asle J. Gronna of North Dakota

A successful banker, newspaper owner, and farm machinery dealer before entering politics, Gronna's progressivism sprang from his antipathy to eastern industrialists and financiers whom he blamed for North Dakota's subordinate political and economic status. His opposition to the Treaty derived in part from this same antipathy. Lethargic-looking, frequently unshaven, hair hanging down over his forehead, wearing a massive walrus moustache, he had the same qualities of courage and tenacity as his frequent companions, La Follette and Norris, though without their overall ability. He was not, as the press sometimes viewed him, "a La Follette echo."

Hiram W. Johnson of California

Johnson has been aptly called the "noise" of the battalion of death. Neither a polished orator nor an agile parliamentarian, but one of the greatest stump speakers of his time, he tracked the country in 1919-1920 in an effort to mobilize anti-League opinion and simultaneously promote his Presidential ambitions. Johnson was earnest and aggressive on the platform, substituting force for finesse, making his points in a harsh, rasping voice, then driving them home with a swinging right arm as a carpenter might pound a nail. A California lawyer who fought the Southern Pacific Railroad machine, later a progressive Governor of the state, and in 1912 Roosevelt's running mate, he came back to the Republican party in 1916 as senator-elect. Johnson remained in the Senate until 1945, announcing from his deathbed his opposition to the United Nations.

Philander C. Knox of Pennsylvania

Knox was one of the two or three most important irreconcilables, marking himself early in the debates as the leading spokesman for those bitter-enders who were nationalists but not isolationists; who would accept, even promote, some form of coalition with America's wartime allies. He commanded respect for his brains and experience. He had been a corporation counsel to Henry Clay Frick and other big industrialists (contacts which proved useful to the irreconcilables), Secretary of State under Taft, Attorney General under Roosevelt, and a Senator for four years in between Cabinet positions. As Secretary of State he had tried to insure economic and political stability at home and abroad through the expansion of American economic activity overseas. "Dollar Diplomacy" created more problems than it solved, and Knox received much of the blame. Although inept and largely unsuccessful in the State Department, his criticisms of the Treaty deserve a more sympathetic judgment. Personally, Knox was considered cold and unapproachable. Short of stature, with a round and boyish face (Roosevelt said he looked like a "sawed-off cherub"), he seemed to compensate for his unimposing appearance by assuming an air of excessive dignity on the floor.

Robert M. La Follette of Wisconsin
La Follette was widely recognized as the greatest progressive of his time. In 1912 Woodrow Wilson described him as an "indomitable" foe of corruption, special privilege, and moral and political depravity in American life. He looked like the battler he was: short and solidly built, his large head often thrown back in what opponents called a defiant pose. His speeches were conscientiously researched, laden with statistics, and delivered with force and conviction. But for all his brilliance, La Follette, like Norris and Gronna, played a relatively minor role in the irreconcilables' fight. Because of their vote against the war, these three were still regarded in 1919 as pariahs, even by most of their colleagues in the Republican party.

Joseph Medill McCormick of Illinois
McCormick was regarded as one of the most promising young Republicans in years. Well informed on European politics, fluent in the French language and adequate in Spanish (as a youth he had accompanied his father, Robert S. McCormick, on ambassadorial missions to various European capitols), boasting a wide circle of friends, many connections as the result of having been publisher of the *Chicago Tribune,* and a politically astute wife (Ruth Hanna, daughter of Mark Hanna), he was expected to go far. A close friend of Theodore Roosevelt, whom he had supported in 1912, McCormick subsequently helped lead the insurgents back to the fold, thus partially placating the Old Guard. His outlook on foreign affairs was almost totally Rooseveltian. His special contributions to the irreconcilables' cause were as a money-raiser and as a coordinator of their speaking activities.

George H. Moses of New Hampshire
Moses came to the Senate unheralded. A former newspaperman—editor of the *Concord Monitor and Statesman*—his one previous position of importance had been Minister to Greece from 1909 to 1912. He quickly made a place for himself in the Senate. His skills as a parliamentarian, plus his staunch conservatism and party loyalty, caused Henry Cabot Lodge to favor him with choice committee assignments, notably a place on the Foreign Relations Committee. Not an effective speaker, his role in the League fight was to serve as a liaison between Lodge and the bitter-enders.

George W. Norris of Nebraska
Norris in 1919 had not yet achieved the outstanding reputation as a progressive he was to enjoy in later years, but even at this time he had earned great respect for his ability. Nobody could forget the successful

attack he had made as a young congressman on the powerful Speaker of the House, Joe Cannon. Closely identified in political outlook with La Follette, Norris lacked the dynamic and colorful personality of his friend from Wisconsin. Nor did he have the oratorical powers of many of the irreconcilables. Frank, friendly, and open in manner, hard working and intelligent, his leadership was of the quiet kind that most impressed one after observing him over a long career.

Miles Poindexter of Washington

Poindexter was one of the early and most active opponents of the League, and he was never far from the center of action throughout the fight. He had been a Bull Moose Progressive who, during World War I, returned to the Republican party and also moved far to the right. As foreign affairs absorbed more of his attention, he began to attack Wilson and those he associated with the President: pacifists, anarchists, Bolsheviks, socialists, and organized labor. Tall, lean, and big-jawed, he was both ambitious and aggressive. Similarly he glorified the drama and virtue of war and military life.

James A. Reed of Missouri

Like several of the irreconcilables, Reed was something of an iconoclast, disdainful of party discipline, more comfortable in opposing others' ideas than in presenting his own. At one time a district attorney in Kansas City, he had compiled an outstanding record and, in the eyes of his critics, acquired a prosecution complex in the process. Those who witnessed him in the Senate testified to his brilliance. Vice President Thomas Marshall said he was the greatest public debater he had ever heard. Eloquent in delivering a set speech, he was even more effective in give-and-take debate. Few men who clashed with him on the floor remained unscathed by his sarcasm and invective. No one looked more like a statesman; tall, broad shouldered, blue eyes, steel gray hair, ruggedly handsome features, he stood out wherever he appeared. Before 1917 he had usually supported the President's domestic legislation, but he became increasingly disenchanted as Wilson attempted to implement his international goals. The two men had also disagreed in the past over patronage appointments in Missouri. While personal animosity toward Wilson probably exacerbated Reed's opposition to the Treaty, there is no reason to believe it was the main cause of it.

Lawrence Y. Sherman of Illinois

Sherman was nearing the end of his career by the time of the League fight. Suffering acutely from a failing sense of hearing that impaired his effectiveness, he had decided not to seek reelection in 1920. He was Lincolnesque in appearance, outwardly sour in spirit, and vitriolic in speech. He also had a deserved reputation for obstinacy. "Most of my experience has been devoted to killing bills rather than promoting them, even when I have been with the majority in control of legislative bodies." He believed that a senator could accomplish more by "incontinently whaling the life out of everything" that came before him than by attempting to pass all kinds of legislation. A fellow irreconcilable described him as "a sort of Ishmaelite in the Senate," and Sherman admitted as much.

Charles S. Thomas of Colorado
It was Thomas's skepticism which most sharply characterized not only his doubts about a league of nations but his general attitude as well. He distrusted senators of both parties who claimed nonpolitical motives for their stand on the Treaty, and he refused to identify himself publicly with the irreconcilables, or any other faction, or to participate in their private conferences. He had always been a nonconformist: a young mining lawyer who attacked the venality of the legal profession, a critic of both the railroad brotherhood and their corporate foes, an ardent bimettalist long after his party had abandoned the cause, and a senator who was suspicious if not scornful of most of his colleagues. One of his final acts, in 1933, was to defy the government's ban on the hoarding of gold. Thomas's fight against the Treaty was an individual, almost a lonely effort.

BIBLIOGRAPHICAL ESSAY

Government Documents

The most important source was the *Congressional Record.* In all I consulted some seventy-nine volumes, from the Sixty-third through the Sixty-sixth Congresses. With a few exceptions the irreconcilables spoke extensively and candidly. In comparing their Senate speeches to their private correspondence, one finds no significant contradictions in their ideas. While the index of the *Record* is usually accurate, it is not as thorough as it might be, and therefore it is possible to find comments on the League of Nations buried in speeches on unrelated subjects.

The Foreign Relations Committee's hearings on the Treaty may be followed in *Treaty of Peace with Germany, Hearings before the Committee on Foreign Relations, United States Senate.* Senate Document No. 106, 66th Cong., 1st sess. (Washington, D.C., 1919). The bulk of the testimony came from ethnic or racial groups and proved largely irrelevant for my purposes. Highlighting the hearings were the appearances of Wilson, Secretary of State Lansing, and William Bullitt.

A fairly scarce and infrequently used but valuable document is the *Proceedings of the Committee on Foreign Relations, United States Senate, from the Sixty-Third Congress (Beginning April 1, 1913), to the Sixty-Seventh Congress (Ending March 3, 1923)* (Washington, D.C., 1923). The *Proceedings* shows the votes of the Committee on Resolutions, such as Knox's "New American Doctrine," which never reached the floor for a vote by the full Senate.

Manuscripts

Most of the irreconcilables left personal papers, in varying degrees of completeness. The best collection is that of William E. Borah (Library of Congress). Borah's correspondents included a wide range of individuals; he wrote many more personal letters than one would have expected. Other collections of great value are those of Hiram Johnson (Bancroft Library, University of California); Medill McCormick (in possession of his daughter, Mrs. Garvin E. Tankersley, Washington,

D. C.); Miles Poindexter (Alderman Library, University of Virginia); and Lawrence Y. Sherman (in possession of his daughter, Mrs. Marion W. Graham, Daytona Beach, Florida). Less revealing are the Papers of Philander C. Knox (Library of Congress) and George W. Norris (Library of Congress), both of which appear to have been culled of potentially important documents. The Charles S. Thomas Papers (State Historical Society of Colorado, Denver) contain the senator's unpublished autobiography, while the Papers of Joseph France (University of Maryland Library) and James A. Reed (in possession of his wife, Mrs. James A. Reed, Kansas City, Missouri) are limited mainly to newspaper clippings and scrapbooks. The George Moses Papers (New Hampshire Historical Society, Concord) have only a few items of interest. Fola La Follette graciously allowed me to examine certain letters of her father, Robert M. La Follette, on condition that I not quote from them. They corroborated what I found in other sources, including the biography of the senator by Fola and Belle Case La Follette.

The papers of nonirreconcilable senators are abundant. Invaluable, of course, are the Henry Cabot Lodge Papers (Massachusetts Historical Society, Boston). I also used the Papers of Warren G. Harding (Ohio Historical Society, Columbus), Charles McNary (Library of Congress), Harry New (Indiana State Library, Indianapolis), Key Pittman (Library of Congress), and Thomas J. Walsh (Library of Congress).

Still other collections that proved useful were those of Chandler Anderson (Library of Congress), James E. Babb (Yale University Library), James Beck (Princeton University Library), Albert J. Beveridge (Library of Congress), William Jennings Bryan (Library of Congress), Raymond Clapper (Library of Congress), Will Hays (Indiana State Library, Indianapolis), Edward M. House (Yale University Library), Salmon O. Levinson (University of Chicago Library), Isaac Lionberger (Missouri Historical Society, St. Louis), Breckenridge Long (Library of Congress), George Wharton Pepper (University of Pennsylvania Library), Elihu Root (Library of Congress), Chester H. Rowell (Bancroft Library, University of California), Henry L. Stimson (Yale University Library), William Howard Taft (Library of Congress), Henry Watterson (Library of Congress), and Woodrow Wilson (Library of Congress). Of the foregoing, the Beveridge Papers stand out. The former senator was a key adviser to the bitter-enders and exchanged dozens of letters with them. Only slightly less valuable are the Root Papers, which demonstrate Root's influence on Lodge and, indirectly, on some of the irreconcilables.

I was disappointed at not locating more manuscript materials on the League for the Preservation of American Independence, the irreconcilables' propaganda organization. Neither the Papers of George Wharton Pepper, the League's director, nor those of Henry Watterson, the League's president, yielded much. The Borah, Beveridge, Lodge, and Sherman Papers have scattered letters concerning the organization, and there is a small collection of pamphlets on the Independence League in the Widener Library, Harvard University.

Newspapers and Magazines

I followed the daily accounts of the League fight in several newspapers: *Boston Evening Transcript, Chicago Tribune, Christian Science Monitor, Louisville Courier-Journal, New York Herald Tribune, New York Sun, New York Times, Philadelphia Public Ledger,* and *Washington Post.* A few of these deserve special mention. The *New York Times,* which favored the League, had the most thorough coverage of events; the *New York Herald Tribune*'s Washington correspondent, Carter Field, provided more insights and background than any other single reporter; the *Boston Evening Transcript* was important because its editor, James Williams, maintained close relations with the irreconcilables; and the *New York Sun*'s owner, Frank Munsey, corresponded frequently with the irreconcilables and gave them much favorable publicity in his paper.

In addition, I spotchecked several other newspapers when Congress was out of session and the irreconcilables were traveling across the country filling speaking engagements, or when there were crucial points in the fight. These included the *Baltimore American, Brooklyn Daily Eagle, Buffalo Courier, Chicago Post, Hartford Daily Courant, Kansas City Star, New Haven Courier-Journal, New York Evening Post, Philadelphia North American, St. Louis Globe-Democrat, St. Louis Republic, San Francisco Examiner, Syracuse Journal,* and *Washington Star.* Finally, I utilized newspaper clippings in the personal papers of the irreconcilables.

Magazines were less helpful. I gained some clarification of La Follette's views, however, from *La Follette's Magazine. Harvey's Weekly,* edited by the anti-League George Harvey, furnished always colorful editorials. Many articles and editorials sympathetic to the irreconcilables appeared in *The New Republic,* the best of which is by William Hard, "The Irreconcilables," 22 (March 31, 1920). The most comprehensive view of press reaction to the League is in the *Literary Digest.*

The bitter-enders contributed occasional articles to newspapers and magazines. Generally they said little that could not be found in their Senate speeches, but I did benefit from the following: Joseph France, "American Idealism in the War," *Annals of the American Academy of Political and Social Science* 78 (July, 1918); Bert Fernald, "Will Nationality Survive?" *The Forum* 60 (October, 1919); and Lawrence Y. Sherman, "The Aims of the Republican Congress," *The Forum* 60 (December, 1918).

Autobiographies, Diaries, and Published Papers

Reminiscences often provide glimpses into the personalities of the drama, but seldom are very accurate about specific events. Only two irreconcilables—La Follette and Norris—published autobiographies and La Follette's stopped in 1911. Norris's *Fighting Liberal* (New York, 1945) has a superficial chapter on the defeat of the League. Royal W. France, in *My Native Grounds* (New York, 1957), sheds some light on his brother, the irreconcilable senator Joseph I. France. *A Many-Colored Toga: The Diary of Henry Fountain Ashurst* (Tucson, Ariz., 1962) is by the Arizona senator who clashed frequently with the battalion of death. Woodrow Wilson's Vice President, Thomas R. Marshall, gives some sparkling descriptions of the bitter-enders in his *Recollections* (Indianapolis, Ind., 1925). Lee Meriwether, *My First Ninety-Eight Years, 1862-1960* (Columbia, Mo., 1960), briefly discusses his relationship to James Reed and his part in the League for the Preservation of American Independence. Alice Roosevelt Longworth, Theodore Roosevelt's daughter, was a frequent visitor to the Senate galleries during the debates. Her *Crowded Hours* (New York, 1933) offers many witty observations. George Wharton Pepper's *Philadelphia Lawyer: An Autobiography* (Philadelphia, 1944) is informative on the League for the Preservation of American Independence. Edith Bolling Wilson, *My Memoir* (Indianapolis, Ind., 1939), recounts the "smelling committee's" visit to Wilson's bedside.

In a special category belongs Henry Cabot Lodge's *The Senate and the League of Nations* (New York, 1925). The book is primarily an attempt to explain and defend his actions. Lodge succeeds in showing the difficulties he faced and brilliantly overcame as majority leader of a party badly split on the League, but he also reveals his rankling ill will toward Wilson.

Secondary Sources

There are only two scholarly, thorough surveys of the League fight: Thomas A. Bailey, *Woodrow Wilson and the Peacemakers* (New York, 1947), published separately as *Woodrow Wilson and the Lost Peace* (New York, 1944) and *Woodrow Wilson and the Great Betrayal* (New York, 1945); and Denna Frank Fleming, *The United States and the League of Nations, 1918-1920* (New York, 1932). They differ sharply in interpretation. Fleming's sympathies clearly lie with Wilson; both the President's ideas and his tactics receive praise, whereas Lodge is the prime villain. Bailey mainly accepts Wilson's concept of collective security, but he assigns major responsibility for the Treaty's defeat to Wilson for his failure to make greater concessions to the Republican reservationists. Scintillatingly written and based on a much broader selection of sources than Fleming's book, Bailey's two volumes have greatly influenced subsequent accounts of the fight.

In contrast to this dearth of comprehensive studies, there are many articles, monographs, and biographies that treat events and individuals as limited parts of the whole story. John Chalmers Vinson, *Defeat of Article Ten of the League of Nations Covenant* (Athens, Ga., 1961), focuses upon what Wilson called the "heart" of the Covenant. A more sweeping analysis of collective security which has some trenchant remarks on the debate over the League is by Roland Stromberg, *Collective Security and American Foreign Policy: From the League of Nations to NATO* (New York, 1963). Stromberg emphasizes ideological differences, either real or felt, between the advocates and opponents of the League, whereas W. Stull Holt, *Treaties Defeated by the Senate*

(Baltimore, Md., 1933), believes that party politics essentially dictated the outcome of the fight. Still another broad interpretation sees Constitutional obstacles—executive-legislative rivalry, suspicion, and jealousy—to have been paramount in explaining what happened. George H. Haynes, *The Senate of the United States: Its History and Practice* (Boston, 1938), expresses this view. Perry Laukhuff, however, attributes the League's defeat primarily to Wilson's physical collapse while on his Western tour. A physically and emotionally healthy President, Laukhuff argues, would have succeeded in his mission. See "The Price of Woodrow Wilson's Illness," *The Virginia Quarterly Review* (Autumn, 1956): 598-610. Selig Adler's *The Isolationist Impulse: Its Twentieth Century Reaction* (New York, 1957) pictures the irreconcilables as part of the isolationist coalition which defeated the Treaty of Versailles.

Other special studies from which I drew information and ideas are Wesley M. Bagby, *The Road to Normalcy: The Presidential Campaign and Election of 1920* (Baltimore, Md., 1962); Ruhl J. Bartlett, *The League to Enforce Peace* (Chapel Hill, N. C., 1944); Alexander De Conde, ed., *Isolation and Security* (Durham, N. C., 1957), an outstanding collection of articles; James F. Eagleton, *James A. Reed and the League of Nations* (Amherst, Mass., 1950); Walter Johnson, *William Allen White's America* (New York, 1947); Warren F. Kuehl, *Seeking World Order, the United States and International Organization to 1920* (Nashville, 1969); Rayford Logan, *The Senate and the Versailles Mandate System* (Washington, D. C., 1945); Seward Livermore, *Politics Is Adjourned: Woodrow Wilson and the War Congress* (Middletown, Conn., 1966); Charles C. Tansill, *America and the Fight for Irish Freedom* (New York, 1957); William A. Williams, *The Tragedy of American Diplomacy* (New York, 1962); Louis A. R. Yates, *The United States and French Security, 1917-1921* (New York, 1957).

There are scores of articles which might be cited. Those most pertinent were Howard W. Allen, "Miles Poindexter and the Progressive Movement," *Pacific Northwest Quarterly* 53 (July, 1962); Waldo W. Braden, "William E. Borah's Senate Speeches on the League of Nations, 1918-1920," *Speech Monographs* 10 (1943); John M. Cooper, "William E. Borah, Political Thespian," *Pacific Northwest Quarterly* 56 (October, 1965); H. Maurice Darling, "Who Kept the United States Out of the League of Nations?" *Canadian Historical Review* 10 (September, 1929): 196-211; Allan Nevins, "Andrew Mellon," *Dictionary of American Biography* (New York, 1958), Supplement Two; Richard Lowitt, "Senator Norris and His 1918 Campaign," *Pacific Northwest Quarterly* 57 (July, 1966); David H. Stratton, "President Wilson's Smelling Committee," *Colorado Quarterly* 1 (Autumn, 1956); Kurt Wimer, "Senator Hitchcock and the League of Nations," *Nebraska History* 44 (September, 1963).

Good biographies of the irreconcilables are few. Borah has attracted more attention than his colleagues, including two competent full-length studies: Claudius O. Johnson, *Borah of Idaho* (New York, 1936), and Marian C. McKenna, *Borah* (Ann Arbor, Mich., 1961). Belle Case La

Follette and Fola La Follette, *Robert M. La Follette*, 2 vols. (New York, 1953), is uncritical but very detailed. Sewell S. Thomas, *Silhouettes of Charles S. Thomas: Colorado Governor and United States Senator* (Caldwell, Idaho, 1959), is a laudatory portrait by the senator's son. A grossly inaccurate and partisan biography by Lee Meriwether, *Jim Reed "Senatorial Immortal"* (Webster Groves, Mo., 1948), has some information on the League for the Preservation of American Independence. Not yet completed is the able work by Richard Lowitt, the first volume of which is *George W. Norris: The Making of a Progressive, 1861-1912* (Syracuse, N. Y., 1963).

John A. Garraty's *Henry Cabot Lodge: A Biography* (New York, 1953) is the only worthwhile biography of Lodge. A distinctive feature is its inclusion of comments by Henry Cabot Lodge, Jr., defending his grandfather against Garraty's criticism. A strong defense of Lodge is made by James E. Hewes, Jr., "Henry Cabot Lodge and the League of Nations," to be published in the *Proceedings* of the American Philosophical Society. Two biographies of Elihu Root, a key figure in the fight, merit praise: Phillip C. Jessup, *Elihu Root*, 2 vols. (New York, 1938), and Richard W. Leopold, *Elihu Root and the Conservative Tradition* (Boston, 1954). Claude Bowers, in *Beveridge and the Progressive Era* (New York, 1932), quotes liberally from the vast Beveridge manuscripts to which he had special access after Beveridge's death in 1927. George Harvey, *Henry Clay Frick* (New York, 1928) contains otherwise unavailable information on financial support of the anti-League cause by Frick and Andrew Mellon.

Biographies of Wilson abound, but none does justice to this tragic period of his career. Arthur S. Link's monumental biography has not yet reached the League fight. Three of his earlier volumes, *Wilson; The Struggle for Neutrality, 1914-1915* (Princeton, N. J., 1960), *Wilson; Confusions and Crises, 1915-1916* (Princeton, N. J., 1964), and *Wilson; Campaigns for Progressivism and Peace, 1916-1917* (Princeton, N. J., 1965 are almost definitive for these years. Link's *Wilson the Diplomatist: A Look at His Major Foreign Policies* (Baltimore, Md., 1957) is a brief, interpretive overview. The best of the completed biographies is Arthur Walworth's *Woodrow Wilson*, 2 vols. (Boston, 1965), second edition revised.

For Wilson's messages to Congress as well as his speeches on his western tour, I relied on the volumes edited by Ray Stannard Baker and William E. Dodd, *The New Democracy: Presidential Messages, Addresses, and Public Papers, 1913-1917* (New York, 1927), Vol. 2, and *War and Peace: Presidential Messages, Addresses, and Public Papers, 1917-1924* (New York, 1927), Vols. 1-2.

John H. Latane, ed., *Development of the League of Nations Idea: Documents and Correspondence of Theodore Marburg*, 2 vols. (New York, 1932) includes a few letters that Marburg received from irreconcilables in response to Marburg's urging of support for the League idea.

Unpublished Sources

I benefited from reading several doctoral dissertations: Joseph Edward Cuddy, "Irish-America and National Isolationism: 1914-1920" (State University of New York at Buffalo, 1965); Archibald John Dodds, "The Public Services of Philander Chase Knox" (University of Pittsburgh, 1950); James Hewes, Jr., "William E. Borah and the Image of Isolationism" (Yale University, 1959); David H. Jennings, "President Wilson's Tour in September, 1919: A Study of Forces Operating During the League of Nations Fight" (Ohio State University, 1959); Jack Kendrick, "The Republican Senate and the League of Nations, 1918-1921" (University of North Carolina, 1952); Franklin Dean Mitchell, "Embattled Democracy: Missouri Democratic Politics, 1918-1932" (University of Missouri, 1964); Paul Willard Morrison, "The Position of the Senators from North Dakota on Isolation, 1889-1920" (University of Colorado, 1954); Aubrey L. Parkman, "David Jayne Hill" (University of Rochester, 1961); Forrest Carlisle Pogue, Jr., "The Monroe Doctrine and the League of Nations" (Clark University, 1939); James Oliver Robertson, "The Progressives in National Republican Politics, 1919 to 1921" (Harvard University, 1964); Robert Seager, "The Progressives and American Foreign Policy, 1898-1917: An Analysis of the Attitudes of the Leaders of the Progressive Movement Toward External Affairs" (Ohio State University, 1955). In addition I used the Master's thesis by Sally B. Geoghegan, "The Political Career of Joseph I. France of Maryland" (University of Maryland, 1955), and the Senior honor's thesis by John McCook Roots, "The Treaty of Versailles in the United States Senate" (Harvard University, 1925).

INDEX

Adams, George Burton: notes Mc-Cormick's prejudice, 84
amendments: reaction to Root's, 87; nature of, 92; Borah on, 114; Johnson on, 114; debate on meaning of, 114; irreconcilable support of, 116; Norris insists on, 120; on restoring Shantung to China, 126; Wilson condemns, 133; reported by Foreign Relations Committee, 139; Foreign Relations Committee reservation on, 140; Foreign Relations Committee's defeated, 140; Hitchcock amendment fails, 143; Walsh amendments fail, 143, 168
Anderson, Chandler: talks to Root, 86
anglophobia: expressed by senators, 61, 192
Appropriations Committee: struggle over chairmanship of, 95-96, 97, 98, 99
Armed-ships bill, 13
Article eight: explanation of, 53
Article eighteen: explanation of, 53
Article eleven: explanation of, 53; questioned by Harding, 124; Wilson on, 129
Article fifteen: Moses faults, 89
Article nineteen: explanation of, 53; mentioned, 106-107
Article seven: source of controversy, 52-53; attacked by irreconcilables, 57, 58, 102
Article sixteen: explanation of, 53; intact, 88
Article ten: heart of covenant, 52; attacks against, 55, 58, 83; and Ireland's independence, 60-61, 102; not revised, 88; linked to Shantung settlement, 106; compared to Knox resolution, 111, 112; Root asks rejection of, 113; explained by Wilson, 124-25; obligations of, debated, 124-25, 126; Wilson attacks reservation to, 130; Foreign Relations Committee amendment to, 140; and

Article ten (continued):
Hitchcock reservations, 141; and compromise talks, 155, 156, 158, 159; reservation on, 165; mentioned, 114, 129, 132
Article twelve: explanation of 53; Poindexter questions, 62-63
Article twenty-six: mentioned, 107
Ashurst, Henry Fountain: on makeup of peace commission, 35n
association of nations. See League of Nations

battalion of death. See irreconcilables
Beck, James: and Round Robin, 72n
Beckham, J.C.W.: equates Knox resolution with Article ten, 112
Beveridge, Albert J.: on election of 1918, 30; assesses Lodge, 91-92; writes to mild reservationists, 122
bipartisan conference: suggested, 151; meetings of, 154-59; irreconcilable disruption of, 156-57; meetings end, 160. See also compromise
bitter-enders. See irreconcilables
Bliss, General Tasker: on peace commission, 34; does not testify on Treaty, 123
Bolshevism. See Russian Revolution
Borah, William E.: of Idaho, Republican, 1; elected to Senate, 4; criticizes Wilson in Lusitania crisis, 5; supports larger navy, 12; explains vote for war, 14; opposes league proposal, 16-17; resolution on Founding Fathers, 20n, 42; amendment for open discussion of peace treaty, 22; and election of 1918, 29; resolution on open sessions on peace treaty, 37-38; on Bolshevism, 40; grouped with Johnson and Reed, 41; attacks league, 42-43, 55, 57; on separation of League and Treaty, 46; questions League sanctions, 50-51; declines Wilson's invitation, 60; interrogates Hitchcock, 61-62; position in March, 1919, 77-78;

Borah, William E. (*continued*):
faith in public opinion, 78; and anti-League propaganda organization, 79; speaking tour, 82; on England and League, 82-83; on Article ten, 88, 165-66; on Monroe Doctrine, 88; advises Reed, 88; on Republican party, 90, 91; promotes national referendum, 91; and Lodge, 92-93, 98, 157; rejects party regularity, 92-93; compared to Wilson, 93; tries to commit party, 93; leads progressive conference, 96; bolt of party unlikely, 99; appeals to hyphenate vote, 102, 103; claims British will dominate League, 102; and Irish-American independence, 102-103; criticized by Thomas, 103; opposes Sherman's religious appeal, 105; criticizes League, 106; charges financial plot behind Treaty, 108; reads Treaty aloud in Senate, 108; wants Root and Taft to testify, 109; and Treaty "leak" inquiry, 110; and Knox resolution, 111, 143, 149; on amendments, 114, 139; opposes any league, 114; reservations inadequate, 114, 122; irresolution as tactic, 114; to reject Treaty, 115; on bolt from party, 117, 157-58; discredits Wilson-mild reservationist talks, 121; urges pressure on mild reservationists, 122; questions Wilson on League, 124; on Allied secret treaties, 124-25; and Wilson's veracity, 125-26; campaigns against League, 131-33; fears Treaty approval, 141; likes Walsh amendment, 142; asks for Senator Swanson's support, 144; opposes Treaty, 144; and Vigilance committee, 152; complains of secret diplomacy, 154; disrupts bipartisan conference, 156-57; condemned by press, 159; on Wilson's statesmanship, 163; and John Maynard Keynes, 165; responds to Simmons, 169; considered for Presidential nomination, 171; accepts Republican plank, 172-73; and Harding's stand on League, 174-75; withdraws support from Harding, 175; on results of election, 176; nationalist, 180; biographical sketch of, 183; mentioned, 128
Borden, Robert: memorandum to, 134
Brandegee, Frank B.: of Connecticut, Republican, 1; elected to Senate, 4;

Brandegee, Frank B. (*continued*):
supports military preparedness, 10, 12, 13; attacks peace progressives, 10-12, 14; nationalist, 41; questions Norris, 56; describes meeting with Wilson, 60; leads interrogation of Wilson, 61; comments on meeting with President, 63; favors filibuster, 67; and Round Robin, 71, 73; clarifies views, 83; request to Chandler Anderson, 86; opposes Covenant, 88-89; and Root, 90, 109; will reject Treaty, 115, 118; suggests jury tampering by Wilson, 121; disagrees with Wilson, 124; questions Article ten, 124; and Bullitt's testimony, 138; speech before final voting, 144; on Lodge reservations, 148-49; disrupts bipartisan conference, 156-57; attacks Lodge, 163-64; reelection of, 175; biographical sketch of, 183-84
British Empire: and Irish question, 82; mentioned, 139
British voting representation: mentioned, 132, 140
Bryan, William Jennings: praises Borah speech, 17*n;* opposes referendum proposal, 153; mentioned, 14
Bullitt, William: before Foreign Relations Committee, 138

Canada: and Executive Council, 134
Catholic Church: will dominate League, Sherman charges, 103-105
Chicago Tribune: poll on League, 89; and Treaty "leak," 108
China: and Shantung settlement, 105-106
Clemenceau, 134
collective security: Borah criticizes concept of, 17; early debate on, 20; at heart of League debate, 124-25. *See also* Article ten
Colt, Le Baron: on Wilson and Article ten, 126*n*
compromise: Senate pressures for, 147; public desire for, 148*n;* and Grey letter, 160-62. *See also* bipartisan conference
Congress, Sixty-fifth: and Senate filibuster, 64-70
Congress, Sixty-sixth: and special session, 32, 33, 33*n*, 60, 90, 100; struggle over organization of, 94-99
Covenant. *See* League of Nations
Cox, James: on League under Democrats, 173; Democratic nominee for

Cox, James (*continued*):
President, 173; on issues of 1920 election, 176; defeated, 176
Cummins, Albert: suggests changes in Round Robin, 72; wants progressive committee structure, 96; mentioned, 122
Curtis, Charles: Republican party whip, 93

Davison, Henry: and Treaty "leak," 110
Democratic party: 1920 platform, 173
Democratic senators: divided, 115; most oppose amendments, 139; support Hitchcock, 141; try to split Republicans, 142; voting on Treaty, 145; those wanting compromise, 147; effect on, of Lansing dismissal, 162-63; appeal to irreconcilables, 168
Dillon, E. J.: critical of peacemakers, 164-65
domestic questions: and reservations, 129, 140, 141
election of 1918: and partisanship, 22, 25, 27; and October appeal, 27-28; results of, 29; effect of, on irreconcilables, 30-31
election of 1920: and Wilson's "solemn referendum," 153-54; campaign and results of, 170-77

Fall, Albert B.: of New Mexico, Republican, 1; elected to Senate, 4; would punish German transgressions, 5; supports preparedness, 12; questions idea of league, 20; reelected in 1918, 29; nationalist, 41; declines Wilson's invitation, 60; signs Round Robin, 73; speaks widely, 82; may reject Treaty, 115; drafts thirty-six amendments, 139; on Walsh amendment, 142; and President's health, 150-51; biographical sketch of, 184
Fernald, Bert M.: of Maine, Republican, 1; elected to Senate, 4; reelected in 1918, 29-30; nationalist, 41; insists on reservations, 121; meets with Wilson, 121-22; announces vote on Treaty, 126; on Treaty and I.L.O., 137; biographical sketch of, 184
filibuster: ending Sixty-fifth Congress, 64-70, 74, 75, 77
Finance Committee: struggle over chairmanship of, 95-96, 97, 98, 99

Foreign Affairs Committee of House: meeting with Wilson, 54, 60, 63
Foreign Relations Committee of Senate: meeting with Wilson, 54, 60, 63; importance of, 91; membership struggle over, 97-99; considers Knox resolution, 111; hears Lansing testimony, 123-24; hearings on Treaty, 123-25; hears Wilson testimony, 124-25; report of the Treaty, 139; proposes reservations, 140; amendments of, defeated, 140
Fourteen Points address: importance to League fight, 21; initial reaction to, 21; attacked by irreconcilables, 24-25; Treaty's violation of, 179
France, Joseph: of Maryland, Republican, 1; elected to Senate, 4; defends war vote, 14; idealism of, 23; on Russian Revolution, 40; joins peace progressives, 41; offers alternatives to Wilson's league proposal, 48-49; views of brotherhood, 54; compared to Wilson, 59; and filibuster, 67, 68, 69, 75; ideas on League, 69; and anti-League propaganda organization, 79; on Executive Council, 134; and plan for world federation, 136-37; on League and Treaty, 136, 140; considered for Presidential nomination, 171; philosophical outlook of, 179-80; biographical sketch of, 184-85
freedom of the seas: 4
free trade: and Fourteen Points, 24, 28; and league proposal, 25
Frelinghuysen, Joseph: opposes League, 90; assists irreconcilables, 103; pressured by Friends of Irish Freedom, 103; opposes compromise, 155-56
Frick, Henry Clay: supports irreconcilables, 81; balks at supporting Johnson, 131
Friends of Irish Freedom: pressure senators, 103; finance irreconcilables' speaking tour, 131

Germany: United States breaks relations with, 13; announces resumption of submarine warfare, 19; signs armistice terms, 34; signs Treaty, 118
Gompers, Samuel: influence on I.L.O., 135
Gore, Thomas P.: supports Knox resolution, 111
Great Britain: on Executive Council, 134. *See also* British Empire
Grey, Sir Edward: visits United

Grey, Sir Edward (*continued*):
States, 160; letter on League fight, 161
Gronna, Asle J.: of North Dakota, Republican, 1; elected to Senate, 4; peace progressive, 6; agrees with La Follette and Norris, 9; view on negotiated peace, 13; votes against war, 14; on filibuster, 66n; speaks out on League, 84; opposes revised covenant, 89; does not fight Lodge, 96; appointed to Committee on Committees, 97; announces vote on Treaty, 126; on Article ten, 137-38; defeated in 1920, 176n; philosophy of a league, 179-80; biographical sketch of, 185; mentioned, 128

Hard, William, 178
Harding, Warren: named to Foreign Relations Committee, 97; questions Wilson on League, 124; on Articles ten and eleven, 124; nominated for President, 171; on League under Republicans, 173; on "association of nations," 174; denounces League, 175-76; wins 1920 election, 176; position on League after election, 177
Hardwick, Thomas: anti-Wilson Democrat, 66; in anti-League organization, 79-80
Harvey, George: criticizes makeup of peace commission, 35; raises money for irreconcilables, 81, 82; and Bullitt's testimony, 138-39
Hays, Will: opposes Norris's re-election, 30; letter from Root, 86; refuses to make statement against compromise, 149; places pressure on Lodge, 160
Hearst, William Randolph: and anti-League organization, 78n
Hitchcock, Gilbert: resolution endorses league idea, 16-17; supports League, 50; debates Borah, 61-62; and Foreign Relations Committee, 98; questions Reed, 101; and Treaty "leak" issue, 110; on Republican divisions, 117; rejects reservations, 118, 144; urges Wilson to see Norris, 120; and interpretive reservations, 129, 141; against Treaty with reservations, 141; purpose of Walsh amendment, 142; offers amendment, 143; urges Wilson to compromise, 147; and President's health, 150; and Lodge, 151; supports referendum proposal, 153;

Hitchcock, Gilbert (*continued*):
and compromise, 154, 156; on Lodge and irreconcilables, 159; mentioned, 19
Holt, Hamilton: and League to Enforce Peace, 15
House, Edward M.: peace commission member, 34; advises Wilson, 59, 118-19; does not testify on Treaty, 123; advises compromise, 147; mentioned, 25
Hughes, Charles Evans: and 1916 election, 159

immigration and League: irreconcilables on, 82
Independence League. *See* League for Preservation of American Independence
International Labor Organization: condemned by Thomas, 126, 140; and Samuel Gompers, 135; La Follette on, 136; Foreign Relations Committee reservation on, 140
interpretive reservations: defined, 114; acceptable to Wilson, 129
Ireland: and Article ten, 60-61
Irish-Americans: importance to League fight, 102
Irish independence: and reservation on, 166
irreconcilables: names of, residence, 1; positions distorted or misunderstood, 2; interpretations of themselves, 2-3; reaction to beginning of war, 4; divisions and disagreements, 4, 17, 22-23, 41, 178, 182; those advocating preparedness, 10; split on neutrality, 10; vote on war declaration, 14; divisions among, in 1917, 14; style of attack, 20; seize initiative, 24; and October appeal, 28-29; on Bolshevism and Allied intervention, 39-40; and isolationism, 41, 180; eleven Round Robin signatories, 73; position in March, 1919, 77; major consensus in March, 1919, 78; organizational problems, 78; financial worries relieved, 81, 82; multiple activities of, 82-83; unfavorable reactions to, 83; effect of speeches and writings, 85-86; on Root amendments, 87; reaction to revised Covenant, 88-89; membership on Foreign Relations Committee, 97, 98, 99; growing strength of, 99; strategy in May, 1919, 100; appeal to hyphenate fears, 102; united on Shantung settlement, 106; at opening of Sixty-sixth Congress,

irreconcilables (continued):
107; miner triumph on Treaty "leak," 108; aided by Root, 110; contradictory statements of, 114; strategy on reservations, 116-17, 122; worried by Wilson's tactics, 121-22; strategy toward Wilson, 123; and Wilson's western tour, 127; effectiveness of trailing Wilson, 133; on amendments, 139; on reservations, 140; on Lodge policy, 141; vote on Treaty, 145; strategy to prevent compromise, 146; appeal to Lodge, 148; appeal to Will Hays, 148; and compromise solution, 149; attitude toward Lodge, 149, 157, 160, 163, 181; and reservationists, 152; fear compromise, 154; disrupt compromise talks, 156-57; condemned by press, 159; threaten to bolt, 159; confidence grows, 159-60; renew criticisms, 165; public support of, 167n on similarities to Wilson, 169; second victory celebration, 170; object to second vote, 170; during 1920 election, 170-71; on 1920 platform, 172; and Harding, 174, 176; philosophical differences discussed, 179-80; realists among, 180; nationalists among, 180; strategy and tactics of, 180-81; appeal to prejudice and emotion, 181; motive for opposing Treaty, 181; questions on collective security, 182; biographical sketches of, 183-88
Isolationism: and irreconcilables, 41
Italy: on Executive Council, 134

Japan: and Shantung settlement, 105-106; on Executive Council, 134
Johnson, Hiram W.: of California, Republican, 1; elected to Senate, 4; attacks Wilson, 20-21; criticizes makeup of peace commission, 35; on President's annual message in 1918, 37; on Bolshevism, 40; grouped with Borah and Reed, 41; on league concept, 43n, 43-44; on separation of League and Treaty, 46; explains Round Robin signatures, 73; speaking tours of, 82, 107; against League, 84, 89; rejects party regularity, 93; and organization of Senate committees, 96; named to Foreign Relations Committee, 98; Presidential ambitions of, 99; attacks Shantung settlement, 106; condemns Article ten, 106; criticizes League, 106; resolution

Johnson, Hiram W. (continued):
on Versailles Treaty's publication, 108; on financial plot behind Treaty, 108; resolution passes Senate, 108; on Knox resolution, 111, 143, 149; on reservations, 114, 140; will reject Treaty, 115; sharply questions Lansing, 123; on Allied secret treaties, 124-25; campaigns against League, 131; trails Wilson, 131-32; on Treaty defeat, 146; response to reservationists, 152; and "irreducible minimum," 155; disrupts bipartisan conference, 156-57; and Presidency, 159; condemned by press, 159; considered for Presidential nomination, 171; and Harding's stand on League, 174-75; nationalist, 180; biographical sketch of, 185; mentioned, 128
Jones, Wesley: wants progressive committee structure, 96; rejects committee assignment, 97

Kellogg, Frank: and Foreign Relations Committee, 97; on reservations, 144-45; and Treaty compromise, 154
Kellogg-Briand Pact: war outlawry suggested, 66n
Kent, William, 30
Kenyon, William: wants progressive committee structure, 96; rejects committee assignment, 97; favors Hiram Johnson, 171; mentioned, 134
Keynes, John Maynard, 164-65
Knox, Philander C.: of Pennsylvania, Republican, 1; elected to Senate, 4; rejects League to Enforce Peace, 20; offers alternatives to league idea, 26; leadership of, 27; criticizes October appeal, 28; nationalist, 41; on American aims at peace conference, 44; wants postponement of league discussion, 44; calls for "New American Doctrine," 44-45, 168; ideas compared to Wilson's, 45; influence of, 45-46; opposes League, 54n; on Poindexter speech, 55n; proposes outlawry of war, 66n; and filibuster ending Sixty-fifth Congress, 66, 67, 70; and Round Robin 71, 72; and anti-League propaganda organization, 79; regarding money from Frick and Mellon, 81; on Foreign Relations Committee membership, 99; influenced by Root, 110; five-part resolution, 110-13; calls for United

Knox, Philander C. (*continued*):
States cooperation with Europe,
111; on separation of League and
Treaty, 111; resolution not brought
to vote, 112; on League's shortcomings, 112; on Monroe Doctrine,
112; on Root's reservations, 114;
questions Wilson on League, 124-
25; attacks Treaty's terms for
Germany, 126; and Bullitt's testimony, 138; resolution opposed by
Hitchcock, 143; opposes Hitchcock
amendment, 143; introduces resolution, 149-50; disrupts bipartisan
conference, 156-57; on Grey letter,
161; criticizes treaty, 165; on "New
American Doctrine," 168; considered for Presidential nomination
in 1920, 171; as realist, 180; biographical sketch of, 185-86

La Follette, Robert M.: of Wisconsin,
Republican, 1; elected to Senate, 4;
peace progressive, 6; proposes international tribunal, 7; favors arms
limitation, 7; proposes international
conference of neutrals, 7-8; argues
for neutrality, 7-8; favors freedom
of the seas, 8; supports peace without victory, 8, 18; for self-determination, 8; supports Wilson's neutrality policy, 8; view on negotiated
peace, 13; votes against war, 14;
attacks October appeal, 28; alleged
disloyalty of, 31, 32; agreement
with Lodge, 32; on Wilson's power,
38; distrusts Allies, 48; favors
special session of Congress, 65; on
filibuster, 65-70 passim, 75; not a
signatory of Round Robin, 73; apprehensive about Treaty, 84, 89;
does not fight Lodge, 96, 96n; attacks Treaty's harsh terms for Germany, 105; on secret diplomacy,
108-109; announces vote on Treaty,
126; disputes Wilson's facts, 126;
on progressive legislation, 134-35;
on International Labor Organization, 136; supports Walsh amendment, 143; considered for Presidential nomination, 171; and Republican party in 1920, 174n; philosophy of, toward League, 19; biographical sketch of, 186

Lamont, Thomas: and Treaty "leak,"
110

Lansing, Robert: peace commission
member, 34; differs with Wilson on
Treaty, 35; testifies on Treaty, 123-
24; quoted by Bullitt, 138, dismissal of, 162

League for Preservation of American
Independence: organization and
goals of, 6n, 7, 78-79; partisan
character of, 79-80; structure and
tactics of, 80-81; financial support
of, 81; as ally of League opponents,
90; sponsors irreconcilable speaking
tours, 107, 131

League of Nations: Wilson proposes,
15; congressional reaction to Wilson's proposal of, 15-17, 89; idea
attacked by irreconcilables, 41-43;
debate on enforcement of, 49-51;
controversial articles of, 53; on
withdrawal, 53; and Monroe Doctrine, 53; question of constitutionality, 82; and Irish issue, 82;
demands for modification of, 86;
revision of, 87-88; Reed criticizes,
100-101; Sherman criticizes, 103-
104; attacked as reactionary, 106-
107; popularity of, waning, 107;
separation from Treaty, 113; interpreted by Wilson, 124-25; Executive Council of, 134; vote on, 145;
role in 1920 elections, 176-77; as
seen by irreconcilables, 179, 182

League to Enforce Peace: founding
of, 15; irreconcilables from counter
organization, 78; poll on Covenant,
89; mentioned, 42, 107, 130

Lenroot, Irvine: on special session, 68;
and Foreign Relations Committee
struggle, 97; named to compromise
committee, 154

Levinson, Salmon: confers with Knox,
66n; mentioned, 90

Lewis, James Hamilton: argues for
League, 49-50

Lloyd George, 134

Lodge, Henry Cabot: and organization of Senate, 31; placates La Follette and Norris, 32; on special session of Congress, 33n, 65; defends
Henry White, 35; on League, 54n,
90-91, 116-17; on Poindexter
speech, 55n; praises Borah and
Reed speeches, 58; meeting with
Wilson, 60; role in Round Robin,
65, 71-75 passim; and Senate filibuster, 66-70 passim, 75; and anti-
League propaganda organization,
79; and Henry White request, 86;
major concerns of, 90; relations
with Borah, 90, 92, 93; and party
unity, 90, 93, 94, 141; progressives
question leadership of 94; conservatism of, 95; struggle with progressive Republicans, 95-99; ap-
points Foreign Relations Committee, 97, 98, 99; compromise with

Lodge, Henry Cabot (*continued*):
Democrats, 103; opposes Sherman's religious appeal, 105; sees prepublication copy of Treaty, 108; and Treaty "leak" 110; and Knox resolution, 111, 112-13; reaction to Root's letter, 113n; prefers reservations, 117; and Borah, 122; meets mild reservationists, 122; strategy toward irreconcilables, 122-23; delays Treaty consideration, 123; invites Wilson to testify, 124; on growing support for reservations, 128; benefits from Wilson's tour, 133; and Bullitt's testimony, 138; endorses amendments, 139; on Walsh amendment, 142-43; on article ten reservation, 143; reply to Root on concessions, 149; and reservationists, 151-52; and compromise, 151-53, 154-60 passim; and pro-Treaty forces, 152; berated by irreconcilables, 157; consults with irreconcilables, 158; and 1920 election, 159; resentful toward irreconcilables, 160; changes in his reservations, 163; defends himself, 164; denies Simmons's charge, 168-69; and second vote, 170; addresses Republican convention, 172; as mediator, 179; mentioned, 109, 130, 140

Lodge reservations: distinct from interpretive reservations, 114; Brandegee on, 148-49; and irreconcilables, 157; voting on revised set of, 165. *See also* reservations to Treaty; Foreign Relations Committee of Senate; Lodge, Henry Cabot

Longworth, Alice Roosevelt: victory celebrations of, 1, 145; mentioned, 134

Lowell, A. Lawrence: and League to Enforce Peace, 15

McAdoo, William Gibbs: and election of 1918, 29

McCormick, Joseph Medill: of Illinois, Republican, 1; elected to Senate, 4; criticizes Wilson, 20; and election of 1918, 29, 30, 31; nationalist, 41; early views on a league, 48; solicits signatures for Round Robin, 72n; raises money for League defeat, 81; speaking tour of, 82, 84 on Covenant, 88; and organization of Senate committees, 96; on stacked Foreign Relations Committee, 98; coordinates irreconcilable speaking tours, 107; may reject Treaty, 115; com-

McCormick, Joseph Medill (*cont.*):
ments on Wilson's speech, 119; campaigns against League, 131 32; likes Walsh amendment, 142; disrupts bipartisan conference, 156-57; criticizes Treaty's economic provision, 165; biographical sketch of, 186

McCumber, Porter: Republican supporter of League of Nations, 35n; on Foreign Relations Committee, 97; supports Knox resolution, 111, 112; prefers mild reservations, 115; questions Wilson on League, 124, 125, 126; supports strong reservations, 141-42

McKellar, Kenneth: denounces Knox resolution, 112; supports Hitchcock amendment, 143; and compromise negotiations, 154

McNary, Charles: wants progressive committee chairman, 96; and compromise talks, 156n; supports Johnson for Presidency, 171

mandates: Foreign Relations Committee reservation on, 140

mandatories: and revised League, 88

Marshall, Thomas: on Sherman's oratory, 70; adjourns Senate *sine Deo*, 70; rules on committee organization, 98; adjourns Congress, 145; mentioned, 58

Martin, Thomas: on special session of Congress, 60, 68

Mellon, Andrew: supports irreconcilables, 81; mentioned, 131

Meriwether, Lee: and anti-League organization, 81

mild reservationists: newspapers identify, 100; wanted League, 115; meet with Wilson, 121-22; reject interpretive reservations, 122; Wilson's explanation unsatisfactory to, 126; most oppose amendments, 139; support Foreign Relations Committee reservations, 141; Kellogg speaks for, 144-45; pressure Lodge, 147; on charges in reservations, 151; win concessions from Lodge, 154; mentioned, 115, 116, 117, 130

military preparedness. *See* preparedness

Monroe Doctrine: Borah's view of, 17; Borah notes absence of, 55; discussed at White House conference, 60, 61; League exempts, 88; discussed by Philander Knox, 112; Root's suggestion on, 113; and Foreign Relations Committee, 140; and Hitchcock reservations, 141;

Monroe Doctrine (*continued*):
and compromise talks, 155, 158; reservation intact, 166; mentioned, 79, 129

Morgan, J. P.: and Treaty "leak," 110

Moses, George: of New Hampshire, Republican, 1; elected to Senate, 4; and election of 1918, 29, 30; nationalist, 41; and anti-League propaganda organization, 79; speaks widely, 82; opposes Article fifteen, 89; offers *modus vivendi* to progressives, 96; named to Foreign Relations Committee, 97; may reject Treaty, 115; and President's health, 150-51; summons Lodge, 156; disrupts bipartisan conference, 156-57; on Treaty's terms, 165; reelection of, 175; biographical sketch of, 186

Munsey, Frank: friend of irreconcilables, 61

nationalism: and irreconcilables, 41

neutrality: irreconcilables' early views, 5; irreconcilables divided on, 5-6; mentioned, 4

New, Harry: solicits signatures for Round Robin, 72n; and anti-League propaganda organization, 79; opposes League, 90; named to Foreign Relations Committee, 97; named to compromise committee, 154; and compromise talks, 155, 156

"New American Doctrine": Knox proposes, 44-45, 168. *See also* Knox, Philander C.

Norris, George W.: of Nebraska, Republican, 1; elected to Senate, 4; peace progressive, 6; favors neutrality, 8; proposes international court of arbitration, 8; favors arms limitation, 8; proposes international navy, 8-9; view on negotiated peace, 13; speech on war message, 14; votes against war, 14; defends Wilson's motives, 19; and election of 1918, 29, 30, 31; resolution democratizing committee structure, 31, 32; challenges Poindexter, 56; indecision about League, 57, 84; opposes filibuster, 66n; on not signing Round Robin, 73; approval of League, 84-85; and organization of Senate committees, 96; opposes Knox resolution, 112; likely to accept Treaty, 115; wants reservations, 118; fairest-minded Republican irreconcilable, 119; attacks Treaty, 119-20; declines invitation

Norris, George W. (*continued*):
to see Wilson, 120; consistent in alternatives, 121; corrects Wilson, 130; attacks Wilson's European trip, 135; on Treaty with amendments, 140; supports Walsh amendment, 143; critical of Lansing dismissal, 162; philosophy of a league, 179-80; biographical sketch of, 186-87; mentioned, 128

October appeal: effect of, on League fight, 27-29

Owen, Robert: and compromise negotiations, 154

peace commission: debate on makeup of, 34-36; political balance criticized, 34; men chosen for, 34; lacks Senate member, 35; McCormick charges partisan character of, 98

peace progressives: on preparedness, 5, 6-7, 13; support neutrality, 6; disillusionment with Wilson, 6; criticize war, 6-7; on secret diplomacy, 7; on nation's security, 7; cite benefits from neutrality, 7; prewar peace proposals, 7-10; attitude toward sanctions, 9; domestic reforms of, 9-10; idealism of, 10; filibuster on armed-ships bill, 13; favor Wilson's ideals, 22-23; party loyalty questioned, 31; joined by Joseph France, 41; on brotherhood, 54; reveal views, 84-85; criticizes League, 106; on Treaty, 140, 179; mentioned, 94

"peace without victory" address: Wilson delivers, 18; irreconcilable reaction to, 18

Penrose, Boies: favors filibuster, 67; and Finance Committee chairmanship, 95-96; named chairman of Finance Committee, 98

Pepper, George Wharton: directs anti-League organization, 79, 80; consults Root, 90

Pinchot, Amos, 125

Pittman, Key: suggests senators for peace commission, 36; denounces Knox proposal, 49; on Borah speech, 58; on Senate filibuster, 65, 66; on Walsh amendment, 142, 143

Poindexter, Miles: of Washington, Republican, 1; elected to Senate, 4; attacks peace progressives, 10, 12; advocates military preparedness, 10, 12, 13; opposes idealistic internationalism, 23; fears "free trade

Poindexter, Miles (*continued*):
league," 25; attacks Bolshevism, 39-40; nationalist, 41; early views on a league, 48; supports continued alliance system, 55; and withdrawal from League, 55, 56; attacks League, 55-56; and moral force, 56; questions Hitchcock, 62-63; position in March, 1919, 78; and anti-League propaganda organization, 78, 79; speaking tour, 82; will reject Treaty, 115; campaigns against League, 131; calls President pro-German, 132; disrupts bipartisan conference, 156-57; on Great Britain and Grey letter, 161; considered for Presidential nomination, 171; biographical sketch of, 187; mentioned, 128

Pope Benedict XV, 104

preparedness: raises questions, 4, 5; peace progressives oppose, 5; those irreconcilables advocating, 10. *See also* individual irreconcilables

progressive Republicans: oppose conservative committee structure, 95-99

public opinion: and irreconcilables' speeches, 85; and polls on League, 89; and Wilson's western tour, 133; and compromise on Treaty, 147, 148n, 154

racism: Reed appeals to, 100-101; in League fight, 103

Ransdell, Joseph: urges Treaty passage, 169

Reed, James A.: of Missouri, Democrat, 1; elected to Senate, 4; views on preparedness, 12, 13n; attacks Norris, 14; attacks league, 18, 41-42, 43, 58; on President's annual message, 1918, 37; grouped with Borah and Johnson, 41; does not sign Round Robin, 73; position in March, 1919, 77-78; and anti-League propaganda organization, 79, 80; speaking tour, 82, 83; objections to Article ten, 83; telegram to Borah, 88; on voting system, 88; appeals to racial prejudice, 88, 100-101, 102; offers alternatives to League, 102; appeals to religious prejudice, 105; will reject League, 115; campaigns against League, 131; denounces President, 132; on Canada and the League, 134; calls reservations cowardly, 141; likes Walsh amendment, 142; on compromise talks, 155; on Grey letter, 162;

Reed, James A. (*continued*):
refused seat, 173-74; during campaign and election, 174; Harding's view of, 176; nationalist, 180; appealed to prejudice and emotion, 181; biographical sketch of, 187; mentioned, 128

referendum on League: promoted by Borah, 91; supported by Wilson, 153;

religious issue: injected into League debate, 103-105

representation on commissions: foreign Relations Committee reservation on, 140

Republicans: and control of Sixty-sixth Congress, 32-33; need for unity among, 90-91; and organization of Senate, 90-91; progressive senators, 94; splits among, 94, 95; struggle over Senate organization, 94-99; progressive senators unite, 95; Hitchcock reservations unacceptable to, 141; support Lodge, 141; votes on Treaty, 145; unity in 1920 election, 170-73; 1920 platform, 172; and Harding's stand on League, 174-75

reservationists: benefit most from Wilson's tour, 133; appeal to irreconcilables, 167; mentioned, 133-34. *See also* strong reservationists; mild reservationists

reservations to Treaty: nature of, 92; Johnson on, 114; Borah on, 114; as distinct from interpretive reservations, 114; debate on meaning of, 114; irreconcilable support of, 116; discussed, 127; Wilson condemns, 133; fourteen voted through, 141; Reed calls cowardly, 141; seven remain intact, 166; possible weakening of, 179; mentioned, 130

Robinson, Joseph: challenges Reed to reelection contest, 102

Roosevelt, Theodore: praises Borah speech, 17n; urges attack on Fourteen Points, 25; and 1918 election, 27, 28; opposes Norris, 30; death of, 95

Root, Elihu: rejected for peace commission, 34; proposes amendments, 86; letter to Lodge, 86; letter to Will Hays, 86-87; and revised Covenant, 87, 90; approves Independence League, 90; favors Senate amendments, 90; involved in League fight, 99; and Treaty "leak," 109, 110; relationship to irreconcilables, 109-10; and Article

Root, Elihu (*continued*):
ten, 113; advises Lodge, 113, 147;
suggests strategy, 113; approach to
League, 113; influence on reservations, 140; drafts platform plank,
172
Round Robin: origin of, 26, 70-71;
discussed, 70-75; mentioned, 77,
97, 98, 140
Russia: Joseph France's views on, 69
Russian Revolution: allied intervention
in, 39; irreconcilable reaction to,
39-40
secret diplomacy: peace progressives
oppose, 7; and Versailles Treaty's
publication, 106-107; mentioned,
4
self-determination: and Irish independence, 166
Senate: constitutional role in treaty-
making, 4, 22; organization of, 32-
33. *See also* Congress
Shafroth, John: on international court,
20
Shantung settlement: provokes loudest
outcry, 105; provisions of, in Treaty,
105-106; Norris considers as indefensible, 120; Lansing testifies
on, 123-24; Wilson on, 124; on
restoring province to China, 126;
Foreign Relations Committee reservation on, 140; mentioned, 132,
139
Sherman, Lawrence Y.: of Illinois,
Republican, 1; elected to Senate, 4;
views on preparedness, 12; on
"peace without victory" address, 18;
doubts Wilson's motives, 19; criticizes October appeal, 28; on
organizing Senate, 31n; on election
of 1918, 33; on Wilson at peace
conference, 37; nationalist, 41; on
idea of a league, 48; attacks League
Covenant, 55; resolution on treaty-
making, 57; replies to Wilson attack, 64, 75; helps lead filibuster,
66-70 passim; threatens bolt of
party, 67, 157; position in March,
1919, 78; speaks widely, 82; on
mandate system, 88; appeals to
religious prejudice, 103-105, 181;
and religious beliefs, 104; calls
Treaty of Versailles Godless, 105;
will reject Treaty, 105; on President and Mrs. Wilson, 133-34; for
amendments, 139; speech before
final voting, 144; disrupts bipartisan conference, 156-57; critical of
Lansing dismissal, 162; biographical
sketch of, 187-88

Simmons, Furnifold: and compromise negotiations, 154; prevents
disruption, 155; and Article ten
reservation, 159n; on Lodge and
compromise, 168-69; mentioned, 25
six votes to one issue: and compromise
talks, 155; mentioned, 52, 53. *See
also* Article seven
Small, Robert: reporter for *Philadelphia Public Ledger*, 123
Smelling Committee: calls on Wilson, 150-51
strong reservationists: newspapers
identify, 100; discussed, 115; a
few oppose amendments, 139; and
compromise talks, 154; mentioned,
115, 116. *See also* mild reservationists; reservationists
Swanson, Claude: objects to Round
Robin resolution, 73; Borah visits,
144
Sutherland, Howard: and anti-League
propaganda organization, 79

Taft, William Howard: and League
to Enforce Peace, 15; drafts Article
ten reservation, 159; enters campaign, 175; mentioned, 109
Thomas, Charles S.: of Colorado,
Democrat, 1; elected to Senate, 4;
views on preparedness, 12, 13n; on
"peace without victory" address,
18; speech on peace settlement, 18-
19; on critics of Wilson's decision,
34n; nationalist, 41; questions
Senate's treaty-making role, 46;
ineffectiveness of moral force, 47;
on tariff reduction, 47; opposes
open diplomacy, 47; answer to
peacekeeping problems, 47; and
Round Robin, 73, 74; speaking tour,
82, 83; charges Foreign Relations
Committee "stacked," 98; criticizes
Borah's hyphenate appeal, 103;
denounces Sherman's religious appeal, 104; on Knox resolution, 111-
12; supports amended Treaty, 115;
meets with Wilson, 120, 121;
criticizes Treaty's terms for Germany, 120-21; favors league of
English-speaking peoples, 121;
condemns International Labor
Organization, 126, 140; against
most amendments, 139-40; re-
submits McCumber reservation,
142n; defeated on independent
ticket, 173; biographical sketch of,
188; mentioned, 128, 135
Treaty of Guarantee: some irreconcilables favor, 180

Treaty of Versailles: explanations of defeat, 2; debate over, foreshadowed, 20; irreconcilables begin attacking, 105; Shantung provisions opposed, 105-106; terms kept secret, 107-108; "leak" issue, 107-10; business attitude toward, 108*n;* separation from League, 115-16 irreconcilable approach to, 116; losing favor, 133; votes on, 145; reason for failure, 145; as issue in 1920 election, 153; public opinion and, 154; responsibility for defeat of, 167; final vote on, 169-70; motion to reconsider, 170; final Congressional decision on, 177; irreconcilable part in defeat of, 181; mentioned, 1. *See also* League of Nations

Tumulty, Joseph: support for League of Nations, 46*n;* on Borah speech, 57-58; on opposition to League, 85; on religious prejudice and League, 104; urges attack on Knox resolution, 113; mentioned, 65, 170

Underwood, Oscar: on compromise, 147, 151; supports referendum proposal, 153

Walsh, Thomas: debates Borah, 51; on Republican divisions, 58*n;* advises Wilson, 63*n;* strategy to split Republicans, 142, 168; effects of amendment, 143; and compromise negotiations, 154; urges Treaty passage, 169

Warren, Francis: committee chairmanship struggle, 95-96; named chairman of Appropriations Committee, 98

Watterson, Henry: president of anti-League organization, 79

White, Henry: praises Borah speech, 17*n;* peace commissioner, 34; asks Lodge advice, 86, 109; does not testify on Treaty, 123

White, William Allen: finds League unpopular, 107

Williams, John Sharp: challenges irreconcilables, 49; on Knox resolution, 111; questions Borah, 139

Wilson, Woodrow: proclamation of neutrality, 4; severs relations with Germany, 13; on peace progressives, 13, 32; delivers war message, 14; preposes association of nations, 15; league proposal attacked, 15-17; proposes "peace without victory,"

Wilson, Woodrow (*continued*):
18; meets growing opposition, 19, 20-21; Fourteen Points address, 21; explains free trade and league idea, 25; attacks critics of league idea, 25-26; issues "October appeal," 27-28; opposes Fall's reelection, 29-30; and special session of Congress, 33*n*, 60, 64, 90, 94; attends peace conference, 34, 36, 39; and intervention in Russia, 39; reads completed Covenant, 51; explains League Covenant, 53-54; requests meeting with senators, 54; Boston speech on League, 54, 59; attacks Republicans, 54; returns from Peace Conference, 59; meets with Foreign Relations Committee, 60-61; explains League's relationship to Monroe Doctrine, 61; speaks to Democratic National Committee, 63; criticizes filibuster and Round Robin, 74-76; pledges no separation of Treaty and League, 75; and revisions in League, 87-88; compared to Borah, 93; aids Lodge, 95; neglects Republican progressives, 95; and Shantung settlement, 106, 124; and Treaty "leak," 108, 110; rejects attack on Knox resolution, 113; replies to Root reservations, 118; delivers message on Treaty, 118, 119; replies to House, 119; conciliates senators, 120; invites Norris to White House, 120; meets with Thomas, 120, 121; meets with Fernald, 121-22; meets with mild reservationists, 121-22; and strategy on reservations, 122; response to Harding, 124; contradicts Lansing, 124; testifies on Treaty, 124-25, 126; on Allied secret treaties, 125-26; will appeal to people, 127; opposition to amendments and reservations, 127; western tour of, 128-30, 132; interpretive reservations proposes, 128; suffers thrombosis, 131; own worst enemy, 133; and Bullitt's testimony, 138; letter to Hitchcock, 143; against Foreign Relations Committee reservations, 143; Cabinet advises compromise, 147; annual message of, 1919, 150; and Smelling Committee, 150-51; and compromise, 151; on League and 1920 election, 153; and reservations, 153, 166, 179; threatened revolt against, 154; and 1916 election, 159; rejects Article ten

Wilson, Woodrow (*continued*):
reservation, 159n; withdraws from
consideration, 173; demagoguery of,
181; mentioned, 77, 78, 141
Wilson, Mrs. Woodrow: on Senator
Fall, 150
Wilson's western tour, 128-30, 132
withdrawal from League: Poindexter
wants provision for, 56; provision

withdrawal from League (*cont.*):
for, 87-88; Root's suggestion for,
113; Foreign Relations Committee
reservation on, 140; and Hitchcock reservations, 141; substantive
change defeated, 166; mentioned,
129
Wood, Henry Wise: and anti-League
organization, 78-79